A READER'S GUIDE TO ERNEST HEMINGWAY

A READER'S GUIDE TO ERNEST HEMINGWAY

by Arthur Waldhorn

FARRAR, STRAUS AND GIROUX

NEW YORK

SECOND PRINTING, 1973

Published simultaneously in Canada by
Doubleday Canada Ltd., Toronto
Printed in the United States of America
Designed by Herb Johnson

For Jesse

Acknowledgments

Quotations from the following works of Ernest Hemingway are fully protected by United States and international copyright: *Across the River and Into the Trees, A Farewell to Arms, By-Line, Death in the Afternoon, For Whom the Bell Tolls, Green Hills of Africa, Islands in the Stream, The Old Man and the Sea, The Short Stories of Ernest Hemingway, The Sun Also Rises, The Torrents of Spring, To Have and Have Not.* Quotations are used by permission of Charles Scribner's Sons, the Executors of the Ernest Hemingway Estate, Alfred Rice, Esq., and Jonathan Cape, Ltd.

"Two Poems to Mary," copyright © 1965, by The Atlantic Monthly Company, Boston, Mass. Reprinted with permission.

CITATIONS

Page references are cited in the text and are made to the following editions, all published by Charles Scribner's Sons:
The Torrents of Spring, in *The Hemingway Reader* (1953)
The Sun Also Rises (1954; identical with Scribner Library series paperback, 1960)
A Farewell to Arms (1949; identical with SL series paperback, 1962)
Death in the Afternoon (1932; identical with 1955 reprint)

Green Hills of Africa (1935; identical with SL series paperback, 1963)

To Have and Have Not (1937; identical with 1953 reprint)

For Whom the Bell Tolls (1940; identical with SL series paperback, 1960)

Across the River and Into the Trees (1950)

The Old Man and the Sea (1952; identical with SL series paperback, 1965)

A Moveable Feast (1964)

By-Line (1967)

Islands in the Stream (1970)

All page references to the collected short stories are to *The Fifth Column and the First Forty-Nine Stories* (1938), *not* to the separate editions. The Modern Library edition (1942) has identical pagination.

Preface

Hemingway's place in American letters is permanent—that much is sure. What is needed is a continuing analysis that may enable us to understand more fully than we do now why he deserves that place. In the decade since his death, scholars and critics have labored toward answers. The "authorized" biography has appeared as well as at least a half-dozen book-length critical studies and a half-thousand notes and essays. Yet the task remains undone, the genius of Hemingway's art (and, it may be added, its relationship to his life) still not fully accounted for, the sources of his enduring appeal still not fully interpreted.

This book is intended for general and literary readers who share an interest in these problems and who may profit from the presence of a "guide" to point out along the way some possible—as well as impossible—explanations. The direction proceeds from panoramic to close-up. Part I discusses, in turn, Hemingway's life, his sense of the world and how to live in it, and his style. In this introduction, I have risked some generalizations about the man and his work that, I hope, will suggest rather than define relationships between Hemingway's life and his art. How some of the patterns in Hemingway's writing take particular shape emerges in Part II, where individual works are analyzed in detail. The novels and the non-fiction books are studied in chronological order. Except for the earliest published stories and "The Snows of Kiliman-jaro" and "The Short Happy Life of Francis Macomber," which are located chronologically, Hemingway's other short stories are interspersed where relevant. All the "collected" stories receive attention—sometimes detailed, sometimes passing—and several of the uncollected stories as well. I have lumped together in a single chapter—without regard to chronology—journalism, poetry, satire, and drama. The Notes, collected at the back of the book, are full and attempt to account, when pertinent, for the most important critical attitudes taken by Hemingway's critics. The Bibliography is annotated.

Many have helped me to write this book. I owe a debt to the scholars and critics of Hemingway who have served as my guides in the past, and as well to the undergraduate and graduate students whose crisp queries and fresh perceptions sharpened my sense of obligation as a guide. I have particular obligations too. I wish to thank Major-General C. T. Lanham (U.S.A., Ret.) and Professor Carlos Baker for granting me permission to read Hemingway's unpublished correspondence, and Alexander P. Clark, Curator of Manuscripts at the Princeton University Library, for his courtesy and assistance. My thanks too to Troy Petrie of the Humanities Library of the City College for his constant interest and help. I am indebted to the City College Research Fund for grants, and to Henry Robbins, a patient and perceptive editor.

Among my colleagues and students who assisted in various ways, my gratitude to Philippe Citron, Richard Goldstone, Theodore Gross, Leo Hamalian, Karl Malkoff, Rima Rudd, Sondra Stigen, John C. Thirlwall, and Frederic Tuten. To Edmond Volpe and Arthur Zeiger, colleagues and friends who saved me once more from infelicities and excess, once more my thanks. And to Philip Young—who surely needs no guide to the subject—my sincerest appreciation for his painstaking and invaluable criticism of the entire manuscript.

Finally, a special award for "grace under pressure" to Steve, the apprentice, and Hilda, the exemplar.

ARTHUR WALDHORN

The City College of the City University of New York
August 1971

Contents

PART ONE

PART TWO

PART ONE

I

Life

"Madame, it is always a mistake to know an author," Ernest Hemingway warns the Old Lady in *Death in the Afternoon* [144]. About his preference for working in the morning or writing with a number 2 pencil, or his tastes in food, drink, guns, music, and art, Hemingway was never reticent. But when the questions touched feeling and motive, his responses were always elusive or coldly negative: "Let's give my life a miss." He wanted no biography written during his lifetime and hoped that none would be written until a century after his death. Only three years before he died, he wrote a codicil to his will insisting that none of his many letters ever be published. Nevertheless, Hemingway drew more attention to himself as a *man* and has had more non-literary copy written about him than any other American writer in the twentieth century.

One simple but compelling reason was his life style, as dramatic as his prose but far more baroque. For more than thirty of his forty years as a famous writer, his other "careers" as hunter, fisherman, skier, boxer, reporter, soldier, bull-ring and saloon *aficionado* were enthusiastically recorded by gossip columnists and mass-circulation magazines. In each decade his life style altered in details, but the essential pattern prevailed: Hemingway took the risks young men dream of taking and older men nostalgically wish they had taken. A youth from a safely bourgeois home in the Midwest, schooled to follow in that tradition, he opted for a wholly different and more perilous way.

The penalties for taking risks run high and Hemingway paid them. In war and peace, he was racked by disease and suffered hundreds of wounds—skull fracture, concussions, internal injuries. But, as he said, "My luck, she is running very good." He survived them all, all except the last, self-inflicted wound. There were other rewards too. People, for example. He formed extraordinary friendships (but carried on endless feuds with many friends).[1] (See Notes, p. 223 ff.) He mingled intimately with Gary Cooper and Marlene Dietrich but as well with hunting guides in Africa, bullfighters in Spain, bartenders in Paris, and fishermen in Havana. To countless GI's in France and Germany, he was self-identified as "Ernie Hemorrhoid, the poor man's Pyle." Moreover, he had four wives and a lot of money, more than a million dollars when he died.

So narrow a view of Hemingway the man tells little of the entire story, but it serves to place him at the outset where, as a man, he belongs—in the romantic tradition. Like Wordsworth, he preferred the common people; like Keats, he loved the sensuous and seemed "half in love with easeful death"; and like Byron most of all, he affected the heroic posture, Promethean rebel against the conventions of society. But such parallels are also too facile. Hemingway lived as an American in the twentieth century and his life (as well as his work) sounds the familiar notes of his violent time and his restless people: loneliness, alienation, and disillusion. Somehow, Hemingway's experience promised a triumph of the soul despite terror, seemed to assure that heroism was still possible, and that the artist knew the way.

One hears in all this the not-too-distant brassy ring of glamour and success. But there is a deeper resonance as well, its source the relationship between the man and his work. To his sympathizers, he was, as one said when Hemingway died, "a man who lived it up to write it down." To his antagonists, what he wrote obscured rather than revealed the truth about the man. Gertrude Stein, for example, disenchanted with her former protégé, wrote in 1933 that she would love to read the "real story of Hemingway, not those he writes, but the confessions of the real Ernest Hemingway . . . but alas he never will. After all, as he himself once murmured, there is the career, the career." 2 Both observers are myopic because they fail to perceive arbitrary and necessary distinctions between the life and the work. It is certainly true that at times (especially in the thirties) the "career" became outrageously disproportionate to the work, as if an excess of adventure compensated for a paucity of art. And the work too is sometimes self-conscious and postured; as Edmund Wilson remarked, Hemingway is "the worst invented character to be found in the author's work." 3 Nevertheless, it should become clear that as Hemingway projects his world, his public and literary images fuse kaleidoscopically. The perspective becomes myriad, but always there is a wholeness, an organic interdependence that suggests, as Malcolm Cowley wrote more prophetically than he knew in 1944, "a sense of an inner and an outer world that for twenty years were moving together toward the same disaster." 4

From the outset, Hemingway's characters are vised in a world of natural and human violence, struggling to survive and to assert the integrity of self. The conflict is intense, the rules of battle merciless and strictly enforced. Love, war, and sports (usually bloody ones) are the games his heroes play and, in conventional terms, lose. From the earliest stories to the latest, the hero ends as victim. "All stories, if continued far enough, end in death," Hemingway writes in *Death in the Afternoon*, "and he is no true story teller who would keep that from you" [122].

Love, war, and sports were Hemingway's life games too, played vigorously and tenaciously from his youth. Like his protagonists, he suffered physical as well as emotional scars and, like them, tried to manifest "grace under pressure." 5 The beginnings were deceptively undramatic. One of his high-school teachers in the then prosperous, middle-class Chicago suburb of Oak Park wondered some years ago "how a boy brought up in Christian and Puritan nurture should know and write so well of the devil and the underworld." [6] Similarly naïve Midwesterners drift through the pages of Hemingway's fiction, inevitably missing the point of their experiences. Yet Hemingway's eighteen years in Oak Park were not on the surface hellish.

Ernest Miller Hemingway was born July 21, 1899, the second of six children. His mother made the boy practice the cello; his father taught him to fish and to shoot. Nothing hinted at trauma. At high school, class of 1917, he was a prototypically zealous and competitive all-American boy: good student, all-around athlete (swimmer, football player, riflist, and, privately, a student at the local boxing gymnasium), debater, cellist in the school orchestra, editor of the school newspaper, *Trapeze,* and contributor of stories (that already hint at his mature style) and poems to the literary magazine, *Tabula.* He went off occasionally on hitchhiking trips, and once even hid hmself from the law after shooting a blue heron on a game preserve.[7] To some critics, Hemingway's expeditions away from home attest to the normality of his boyhood; to others they symbolize his early rebellion against the norms of Oak Park and reflect the tensions of his home life.

Certainly his parents had sharply divergent interests that stirred ambivalent responses in him and some antagonism toward one another. Marcelline Sanford, a sister two years his senior but raised as Hemingway's twin, testifies that her parents "loved each other deeply," but admits that they "frequently got on each other's nerves." [8] A Congregationalist and obsessively religious woman (she named her four daughters after saints) but also an artistic one,[9] Grace Hall Hemingway shaped a home environment rather like a church-organized cultural salon. Clarence Edmonds Hemingway, a prominent physician and an ardent, disciplined sportsman and amateur naturalist, introduced his son to the excitement of the out-of-doors. During summers at their lakeside house near Petoskey in northern Michigan, Dr. Hemingway occasionally took his son along on professional visits across Walloon Lake to the Ojibway Indians; more often they fished and hunted together. Their bond was close, though the father was a strict disciplinarian and even more rigid and puritanic than Mrs. Hemingway.

What each of his parents transmitted to him is at least superficially clear. His appetite for the out-of-doors and the discipline and courage of the athlete never abated. Neither did his love for music (though he hated having to study the cello) and the arts. He cherished Bach and Mozart, stressing what he had learned about writing from "the study of harmony and counterpoint"; and, he added, "I learn as much from painters how to write as from writers." [10] Nothing in the available data of Hemingway's boyhood and adolescence in Oak Park augurs other than a reasonable expectation of a well-adjusted adulthood. Yet when one turns to the fiction of this extraordinarily autobiographical writer, one notes several Nick Adams stories written about those years ("Indian Camp," "The Doctor and the Doctor's Wife," "The End of Something," "The Three-Day Blow," "The Battler," and "The Killers") that record patterns of violence and fear, confusion and disillusion—and loneliness, the quality his classmates coupled with his versatility as most characteristic of him.

Two months before his graduation, the United States had entered the war. "College, war, and work were the choices that confronted him," Carlos Baker writes, and Hemingway's choice was work. Defective vision in his left eye made war an unlikely experience anyhow. In October 1917, he began an assignment as a cub reporter on the *Kansas City Star*, then one of the best American newspapers. For six months he covered hospital and police-station beats, absorbing also excellent professional advice from the *Star*'s fine editor, C. G. (Pete) Wellington.[11] At the *Star*, Hemingway learned for the first time that style, like life, must be disciplined. "Use short sentences," read the *Star*'s famed style sheet. "Use short first

paragraphs. Use vigorous English. Be positive, not negative."
Within a remarkably short time, Hemingway learned to
transmute journalistic rules to literary principle.

But the war became increasingly tempting to Hemingway,[12] and in late May of 1918 he began that adventure. Of
the first two months he spent in Italy as a volunteer Red
Cross ambulance driver, he was at the front for only a week.
Just after midnight at the end of that week, while passing
bars of chocolate to Italian soldiers at Fossalta di Piave in
northeastern Italy, Hemingway was hit by fragments of an
Austrian trench mortar shell. The soldier beside him was
killed, another just beyond badly wounded. As he dragged
the wounded man to a rear area, Hemingway was hit in the
knee by machine-gun bullets; by the time they reached sanc-
tuary, the wounded man was already dead. At the hospital in
Milan where he spent the next three months, Hemingway un-
derwent a dozen operations to remove most of the more than
two hundred shell fragments lodged in his legs and body.
When he was hit, Hemingway was two weeks short of his
nineteenth birthday.[13]

Early in the 1950's Hemingway said, "Any experience of
war is invaluable to a writer. But it is destructive if he has
too much." [14] The explosion that shattered Hemingway's body
metaphorically penetrated his mind too. There its effects
were longer-lived and more far-reaching. One immediate effect was insomnia and a total inability to sleep in the dark.
Five years later, living in Paris with his wife, Hemingway
could still not sleep without a light on. The sleepless man appears everywhere in Hemingway's fiction. Jake Barnes in *The
Sun Also Rises*, Frederic Henry in *A Farewell to Arms*, Nick
Adams, Mr. Frazer in "The Gambler, the Nun, and the
Radio," Harry in "The Snows of Kilimanjaro," and the old
waiter in "A Clean, Well-Lighted Place" are among those
who suffer insomnia and dread the dark.

"After all, it's only insomnia. Many must have it," says the
old waiter. Insomnia is a symptom of the agonizing syndrome
that tormented Hemingway, his protagonists, and ("Many

must have it") his fellow man. In a brilliantly reasoned psychological analysis of Hemingway's personality, Philip Young
argues that the trauma of his war wound released more emotion than he could rationally control. Repeatedly and obsessively in his later years, Hemingway sought analogous
experiences to exorcise that trauma or, failing that, by contin-
ually reliving the event through his writing rather than thinking about it, to control the anxiety it evoked.[15]

Hemingway's art, not his trauma, is the ultimate concern,
as Young wisely admits. Yet, within limits, Young's theory of
personality helps to reconcile the man and his work. Furthermore, it lends special significance to Hemingway's observation about war and the artist. What made his war experience
"invaluable" was more than the splendid recording in *A Farewell to Arms* and several short stories of the social, emotional,
and ethical implications of war: it burned into his psyche a
vision of man's fate that afterwards seared almost everything
he wrote. The fragmenting trench mortar became a synec-
doche for the destructive force of a v 'nt world, and Hemingway and his protagonists symbols   ded mankind
searching for some way to survive. He   st ready to
translate that sense of life into literature.

During the five years after he acquired   'ge of
courage, Hemingway worked slowly but pu   ard
his career as a writer. Oak Park welcomed its   -
tically, but Hemingway's parents—especially
lost patience with a young man who showed no
yond writing and who seemed too willing to let the family
provide for him. For a while, Hemingway wrote features for
The Toronto Daily Star and *Star Weekly*. Shortly after his
twenty-first birthday, his sister Marcelline writes, his mother
issued an ultimatum that he find a regular job or move out.[16]
Hemingway moved out, to Chicago, and worked for a year as
editor of *The Cooperative Commonwealth*, a house organ for
an investment co-operative. That winter, he met Sherwood
Anderson, his first important literary acquaintance, and,
through Anderson, other members of the "Chicago Group." At

the same time, he met and fell in love with Hadley Richardson, a beautiful redhead, eight years older than he. Hemingway and Hadley were married in September 1921, honeymooned at the family cottage, then left for Toronto, where he continued for a few more months as a feature writer.

But it was Europe and leisure to write that he really wanted. Boldly, the Hemingways determined to chance a part-time journalistic assignment abroad. For the next two years, Hemingway became the *Star's* roving European correspondent, headquartered in Paris but filing by-lined reports of international conferences at Genoa and Lausanne, and taut, dramatic dispatches about the Greco-Turkish War. Also, he wrote casual but sharply observed impressions about skiing in Switzerland, bullfighting in Spain, and postwar life in Germany. The technique of the cable—compressed, tense—now worked even more potently on a style already affected by his earlier journalistic training, as well as by a predisposition for terseness.

Meanwhile, he worked at his fiction and poetry, trying without success (as he had since 1918) to find a publisher to accept one of his pieces. In 1922, a rapid succession of events quickened his hopes and then plunged him into despair. Armed with a letter of introduction from Sherwood Anderson, he had presented himself and his writing to Gertrude Stein, whose salon in rue de Fleurus was the artistic hub of expatriates like Ezra Pound, James Joyce, and Ford Madox Ford. Stein liked the young man with the almost Continental manner and "passionately interested" eyes and encouraged him as a writer, warning him, however, that he should give up journalism altogether and rewrite his prose more economically: "There is a great deal of description in this and not particularly good description. Begin over again and concentrate." Ezra Pound, too, liked the newly arrived writer, walked and boxed with him, and urged him to go on with his poetry. In May and June, Hemingway's first published work appeared —a two-page satirical fable, "A Divine Gesture," and a four-line poem, "Ultimately," the latter printed to complete a page that featured a six-stanza poem by William Faulkner. *The Double Dealer,* a New Orleans magazine, had printed both works, and once more he owed his good fortune to Sherwood Anderson.

The disaster occurred late in 1922 while he was covering the peace conference at Lausanne. En route to meet him there, Hadley was to bring a suitcase in which she had packed nearly all his manuscripts (a few others were in the mail). At the Gare de Lyon in Paris, she left the suitcase unguarded in her compartment for a few moments and returned to find it gone. Years later, Hemingway wrote to Carlos Baker that the episode pained him so that he "would almost have resorted to surgery in order to forget it." [17] With no alternative, Hemingway started afresh, this time with startling success. In 1923, several of his pieces were accepted. Harriet Monroe took six short poems for *Poetry* (published in January 1924); [18] Margaret Anderson and Jane Heap accepted for *The Little Review* (April 1923) six of the eighteen sketches that would appear in January of the following year as *in our time;* and Robert McAlmon published Hemingway's first book in the summer of 1923, *Three Stories and Ten Poems* (the stories were "Up in Michigan," "My Old Man," and "Out of Season").

However assured the future seemed, real obstacles blocked the way. Hadley was pregnant and the Hemingways had almost no money. They agreed to return to Toronto for two years, where he would earn enough money to return to Paris, and then do nothing but write. Thus they left Paris in August 1923. John Hadley ("Bumby") Hemingway was born in October, but by January 1924 the Hemingways had returned to Paris and Montparnasse, settling into an apartment in rue Notre Dame des Champs. Again the steps toward success were delayed because Hemingway had to continue working part-time to support his family. He avoided the sybaritic life of Montmartre, nearly starved himself, as he tells in *A Moveable Feast,* but kept at his writing. He was, as Gertrude Stein observed, "very earnestly at work making himself a writer." [19]

The breakthrough came in 1925—probably because two influential supporters made it possible. Even before he met Hemingway, Scott Fitzgerald had been impressed by what Edmund Wilson had shown him of Hemingway's writing and had urged Maxwell Perkins at Scribner's to ask for more. Perkins wrote, but through a series of delays and mailing errors, his letter arrived ten days after Hemingway received and accepted from Boni and Liveright, Sherwood Anderson's publishers, an offer of a two-hundred-dollar advance for *In Our Time*, a collection of short stories which included the earlier sketches published as *in our time*, and an option on his next two books.[20]

Financially, *In Our Time* was a failure, as was its successor, *The Torrents of Spring*, a satirical parody of Sherwood Anderson's writing, but they brought Hemingway to the attention of major American reviewers like Allen Tate, Paul Rosenfeld, and Louis Kronenberger, each of whom proclaimed the arrival of a fresh new voice in American letters. Once more, however, it was Fitzgerald who spoke most forcibly about Hemingway's talent. In an essay called "How to Waste Material: A Note on My Generation," [21] Fitzgerald attacked those writers of the Establishment—especially H. L. Mencken and Sherwood Anderson—whose "compulsion to write 'significantly' about America" was "insincere because it is not a compulsion found in themselves." The expatriate, Fitzgerald argued, had the advantage of being able to discover for himself an "incorruptible style" and "the catharsis of a passionate emotion." As his prime example of a writer who was "temperamentally new" and possessed of both qualities, Fitzgerald cited Ernest Hemingway and *In Our Time*. Fitzgerald's essay appeared in May; five months later Hemingway justified Fitzgerald's praise beyond question.

With Scribner's publication of *The Sun Also Rises* in October 1926,[22] Hemingway, not yet thirty, became an established literary figure. Sales were impressive for a first novel, and reviews were enthusiastic. Near the end of his life, Hemingway recollected these years—1921–26—celebrating in *A*

Moveable Feast the dreams, the discipline, and the disasters. The dream is pastoral: the innocence of his love for Hadley; the beauty of place—Paris and the Voralberg; the affection of friends. Discipline, imaged as hunger, spurs him competitively and pitilessly toward success but also toward mastery of a literary style. Disaster is the nightmare reality that follows on the heels of success, shattering the dream and crumbling the discipline, leaving only lust, surfeit, and disillusion. Illness, physical and mental, probably intensified the sweetness and the bitterness of an aging man's nostalgia. Yet there is also a sense that Hemingway knew at last that the early period in Paris was the time when man and artist most happily merged. By the time he published *In Our Time, The Sun Also Rises*, and, by 1929, *A Farewell to Arms*, Hemingway had experienced all he needed to form his vision of man's fate and had forged a literary style absolutely expressive of it. Although his artistic development was not ended, what he was to write thereafter would, at its best, refine and polish his craft and play variations on themes he had already sounded.

What sustains the drama of the next two or three decades —apart from the sequence of almost incredible episodes—is in some measure the remarkable flexibility with which Hemingway adjusted his public image to the special demands of changing times. That he could do so accounts for the mass personal appeal he generated—whether as the benign "Papa" or as the pugnacious "Champ." More absorbing, however, is the inward drama. As his fame swelled from a ripple to a torrent, Hemingway's sensibility seemed to wallow in the trough. In the early work, terror and beauty are too intimate to be stated: they are communicated only as feeling, rigidly disciplined. The artist controls the image of the man. In the later work, the delicacy of restrained feeling is often dissipated in statement that almost parodies the emotion. Therein lies the force of the inward drama. For almost as if to atone, the man overcompensates in life for his failure in art. His behavior in the real world continues to reflect his preoccupation with the tragedy of experience and his compelling need to

combat the hostility of the universe, to affirm his own identity. But the actions are so obviously statements that they
become—because they are so blatantly and determinedly
heroic—comic, embarrassing, even at times boring. If, then,
the twenties are the years of art as adventure, the thirties and
forties are the years of the artist as adventurer. The vision remains unaltered; only the discipline slackens.

In the years between the publication of *The Sun Also Rises*
and *A Farewell to Arms,* Hemingway, divorced by Hadley,
married Pauline Pfeiffer, a former fashion editor for *Vogue.*
They returned to the United States and settled in Key West,
where Hemingway completed and published in 1927 his
second collection of short stories, *Men Without Women.*
In 1928, as he worked on the first draft of *A Farewell to
Arms,* Pauline gave birth to the first of their two sons; as he
revised the completed draft, he learned that his father, ill
with diabetes, and depressed by economic reversals, had
committed suicide, using his own father's Civil War revolver.
Twenty years later, in an introduction to an illustrated edition of *A Farewell to Arms,* Hemingway wrote that he recalled "the fine times and the bad times we had in that year,"
but went on to note that he was "living in the book" and
"was happier than I had ever been." [23]

The early thirties were a time of financial success, marital
harmony, and high adventure. These were the years of duck
and elk shooting in Wyoming and Montana, of big-game
hunting in Africa, and of fishing the waters off Key West and
Bimini aboard his custom-built cruiser, the *Pilar.* They were
also the years of the Depression. But to a nation demoralized
by economic disaster, Hemingway seemed more than a Boy
Scout gone berserk. The twenty-three lively but slick articles
about hunting and fishing he wrote for *Esquire* magazine between 1934 and 1936 offered vicarious escape for the urban
victims of a depression.[24] In Hemingway's rugged face and
powerful torso, they discerned the lineaments of a hero in a
time of defeated men; in the clipped rhythms of his under-

stated prose and laconic dialogue a model for demonstrating "grace under pressure." Two non-fiction books published in these years reinforced the image. *Death in the Afternoon* (1932), a homage to the ritual of bullfighting, and *Green Hills of Africa* (1935), an account of a safari, rehearse the tragedy of man and beast but celebrate—almost desperately—the triumphant dignity of human courage.

The early thirties were also years in which Hemingway wrote relatively little fiction. During a comparable period in the twenties, Hemingway had published two novels, thirty-five stories, a parody, and several poems, in addition to a considerable journalistic production. His only major book during the first half of the thirties was *Winner Take Nothing* (1933), a collection of fourteen short stories.[25] In 1936, however, Hemingway published one of his finest stories, "The Snows of Kilimanjaro," in which he has his author hero berate himself for not writing the stories it was "his duty to write of."

From 1937 until the end of World War II, Hemingway, still the artist as adventurer, altered his mien. Beginning with Harry Morgan's dying words in *To Have and Have Not* (1937)—"One man alone ain't got . . . no bloody f——ing chance"—Hemingway and his characters sacrifice their privacy to the collective obligations engendered by world crises. On the surface at least, the Depression and the Spanish Civil War had shattered Hemingway's long-held belief that "anybody is cheating who takes politics as a way out" of the writer's essential task: "to write straight honest prose on human beings." [26] Leftist critics had long ridiculed what they regarded as his hedonistic isolationism and welcomed the change. In fact, Hemingway had not in his fiction swerved to the left, and the road his characters travel is the familiar one —dangerous, lonely, its terminus a dead end. They had re-entered the world because democracy was probably better than Fascism, but though they were among men, they were not of them. The same remained true of Hemingway. Whatever wars he would engage in were to become *his* wars, and he fought them as he always had, on his own terms and for his own reasons.

Early in 1937, Hemingway went to Spain. Officially a correspondent for the North American Newspaper Alliance, he was not an impartial observer. He went into debt to buy ambulances for the Loyalists, attacked Fascism in an address before the Second National Congress of American Writers, helped to prepare the pro-Loyalist film, *The Spanish Earth* (1938), and wrote *The Fifth Column* (1938), his only full-length play, about the conflict. In 1939, at Finca Vigia ("Lookout Farm"), a hilltop house on an estate he had purchased in the outskirts of Havana, Hemingway worked on his major novelistic statement about Fascism, democracy, and the individual, *For Whom the Bell Tolls* (1940).

A few days after the novel appeared, Pauline Pfeiffer divorced him for desertion. Within a week, Hemingway had married his third St. Louis-born wife, Martha Gellhorn, a novelist and journalist to whom he was wed for five years. For the first two years of their marriage, they served together as war correspondents in China, Hemingway filing reports for the now defunct New York newspaper, *PM*. In his dispatches, Hemingway thought a war between Japan, England, and the United States unlikely but not impossible. He added, prophetically, that war would become inevitable if Japan attacked American bases in the Pacific or Southeast Asia.

From 1942 until he was assigned to General Patton's Third Army in 1944 as a civilian correspondent for *Collier's* magazine, Hemingway sailed the *Pilar*—fitted at government expense with communications and demolition equipment—as a Q-boat, an anti-submarine vessel. Although the *Pilar* never encountered a submarine (had it done so, Hemingway's self-imposed orders were to drop grenades and short-fused bombs down the conning tower), Hemingway's reports may have helped the navy to locate and sink several U-boats and he was decorated for his services. In England in 1944, Hemingway flew unscathed on several combat missions with the R.A.F. but suffered head and knee injuries in an automobile accident during a London blackout. Several newspapers printed his obituary, but shortly thereafter, on D-day, at Fox Green Beach in Normandy, Hemingway went ashore to watch the action for several minutes before returning to his landing craft.

Despite his official assignment to General Patton's army, Hemingway attached himself to the Fourth Infantry Division of the First Army [27] and saw action during the liberation of Paris and the Battle of the Bulge. Although his accounts of his own boldness and valor are either exaggerated or distorted,[28] Hemingway did behave more like a soldier than like a correspondent. He served effectively as a scout and an interrogator at a post outside Paris, gathering intelligence for General Leclerc's advancing army. At even greater personal risk, he fought with small arms in a fierce encounter in Huertgen Forest during the German counter-offensive. Military men regarded him more favorably than did his fellow journalists. Perhaps his brashness offended them, or his lavish tales of having liberated the Travellers Club and the Ritz Hotel with a personal band of partisans.[29] But a group of correspondents preferred charges that Hemingway had violated the regulations of the Geneva Convention affecting war correspondents. After a short hearing, Hemingway was exonerated, and later received the Bronze Star.

At the end of the war, Hemingway was forty-six, his image of himself as a battered but unbowed veteran no longer a pencil sketch but a full-scale portrait in somber oils. What remained? By statement and by action, Hemingway indicated his commitment to a fresh start in life and art. During the war years, he had published only his *PM* reports about the Sino-Japanese War and, for *Collier's*, his dispatches from the European theater of operations.[30] Now he spoke about a vast work-in-progress, a novel about war on "Land, Sea, and Air." As if to emphasize his feeling of renewal, Hemingway divorced Martha Gellhorn late in 1945 and in March 1946 returned to Finca Vigia with his fourth and last wife, Mary Welsh, another journalist, this time Minnesota-born.[31]

Across the River and Into the Trees (1950), Hemingway's first novel since 1940, was not the big one readers had been expecting. A year earlier, he had nearly died from erysipelas. Though the actual cause was an infection from a dust-scratched eye, Hemingway later enlivened the commonplace by telling how a bit of gunshot wadding had entered his eye during a duck-shoot near Venice. While hospitalized, he decided instead to write this shorter book. Circumstances rarely alter criticism and the novel suffered a harsh assault. The gentler critics thought it "tired" or were convinced that Hemingway had more to say; the others, who were overwhelmingly predominant, savaged it as a narcissistic self-parody. In his conspicuously autobiographic portrait of Colonel Richard Cantwell, Hemingway dwelled on his inevitable themes—death, loneliness, love, and courage—crystallized from his experiences of the forties. Henceforth, he plunged progressively deeper into his past, as if searching in nostalgia a cure for artistic impotence.[32] The cycle was nearly closed as the artist as adventurer became the adventurer searching once more for his art.

He returned first to the thirties, the venturesome years of big-game hunting and fishing. In 1953, he went to Africa with Mary on safari. This time, his already too often damaged body was nearly destroyed by successive airplane crashes. In the first accident, in which Mary suffered two broken ribs, Hemingway's liver and kidney were ruptured, his lower spine damaged; in the second, the next day, he suffered the worst of a dozen concussions in his lifetime (the craft was ablaze, the airplane door had jammed, and Hemingway butted the door open with his head) and additional internal injuries. Although his luck was starting to run out, it was still running good, and Hemingway enjoyed reading his obituaries as he recuperated in a hospital in Nairobi.[33] He wrote a long account of his African experience, but all that he published was a two-part serial of second-rate journalism for *Look* maga-zine.

Fishing netted a better haul. Drawing upon a sketch he had written of a Cuban fisherman fifteen years earlier for *Es-quire*, Hemingway recouped his literary losses with *The Old Man and the Sea* (1952), which won him the Pulitzer Prize in the same year and probably helped him to win, in 1954, the Nobel Prize in Literature. Now he pressed harder against the stubborn barrier of the past, pushing toward the twenties, when he had savored the ritual of the bullfight. In 1956, after working enthusiastically with Warner Brothers on the film version of *The Old Man and the Sea*, he went to Spain, hoping to translate the rivalry between two famed toreros, Antonio Ordóñez and Luis Dominguín, into another *Death in the Afternoon*. The product was again a two-part serial-ization called "The Dangerous Summer," this time for *Life* magazine (the rest of the manuscript has never been pub-lished), and again pallid, lifeless, almost dull.

There remained Paris, the Paris of the early twenties and his apprenticeship to art. Even before returning from Spain, Hemingway had begun to sift through a trunkload of note-books from those years and to plan what would be, he told his wife in the jargon of *jai alai*, "biography by *remate*, by reflection." Unsettled by Fidel Castro's triumph when they re-turned, the Hemingways left Finca Vigía and moved to a large chalet in Ketchum, Idaho, where Hemingway reworked and polished his sketches. Mary Hemingway found the type-script in a blue box in his room after his death. "He must have considered the book finished except for the editing," she wrote in an article for *The New York Times*. It was published in 1964 as *A Moveable Feast*.

The ardor of writing must have been excruciating for Hem-ingway in 1960. Physically, he had deteriorated, the massive frame shrunken, the face worn and pained. At the Mayo Clinic, the diagnosis was ominous: hypertension as well as the possibility of diabetes (which had afflicted his father) and hemochromatosis, a rare disease that affects vital organs.

Psychically, he was even worse, almost inarticulate, anxious, severely depressed—"an unsure schoolboy," Seymour Betsky and Leslie Fiedler wrote of him after a visit in November 1960 to invite him as a campus speaker at the University of Montana. By the spring of 1961, he had received twenty-five electric-shock treatments to alleviate his depression.[34] He had just returned to Ketchum from the Mayo Clinic after a month's stay when, on the morning of July 2, 1961, he placed the muzzles of a silver-inlaid shotgun in his mouth and pulled both triggers.

In *Islands in the Stream*, Hemingway's wounded hero, possibly dying, tells himself, "Don't worry about it, boy . . . All your life is just pointed toward it" [464]. Certainly the lure of death pervades Hemingway's adventures in life and art. But it is well to remember that Hemingway held passionately to living as well. What he writes about Paris at the end of *A Moveable Feast* is a metaphor he extended to his own life and to the lives of his characters: "Paris was always worth it and you received return for what you brought to it."[35]

2

The World, the Hero,
and the Code

To summarize Hemingway's sense of the world blunts its force. Generalizations about his heroes and the so-called "code" that patterns their lives also risk the flat thud that simplification entails. But some preliminaries are necessary, if only to clarify Hemingway's rather special understanding of the world, his hero, and code. Once the reader has enough basic information about each, he may more readily appreciate how they interact dramatically and at last cohere to shape Hemingway's essential vision.

Asked once to comment about contemporary themes, Hemingway snapped, "That is a lot of deletion." The themes have always been there, he added—the salient ones: "love, lack of it, death and its occasional temporary avoidance which we describe as life . . ." [1] Only death remains unequivocated in that phrase, as it should, for death, along with its natural ally, violence, is the single reality that most comprehensively expresses Hemingway's sense of the world. The untitled vignettes of his early work, *in our time*, trace the grim image of man as Hemingway observed him at home and abroad— killing or being killed. The subject range is specialized: war, revolution, murder, execution, bullfighting; the outlook a

mordantly ironic echo of *The Book of Common Prayer*—
"Give peace in our time, O Lord." Little occurred in the next
thirty years to compel Hemingway to expand his range. The
world spawned its terrors as before, and there was nothing
new for the sun to rise upon. When men occasionally failed
to destroy one another, nature leaped into the breach: the bi-
ological trap springs on Catherine Barkley in *A Farewell to
Arms* and Harry in "The Snows of Kilimanjaro"; the sharks
destroy the marlin in *The Old Man and the Sea*.

The unalterable, objective fact of physical destruction scars
the surface of Hemingway's world. As Malcolm Cowley has
said, no other writer of our time has presented "such a profu-
sion of corpses . . . so many suffering animals . . ."[2] Yet the
real terror of Hemingway's world lies beneath that surface,
where the agony of the spirit is as profound as that of the
flesh. The semi-literate wife in "One Reader Writes" ad-
dresses a pitiable letter to a doctor whose picture she has
seen in the newspaper, asking whether she will ever be able
to live again with her husband, an ex-serviceman under treatment for "sifilus." In "Homage to Switzerland," divorce and
suicide engage the thoughts of the characters. In "God Rest
You Merry, Gentlemen," a sixteen-year-old boy mutilates himself on Christmas Day to stop his lustful thoughts. William
Campbell, the drug addict in "A Pursuit Race," refuses to
come out from under his bedsheet, too terrified to face whatever unnamed reality terrifies him.

Hemingway is not—despite the insistence of several critics
—a naturalist coolly analyzing the causality of disaster.[3] A
lyric rather than a scientific impulse underlies Hemingway's
documentation, and it is the always nascent *feel* of terror and
anxiety that his imagination projects. Death is a fact, but it is
also a metaphor for the hostile implacability of the universe
toward living and loving. To die in Hemingway's world is
certain; to live and love are at best provisional. "The world
breaks every one," Hemingway wrote in *A Farewell to Arms,*
"and afterward many are strong at the broken places. But
those that will not break it kills. It kills the very good and

the very gentle and the very brave impartially" [258–59]. In *Death in the Afternoon*, he tells the Old Lady that a monogamous bull dies harder than his polygamous fellows, and adds that "all stories of monogamy end in death, and your man who is monogamous while he lives happily, dies in the most lonely fashion . . . If two people love each other, there can be no happy end to it" [122].

Although happy endings are rare in Hemingway's world— even the humor is generally black [4]—courage and endurance are not. His central characters, though bound by death, do not easily surrender their passion for life. For some, there is only desire, spasm, then shadow. After Liz Coates, the hired country girl in "Up in Michigan," loses her virginity, she is "cold and miserable and everything felt gone." Others are more knowing and battle against the darkness that threatens to consume them. Young men like Jake Barnes in *The Sun Also Rises* and Frederic Henry in *A Farewell to Arms,* and older men like Santiago in *The Old Man and the Sea* and the waiter in "A Clean, Well-Lighted Place," acknowledge *nada* ("nothingness") but abhor it and struggle ceaselessly against the void. That contest dramatizes Hemingway's sense of his world and helps to define his heroes.

As Philip Young and Earl Rovit have convincingly demonstrated, two kinds of hero inhabit Hemingway's world.[5] Here they are called "apprentice" and "exemplar." In most of Hemingway's fiction, the apprentice and exemplary heroes are discriminated, their lineaments sharply differentiated. Sometimes—especially in the later work—the features that distinguish each type overlap and blend. Both types of hero try to order their world. But the exemplar has already suffered and subdued many of the afflictions that still await the apprentice: insomnia and a fear of the dark; passivity and dependence (especially on liquor and sex); superstition and a yearning for religion; an inability to stop thinking. Skilled, professional, and charismatic, the exemplar is a necessary presence for the apprentice, whose rite of passage must continue. As a character in fiction, however, the exemplar is more often a static figure, less affecting, and less interesting dramatically and psychologically.

Nick Adams is Hemingway's earliest and most fully developed study of an apprentice, and the stories of his progress from childhood to manhood are a blueprint of an apprentice's initiatory trials. As a child, Nick registers experience but cannot effectively react to it. Instead, as in "Indian Camp," he rationalizes violence (here the agonies of birth and death by suicide) with a defensive conviction of his own immortality. As an adolescent, Nick no longer tries to explain away violence and evil. He simply runs. What comes through to the reader of "The Battler," "The Light of the World," and "The Killers" is that Nick cannot yet cope with brutality and inhumanity.

Fear and flight still attend Nick after he returns wounded from war. But he has now begun consciously to seek therapeutic experiences and to identify and avoid whatever reawakens terror. In one of Hemingway's finest stories, "Big Two-Hearted River," a complex system of covert emotional checks and balances sustains Nick's fragile self-control. Like Hemingway after the war, Nick travels alone to the north Michigan woods. He feels happy because he has "left everything behind, the need for thinking, the need to write . . . It was all back of him." Nick fixes his attention upon the natural scene, and nature provides therapy—it is a "good" place. But Nick rejects the prospect of fishing downstream in the swamp where the big trout swim. Fishing, there, he thinks, "would be a tragic adventure." The swamp is not a "good" place where one feels secure from memory and thought, and Nick still lacks the emotional stamina to abide "bad" places.

Nick is but the first in a long line of apprentices that includes Jake Barnes of *The Sun Also Rises*, Frederic Henry of *A Farewell to Arms*, and Robert Jordan of *For Whom the Bell Tolls*. None of them finds any place wholly "good." Their psychic wounds never fully heal and they never entirely master the art of living with them. Despite their efforts at control, they are obliquely passive: life affects them more than they affect it. Often they seek release through "opiates." Drinking is the "giant-killer," says Mr. Frazer, the insomniac writer convalescing from an automobile accident in "The Gambler, the Nun, and the Radio," a "sovereign opium of the people." Religion, gambling, music, patriotism, education—these too serve, but drinking and sex relieve the pain most effectively, if only temporarily. The aftermath of love lingers, always an ache, whether of frustration, disillusion, or death. But for a brief time, loving isolates the apprentice from society and insulates him from the world. "So if you love this girl as much as you say you do," Robert Jordan reflects, "you had better love her very hard and make up in intensity what the relation will lack in duration and continuity" [168]. The lovers never doubt that death will at last claim them, and it does. But in their idyllic hours together, they create a significant, almost spiritual order of their own.

In *Death in the Afternoon*, Hemingway wrote, "I know only that what is moral is what you feel good after and what is immoral is what you feel bad after" [4]. This is the moral law that operates in most of the love affairs Hemingway describes.[6] Its source is inward, its divinity man, and it sanctions sensibility as well as hedonism. Catherine Barkley in *A Farewell to Arms* feels "married privately," arguing that "You can't be ashamed of something if you're only happy and proud of it." In *For Whom the Bell Tolls*, Robert Jordan and Maria agree that they are "as good as married." Brett Ashley, on the other hand, abandons her young bullfighter in *The Sun Also Rises* because she feels "rotten" about corrupting him and "rather good deciding not to be a bitch . . . It's sort of what we have instead of God" [245].

At best, then, the apprentice attains a working defense that yields moments of pleasure and a functional accommodation to death, loneliness, and *nada*. The alternative is far less tolerable: a surrender to dissolution, whether by the slow grinding of the mills of convention or by one's own hand. Though suicide haunts some of Hemingway's apprentices, only one ever succumbed—the author himself. The others strive toward the life style of the exemplar, who, despite his physical or psychic wounds, has learned how to live in a world in which all victories are Pyrrhic. What matters to the exemplar is the quality of courage with which he faces down death and *nada*. Although the rules that guide the exemplar's behavior are unwritten, they are known, understood, and respected by exemplary and apprentice hero alike. Only the exemplar fulfills the rules in practice as well as intention—rules which, if compiled, would become the "style sheet" or manual of conduct commonly known as the Hemingway "code."

Manuel Garcia, the sick, aging bullfighter in "The Undefeated," is one example of an exemplar living according to the code. Garcia knows the bulls, both what he can do to them and what they can do to him. That knowledge and skill in applying it enable him to perform "the necessary measures without thought. If he thought about it he would be gone" [358]. In the arena, however, Garcia fights badly, draws boos from the crowd, and is gored. Refusing aid, Garcia fights on —drawing wholly from his resources of instinct and pride— and kills the bull before he is carried to the infirmary. He is "undefeated" less because he has killed a bull than because he has won a victory over the public and physical humiliation that might have deprived his life of meaning.[7]

Thus the code does not ask that a hero be fearless or entertain illusions about refuge or escape. But it insists that he discipline and control his dread and, above all, that he behave with unobtrusive though unmistakable dignity. "Don't think about it" (and, by corollary, "Don't talk about it") is its formal injunction to exemplar and apprentice alike. Yet the code is neither mindless nor thoughtless, only resolute in its conviction that action and feeling have greater utility than reason. And it suggests that, like Garcia, a hero have *cojones*.

Though not all exemplary heroes are so attractive as Garcia, they share with him a commitment to the code that assures them honor, dignity, even a quiet grandeur. Cayetano Ruiz, the wounded Mexican gambler in "The Gambler, the Nun, and the Radio," has no "opiates," neither the nun's religion nor Mr. Frazer's liquor or radio, to ease his pain. But he steadfastly refuses to complain about his suffering or to identify the man who shot him for cheating at cards. In "Fifty Grand," a nasty story of an attempted double-cross during an already fixed fight, \the code demands that the exemplar observe to some extent the ritualistic rules of good sportsmanship—even though the game is crooked.\Jack Brennan, a worn-out champion certain he will lose, bets against himself. But when he is deliberately fouled, he refuses to quit. Instead, he fouls Walcott, the challenger, twice in return, losing his championship but winning his "fifty grand." In part, Brennan's motive is simply money: "It's funny how fast you can think when it means that much money" [424]. But the code impels him too. He must honor even a dishonorable agreement.

The courage demanded by the code, then, is something more than a thing unto itself. The code asks of a man that he try to impose meaning where none seems possible, that he try in every gesture he makes to impress his will on the raw material of life.\ Nowhere does Hemingway dramatize this effort more economically or more poignantly than in "A Clean, Well-Lighted Place." The plot is negligible: a deaf old widower sits until late drinking at a Spanish café while two waiters—one young, inconsiderate, eager to get home to his wife; the other older, more compassionate—discuss him. When he leaves, the older waiter stops at a *bodega* (where one must stand while drinking), thinks about the old man's plight and his own, drinks a cup of coffee, and returns home alone to bed and sleeplessness.

Although, as Philip Young writes, the story "involves neither hero nor code," its poetic vision of despair—perhaps the darkest Hemingway ever limned—encompasses all men of sensibility who, like the older waiter and the widowed old man, "need a light for the night." Lacking both the sensibility and the need, the confident, impatient young waiter cruelly wishes that the old man had succeeded in his suicide attempt a week earlier. The young waiter may never achieve sensibility, but as Hemingway shadows forth the world, he will surely know the need. The other two men grope for whatever illuminates the darkness and fills at least some corner of the void. What the old man has is cleanliness and bearing: he drinks without spilling and walks "unsteadily but with dignity." Kindness toward those who share the darkness helps the older waiter temporarily to order his world. He can keep the light on a little longer at the café for those who, like himself, "do not want to go to bed."

But for all of them the respite is always temporary—the café most close, the lights must be turned out—and emptiness rushes in again. "It was all a nothing," the older waiter muses, "and a man was nothing too." He begins a bitter parody of the Lord's Prayer: "Our nada who art in nada . . . deliver us from nada"—but aware that there is no deliverance, he interrupts himself and concludes his prayer with a tart variation of Hail Mary: "Hail nothing full of nothing, nothing is with thee."

"A Clean, Well-Lighted Place" is a superb story and a somber paradigm of the world in which Hemingway's heroes must learn to apply the code. Apprentice and exemplar resemble the older waiter and the old man insofar as all are minor men trapped in a major catastrophe. But unlike the equally lonely and isolated heroes of many novels of the later twentieth century, Hemingway's hero rejects attitudes of ignominy and abasement. Parts of a world are salvageable. A man knows when he does his work well, and earns pleasure and dignity from the knowing and the doing. The feel of a line against the palm, of a hand trailing in water, of pine needles against the cheek; the smell of burnt powder; and the sight of the red mud in the bull ring, or even of an electric light in a clean café—these too form a bulwark against nothingness because they are concrete and immediate, not abstract or eternal like the words Hemingway cites with abhorrence in *A Farewell to Arms: glory, hallow,* and *sacred.* To risk more—love, for example—invites disaster, but the risk is often worth taking, the joys to be savored, the agony to be endured with the courage and dignity that demonstrate "grace under pressure."

Many readers complain about Hemingway's world view, his heroes, and his code.[8] His world, they say, is too grim and too exclusive, ignoring familiar social contexts—family, nation, money, a sense of the past. His hero, Wyndham Lewis wrote, is a "dull-witted, bovine, monosyllabic simpleton." And the morality of the code, Delmore Schwartz argued, holds only "for wartime, for sport, for drinking, and for expatriates."[9] The charge that Hemingway sees the world darkly is fairly stated and it is also fair that we should complain about that world. But, as Philip Young writes, "we should be hard pressed to prove that it is not the one we inhabit." As Hemingway documents his sense of the world, wartime is all the time, the sport is killing or violence, and everyman—because he is spiritually homeless—is an expatriate. Small wonder that he drinks. The great wonder is that he still hungers for life and is capable on so many occasions of tenderness and humaneness, and of the nobility of spirit that animates his tragedy and informs his vision.

3
Style

The true center of Hemingway's literary style—like that of his heroes' life style—is discipline. When Hemingway wishes to control his response to the gap between the world as it is and as he would wish it to be, his expressive mode is often irony.[1] Or, exercising like restraint, he draws upon understated imagery and metaphor to achieve what Harry Levin calls "the authenticity of his lyric cry." Hemingway's imitators capture only his tense sentence rhythms, simple diction, and generally lean expression. What they miss is the rigor that unites style with vision and mood. Unfortunately, Hemingway lapses too. When he does, the stylistic results are disastrous: distance and control dissolve; the tang of irony fades into melodrama or self-pity or sentimentality; and language and lyricism sour. At such times, no parodist can match Hemingway's catastrophic abuse of his own manner.[2] But when, especially in his early work and often in the later, he assumes firm command of the interplay between style and substance, he ranks among the masters.

Many details of Hemingway's style will be considered in the chapters to come. In this brief overview, the purpose is to describe the origins of that style and to point out its characteristics. To gain the effects he wanted and the control he needed, Hemingway had to create whole a style already available to him in many of its parts. Besides what he had learned from his novitiate as a journalist, he absorbed much from already established literary mentors. From Ring Lardner he learned—as early as high school—how to affect a flippant, ironic prose that barely concealed real indignation.[3] Sherwood Anderson's loosely episodic structure and free-flowing vernacular speech rhythms influenced him too, especially in early pieces like "My Old Man." But Anderson's carelessness with words and his bent toward sentimentality were intolerable to an aspiring stylist whose apprentice years as a journalist had already taught him the need for greater rigor. Ezra Pound's advocacy of simplicity, precision, concreteness, and freshness in language was not lost on him either, and he acknowledged Pound as "the man who taught me to distrust adjectives."

"Ezra [Pound] was right half the time," Hemingway once remarked, "and when he was wrong, he was so wrong you were never in any doubt about it. Gertrude was always right."[4] Gertrude Stein was a better teacher, who, Hemingway wrote, "discovered many truths about rhythms and the uses of words in repetition that were valid and valuable."[5] During his regular visits to her salon in Paris, Hemingway absorbed many other truths he would soon incorporate into his own practice: the need for clarity ("so the reader will see it too," as she wrote later in Lectures in America, "and have the same feeling that you had"); the importance of description as explanation and of writing prose that communicates "the emotion of reality."

To his mentors' injunctions, Hemingway added one of his own—that a writer must maintain an "absolute conscience . . . to prevent faking." Faking does not mean, Hemingway explains in Death in the Afternoon, "breaking so-called rules of syntax or grammar to make an effect which can be obtained in no other way" [54]. But when a writer mystifies "where there is no mystery" or injects "a false epic quality" into ordinary prose, he fakes. Fakers, Hemingway insists, are bad writers and "all bad writers are in love with the epic."[6]

Lacking a world whose established and accepted values justified an epic, Hemingway, as Archibald MacLeish said, "whittled a style for his time." It is a conspicuously American style, stressing naturalness of language, syntax that fragments rather than unifies his predominantly simple sentences, and a persistent use of repetition to force the parts into a coherent whole. These characteristics—extraordinarily akin to the mechanics of poetry—are not original with Hemingway. As Richard Bridgman points out, they may be found in the writing of Henry James and Mark Twain. Lardner, Anderson, and Stein worked along similar lines, all seeking a way to link American language with American experience. "To Hemingway," Bridgman writes, "fell the task of joining the two lines leading from Henry James and Mark Twain." [7]

Hemingway's success owes in part to his genius as a consciously disciplined stylist. Nearly as much owes to his vision of man as a creature at bay, haunted by the bogy of violence and the specter of destruction. To delineate such a man, a leisurely, contemplative prose would have been inappropriate. Pressing hard, one upon the other, Hemingway's conjunction-bound simple sentences declare flux and crisis. The static luxury of reflective or introspective discourse would seem an intolerable extravagance when reality demands mobility. During the retreat from Caporetto, Frederic Henry is arrested and made to stand with others awaiting interrogation: "We stood in the rain and were taken out one at a time to be questioned and shot. So far they had shot every one they had questioned. The questioners had that beautiful detachment and devotion to stern justice of men dealing in death without being in any danger of it. They were questioning a full colonel of a line regiment. Three more officers had just been put in with us" [233]. The staccato rhythm increases consciousness of tension, as does the nervous narrative eye darting about. Thinking is minimal, limited to an ironic comment about the "beautiful detachment" of the interrogators. Strain, the dominant motif of the passage, accretes through the incremental, fugal rhythms and crucial words (questioned, questioners, questioning) that afford no relief. Only when Henry breaks away does the freer sentence pattern echo his release: "I looked at the carabinieri. They were looking at the newcomers. The others were looking at the colonel. *I ducked down, pushed between two men, and ran for the river, my head down.* I tripped at the edge and went in with a splash" (italics added).

The constants in Hemingway's style function, then, to express a vision of experience and also to control his hero's emotional response (as well as his own) to that experience. If, as critics have observed, Hemingway's prose is lyric rather than dramatic, it is a reticent, not a confessional lyricism. Even when he narrates from the perspective of the first person, we are privy to what the hero sees and does, rarely to a direct statement of what he feels. In "Big Two-Hearted River," Nick's experience while fishing near the swamp evokes terror. What Hemingway describes, however, is not an emotion—*terror* is never mentioned—but its objective correlatives as Nick and the reader see them: "In the swamp the banks were bare, the big cedars came together overhead, the sun did not come through, except in patches; in the fast deep water, in the half light, the fishing would be tragic. In the swamp fishing was a tragic adventure" [329]. Objective, external, the description relies for its impact upon the controlled release of Nick's response to pure visual stimuli. Not until the rather mysterious word *tragic* does emotion implode upon Nick's and the reader's consciousness.

Why fishing in the swamp might be tragic, Nick does not explain. Hemingway says only, "Nick did not want it. He did not want to go down the stream any further today." As Daniel Fuchs observes in another context, the "docility of the language intensifies the panic."[8] Terror and panic are the life stuff Hemingway writes about here and nearly everywhere in his fiction. Since his apprentice and exemplary heroes alike must learn not to confess inward strife, Hemingway needed a

style compatible with the "code." Reticence is the hallmark of
that style, but a reticence so artful it nearly shouts through silence a testimony of inward torment.

When there is neither tension nor torment, just the joy of
companionship and nature, for example, the sentences open
and expand to reflect wonder and delight. Thus, as Jake
Barnes and Bill Gorton journey by bus to their fishing site,
they drive through a forest of "cork oaks, and the sun came
through the trees in patches, and there were cattle grazing
back in the trees. We went through the forest and the road
came out and turned along a rise of land, and out ahead of us
was a rolling green plain, with dark mountains beyond it . . .
The green plain stretched off. It was cut by fences and the
white of the road showed through the trunks of a double line
of trees that cross the plain toward the north. As we came to
the edge of the rise we saw the red roofs and white houses of
Burguete ahead strung out on the plain, and away off on the
shoulder of the first dark mountain was the gray metal-
sheathed roof of the monastery of Roncesvalles" [108]. Yet,
here too, Hemingway avoids *explaining* that Jake and Bill are
happy, relying instead upon the grace of rhythm and the
bright concreteness of the setting to convey the pleasurable
feeling the men share.

Though he suppresses whatever need not be stated, Hemingway's style is not evasive. He strips away whatever ob-
scures the object that evokes feeling. No euphemisms gloss
the harsh, violent facts of reality. Nor, at his best, does he
embellish them with rhetorical flourishes or elaborate abstractions.[9] By telling without comment and telling in the vernacular, Hemingway avoids direct statement about emotion
without obscuring the intensity of the emotion. Like Robert
Frost, who considered himself a synecdochist, Hemingway
also believed, as he wrote in *Death in the Afternoon*, that
"any part you make will represent the whole if it's made
truly." His adjectives and adverbs, for example, are sparse
and relatively unspecific. What delights is usually *fine, swell,
lovely, very nice,* or *very good;* what appalls may be *rotten* or

damned awful. That they are trite in no way renders them impersonal or ineffectual. Even when trite, the vernacular may suggest deeply felt emotion without wholly revealing all that is felt. For similar reasons, Hemingway curbs the force and diversity of his verbs. Variants of *to be* serve as his dominant form, usually introduced by an expletive: "there is," "there were." Frequently, gerunds replace the anticipated verbs: "The crowd shouted all the time . . . keeping up *whistling* and *yelling*" (italics added), as if to rein the emotive surge of "shouted, whistled, and yelled." It is the noun, as Harry Levin points out, that Hemingway emphasizes because nouns "come closest to things. Stringing them along by means of conjunctions, he approximates the actual flow of experience." [10] As Hemingway's heroes select experience to order chaos, so Hemingway selects his sentence rhythms and parts of speech to mirror reality and, so far as possible, to control its impact upon the spirit.

Because Hemingway's characters dare not fully release their feelings, their unemphatic language communicates feeling without having to define it too explicitly. Subjectivity is never eliminated, only disciplined, controlled. Even when reality is pleasurable rather than miserable, Hemingway imposes restrictions upon the expression of delight. In "Cross-Country Snow," for example, he captures in a single sentence the grace and excitement of a skier's swift descent: "George was coming down in telemark position, kneeling; one leg forward and bent, the other trailing; his sticks hanging like some insect's thin legs, kicking up puffs of snow as they touched the surface and finally the whole kneeling, trailing figure coming around in a beautiful right curve, crouching, the legs shot forward and back, the body leaning out against the swing, the sticks accenting the curve like points of light, all in a wild cloud of snow" [282]. Exhilaration inheres in the rhythm of the sentence, the hesitant cadences at the start of the run marked off by semicolons, the tempo then increasing until sight and motion are abruptly arrested in the swirling last phrase. Except for an occasional image, the bracing

emotional impact is achieved without decoration. The visceral facts *are* the feeling. But when a friend tries to share
with George the thrill of skiing by analyzing it, George
grunts, "Huh . . . It's too swell to talk about."

In Hemingway's dialogue as in his narrative prose, the testimony of feeling is conspicuously minimal. Speech tags are
cut to "he said," "she said," or omitted altogether. To talk
about an emotion is bad form. Echoing George, Wilson, the
hunting guide, admonishes Francis Macomber against dis-
cussing his "feeling of happiness" after Macomber kills a buffalo: "Doesn't do to talk too much about all this. Talk the
whole thing away. No pleasure in anything if you mouth it
up too much." When Jake Barnes protests his love for Brett
Ashley in *The Sun Also Rises*, she says, "Let's not talk. Talking's all bilge."

For Hemingway, as for Mark Twain, the brusque understatement of everyday speech (which may be expressed in
Hemingway as American or Spanish or Italian or even English) is the most efficient way to communicate emotional
truth. "I can lie so much easier in English, it's pitiful," says
Philip Rawlings, the hero of *The Fifth Column*. And those
who lie in Hemingway's fiction, whether to themselves or to
others, often adopt the mannerisms of traditional literary
speech. Contrast, for example, the plausible but imperfect
concern of the lover in "Hills Like White Elephants" with the
simple, though bitter, honesty of the young woman about to
have an abortion:

"I don't want you to do anything that you don't want to
do—"

"Nor that isn't good for me," she said. "I know. Could we
have another beer?"

"All right. But you've got to realize—"

"I realize," the girl said. "Can't we maybe stop talking?"

. . .

"You've got to realize," he said, "that I don't want you to
do it if you don't want to. I'm perfectly willing to go through
with it if it means anything to you."

. . .

"Would you do something for me right now?"

"I'd do anything for you."

"Would you please please please please please please please
stop talking." [374–75]

At its furthest reach, as Richard Bridgman has observed,
Hemingway's dialogue "dwindled down to silence, the other
side of speech." [11] In "The Three-Day Blow," Nick Adams's
friend Bill consoles him about the end of Nick's adolescent affair. After each of Bill's comments, Hemingway notes Nick's
responses, in this sequence: "Nick said nothing" (repeated);
"'Sure,' said Nick"; "'Yes,' said Nick"; "Nick nodded"; "Nick
sat quiet"; "Nick said nothing." Silence is the only response
several of Hemingway's characters can make when they have
been shocked into psychic disorientation, whether by love or
by violence (as in "The Battler") or by the demands of a society whose values they reject (as in "Soldier's Home").
Among contemporary writers of the "apocalyptic" school
(Samuel Beckett, William Burroughs, *et al.*), silence is a
wordless metaphor expressing outrage against the chaos of
the universe and the isolation of the individual. The silences
and near-silences of Hemingway's apprentice and exemplary
heroes herald this protest.

Through reticence and "silence," Hemingway worked toward what he calls in *Green Hills of Africa* "a prose that has
never been written," a prose "much more difficult than poetry." At best his devices never usurp attention but help to
sharpen the focus upon a lyrical, emotional awareness of experience. When Ole Andreson turns to the wall in "The Killers," for example, that familiar symbol of an irresistible obsta-
cle subtly adds to the total image of terror without becoming
an effect for its own sake. Some critics have hunted Hemingway's symbols with unlicensed fervor, finding beasts even
where there is no jungle.[12] Not that there are no objects that
might qualify as symbols. These are not at all hard to find,
some of them drawn from nature: rain (*A Farewell to Arms*)
and snow (*A Farewell to Arms*, "Alpine Idyll," "The Snows of
Kilimanjaro," *For Whom the Bell Tolls*, and several others); a

swamp ("Big Two-Hearted River"); a leopard and a hyena ("The Snows of Kilimanjaro"). Or the item may be a wound (*The Sun Also Rises*), a *coleta*, the bullfighter's pigtail ("The Undefeated"), a bridge (*For Whom the Bell Tolls*), or even short as opposed to long hair on women. But Hemingway does not use symbols like a "symbolist."Rather than artificially impose intellectual significance from without, he allows his meaning to emerge from within. Hemingway never practiced, as Bern Oldsey writes, "the symbolic or mythic overlay. His images and symbols are organic, interior, naturalistic; almost always they come out of the fictional context." [13] Within that framework, Hemingway's symbols resist arbitrary meaning: rain in *A Farewell to Arms* is neither death nor rebirth; snow in "The Snows of Kilimanjaro" and *For Whom the Bell Tolls* is neither purity nor terror—except as each is a metaphor of the ambiguity inherent in the literary context Hemingway describes. Only rarely does Hemingway force a didactic relationship between symbol and meaning. When he does, as when Colonel Cantwell's young mistress in *Across the River and Into the Trees* imagines her lover's mutilated hand to be that of Christ, the result is ludicrous because it imposes likeness where none exists. Santiago's scarred palms in *The Old Man and the Sea*, on the contrary, by suggesting without insisting, add dimension to Hemingway's portrait.

"No good book has ever been written that has in it symbols arrived at beforehand and stuck in," Hemingway told a friend.[14] Though Hemingway avoided sticking symbols in, he knew, as Oldsey says, how to draw them out and shape them to serve the emotions rather than the mind. His allusive titles, for example (*The Sun Also Rises, A Farewell to Arms, For Whom the Bell Tolls*, and the like—drawn from biblical and literary sources), are not merely symbolic clues to transparent meaning. They function, rather, as ironic comments on complex reality, their multiple overtones most effective when heard together with all the harmonies and dissonances that sound throughout the entire work.

Isolated, any of Hemingway's stylistic devices fails. Were

his short sentences conveniently separable from their context, they would deserve no better than the witty popular phrases so often used to describe them—"Stein-stutter," and "crisis in a cable." So too with his dialogue, which is perhaps why he fares so badly on the screen, where he has been represented almost exclusively by his dialogue—and it sounds absurdly artificial. But on the page, where his dialogue has a unique visual authenticity that makes the words look as if they sound, the speech pattern is but one among many facets of Hemingway's expression that fuse to sustain tension and stretch meaning. When he succeeds as a stylist, Hemingway interweaves and crosspatches each strand until it is discernible but not obtrusive. The effect is poetic rather than didactic, even though one feels the near presence of the moralist and the ironist.

Hemingway's stylistic force is more powerful when it is concentrated. The vignettes of *in our time*, or a masterpiece like "A Clean, Well-Lighted Place," exemplify his ability to freeze into permanence fleeting moments of poetic insight, whether into landscape, loneliness, or an act of "grace under pressure." These works are extreme examples of compression. Short stories that range from a dozen pages to thirty ("The Undefeated," "The Light of the World," "Big Two-Hearted River," and "The Snows of Kilimanjaro"), and short novels like *The Sun Also Rises* and *The Old Man and the Sea* (the latter really a novella), afford Hemingway the most comfortable boundaries within which he can control his stylistic resources and match them with his vision. When he strays too ____ limits (especially when he superimposes ____ social or metaphysi- ____ ipline

cally flawed, though ____ sages easily separated as memorable short stories.

Some critics argue, as Mark Spilka does, that Hemingway's style "will not accommodate deep or complex inner conflict," that its very economy derives from "fear of deep affective damage." [15] William Faulkner voiced the complaint of others when, admitting that Hemingway "has done consistently probably the most solid work of all of us," [16] he added that Hemingway ultimately failed because he avoided experimentation and settled for what he early learned to do well. Both charges merit some respect. Hemingway's world lacks the diversity and density of Yoknapatawpha; his characters and creatures are neither Ahabs nor Moby Dicks; and his style does not alter significantly over the years. But Hemingway's delineation of *nada* and his portraits of those who suffer it cannot be dismissed as evasive or superficial. The wasteland is at once myth and reality, and Hemingway, who experienced its reality as a man, as an artist forged a supple and powerful style to express it as a myth. When he is in command of all his resources, he is unrivaled, in Saul Bellow's just phrase, as "the poet of the crippled state."

PART TWO

4

"Three Stories"

AND

in our time

The three stories published in Hemingway's first book along with his ten poems owe much to Sherwood Anderson and Gertrude Stein. Their tutelage is sufficiently apparent to suggest that Hemingway had not yet wholly freed himself of shaping influences. But evidence also abounds that originality lay near at hand.

His clearest debt is stylistic. Simplicity of diction and colloquial speech in each of the stories reflect the precept and practice of both Anderson and Gertrude Stein. Twice in "Up in Michigan," he consciously imitates the device of repetition Miss Stein had used in *Three Lives* to stress and clarify emotion. In a single paragraph, he uses *liked* eight times to reveal Liz Coates's growing desire for Jim Gilmore, then sums all the emotion in the closing sentence with a sudden shift to the gerund: "Liking that made her feel funny." The previous paragraph, as Charles Fenton observes, foreshadows the harsh resolution with its notation that Jim *"liked* her face because it was so jolly but he never thought about her." Elsewhere in the story, with less effect, he rings changes on *think, thought,* and *thinking*. From Gertrude Stein too, Hemingway was still learning to look at landscape like Cézanne: the river in "Out of Season" is "brown and muddy. Off on the right there was a dump heap"; and Horton's Bay in "Up in Michigan" is "blue and bright and usually whitecaps on the lake beyond the point . . ." Anderson's use of a boy's point of view in "I Want to Know Why" seems to have influenced Hemingway in "My Old Man," though he denied it.[1] And the loose, episodic structure of the story is similarly reminiscent of Anderson's narrative method.

The essentials of loneliness, cruelty, tenderness pervasive in Anderson's tales are here too and, as both Oscar Cargill and Philip Young have noted of "Out of Season," so is the ominous sense of deadness and flatness Fitzgerald evoked while narrating the final stages of a broken marriage or love affair. But though Hemingway borrows, he is not slavishly imitative. Many of his subjects are his own. Introduced here for the first time are materials he would return to throughout his career. Sports and the out-of-doors motifs, for example, are figured in the hunting of "Up in Michigan," fishing in "Out of Season," and horse racing in "My Old Man." The physical violence that textures his major works roughs the surface of two of these early stories as well: horse and jockey are killed in "My Old Man"; Liz Coates is more nearly raped than seduced in "Up in Michigan." Psychic pain is even more harsh for the jockey's son when he learns that the dead father he adored had been notoriously corrupt: "Seems like when they get started they don't leave a guy nothing." The boy is Hemingway's first apprentice hero, the ancestor of Nick Adams and, like Nick, tells his own story. Liz Coates, the boy's feminine counterpart and ancestress of Hemingway's passive women, also learns the pain of aftermath when "everything felt gone." The ineffectual, drained husband of "Out of Season" knows that he will probably not fish on the morrow, for his marriage as well as trout fishing has gone "out of season." If he feels "rotten" (the first use of that moral epithet too) after an undescribed quarrel with his wife, Tiny, bettering their relationship is unlikely. That *ur*-bitch character seems to have ample reserves of sallies like the one she launches when her husband lamely continues their illegal fishing expedition: "Of course you haven't the guts to just go back."

These stories, then, are apprentice, not amateur work. "My Old Man" was included in *The Best Stories of 1923* and lingers as a standard choice among anthologists, though it does not truly represent Hemingway's mature narrative patterns. "Up in Michigan," his first published story, shows more of those patterns in its taut narrative tracing of a dark vision. Its only real flaw, as Edmund Wilson pointed out in a contemporary review, is that it left its "rude and primitive people . . . rather shadowy." [2] The same obscureness mars his portraits of the sophisticated couple in the tightly written "Out of Season," but the drunken, uncomprehending guide, Peduzzi, comes through sharp and definite. "I was trying to write then," Hemingway recalled some years later in *Death in the Afternoon*, but ". . . the real thing . . . was beyond me and I was working very hard to get it" [2]. Even as he readied "Three Stories and Ten Poems" for the press, Hemingway was writing the "real thing," the eighteen vignettes published in 1924 as *in our time*,[3] his first unequivocally original work and one of the most original prose works of the decade.

Like the three stories, *in our time* selects subjects destined to be lifelong concerns. To get at the "real thing," he also noted in *Death in the Afternoon*, he had begun "with the simplest things, and one of the simplest things of all and the most fundamental is violent death [2]." Six of the vignettes are about bullfights Hemingway first watched in Madrid after World War I. One (Chapter XII) tells of the goring of a picador's horse, its entrails hanging down and swinging as the picador spurs him on. Another (Chapter II) relates the goring of two matadors and the experience of a third who must battle the remaining five bulls. A third (Chapter XV) reports the crowd's humiliating of a conscientious but incompetent torero, and the others (Chapters XII–XIV) tell of beauty, bravery, and death in the bull ring.

Six more vignettes center upon violence Hemingway saw at first hand or heard about from others during his career as a journalist: the evacuation of the Greeks (Chapter III); the exeution of a half-dozen cabinet ministers, one of them sick with typhoid and sitting in a puddle of water when the volley is fired (Chapter VI); the flight and capture of a cultured young Hungarian Communist refugee (Chapter XI); the palace-bound King of Greece cultivating his garden (Chapter XVIII). And in America, he reports the hanging of a criminal who discomfits his guards by having a bowel movement just as he is about to be hanged (Chapter XVII), and the shooting of two Hungarians by a Chicago policeman who reassures a fellow officer, "They're wops, ain't they. Who the hell is going to make any trouble?" (Chapter IX). The other six vignettes concern World War I, two of them (Chapters IV and V) about "potting" Germans through a wrought-iron grating and as they climb over a garden wall. A drunken French lieutenant (Chapter I) frets that the enemy may spot a kitchen fire though his unit is fifty kilometers from the front; a soldier prays to Jesus during a bombardment (Chapter VIII), but the next night, in bed with a whore, tells nothing of his prayer. A wounded soldier and his nurse in a Milan hospital fall in love and vow to marry after the war when he gets a job back in the States (Chapter X); but during his absence, she gives herself to an Italian major, who abandons her, and the returned soldier gets gonorrhea from a Chicago salesgirl. And a soldier named Nick, shot in the spine (Chapter VII), sits against a wall and tells his comrade that they have made a "separate peace." [4]

Summaries are tiresome, even irritating, when they lack any semblance of narrative pattern. Yet this summary appears without apology, its intention to suggest the apparent discontinuity of *in our time*. In fact, at first glance and superficially, the arbitrary groupings provide more guidance than the text. Each of the vignettes—few longer than a paragraph of 100 to 150 words—seems discrete and, even within its own confines, lacking climax. Traces of Hemingway's heroes and even hints of the "code" may be discerned, but their relevance here is peripheral. Not the hero but his world is what Hemingway attempts to define in *in our time.*

Altering Gertrude Stein's notation that "description is explanation," Tony Tanner suggests that for Hemingway, "description is definition." [5] In most of the vignettes of *in our time,* Hemingway defines the world in a painterly manner, meticulously selecting and arranging pictorial details that register the emotion inherent in each scene. Never explicit, emotion seems almost to surface from within the reader. The eye moves the heart toward horror. Look at Chapter III:

> Minarets stuck up in the rain out of Adrianople across the mud flats. The carts were jammed for thirty miles along the Karagatch road. Water buffalo and cattle were hauling carts through the mud. No end and no beginning. Just carts loaded with everything they owned. The old men and women, soaked through, walked along keeping the cattle moving. The Maritza was running yellow almost up to the bridge. Carts were jammed solid on the bridge with camels bobbing along through them. Greek cavalry herded along the procession. Women and kids were in the carts crouched with mattresses, mirrors, sewing machines, bundles. There was a woman having a kid with a young girl holding a blanket over her and crying. Scared sick looking at it. It rained all through the evacuation. [6]

The structure of the paragraph—though it may not seem so at first glance—is orderly and inevitable: from a distant glimpse of minarets in the rain to a panorama of people and possessions to the climactic scene—the close-up of a terrified girl watching a woman in childbirth; then the eye returns to rain and space. We are never told where to locate the center of emotive force but are led subtly and irreversibly to it by the arrangement of detail, sentence pattern, and diction. The sentences are declarative and short, with three pertinent exceptions. Two sentence fragments occur in sequence but serve slightly different purposes. "No end and no beginning" breaks the rhythm, arresting motion temporarily to allow the reader

to absorb the emotional implications of the scene. "Just carts
. . ." protracts that time lag but also makes a transition from
carts and animals to humanity—"everything *they* owned."
The third sentence fragment—"Scared sick looking at it"—
suspends all motion and turns the eye inward even as it fixes
in awe upon the spectacle of the young girl and the woman.
The strategy of flat statement in the final sentence insulates
the terror as nature's indifference augments man's misery.

Hemingway exercises like control over his diction. Sup-
pressing modifiers, he allows us a chance to discover our own
sentiments. But we are not left wholly free to pursue our own
course. Of four adjectives used, each serves a specific purpose. *Old* delineates the people. *Yellow,* the only color
word in the paragraph, functions variously. The pallor of the
river blends with the drab landscape, its abnormal hue as dis-
tressing and sickly as the setting. Furthermore, the adjective
forces attention upon a sentence deliberately located dead
center in the paragraph, where it effects a transition from the
generalized description of the first half to the concrete details
that follow. Two adjectives are reserved for the dramatic core
of the vignette: the girl is *young* and *sick.* Verbs, as always,
function to direct emotive response but also to avoid possible
misdirection. Thus, the potential exoticism of *minarets* is
snuffed out by the harshness of *stuck.* The gerund, however,
bears the ultimate responsibility for "moving" the reader literally and emotionally. Ten gerunds occur, "one out of every
thirteen words," as Charles Fenton points out, to control
"movement and flow." Four of them cluster about the scene of
the girl and the woman in childbirth: *having, holding, crying,
looking*—a measured progression toward the emotional resolution of Hemingway's earliest handling of the theme of birth
and death.

Though the narrator seems effaced, impersonal, objective,
his lyric impulse dwells just beyond the reader's immediate
consciousness. Even a seemingly obvious intrusion of poetic
effect may pass unnoticed, like the alliteration of "carts
crouched with mattresses, mirrors, sewing machines."

Scarcely aware of the subtle force of art imposed upon him, the reader may shape a response remarkably congruent with Hemingway's purpose.

Most of the vignettes similarly structure visual details into patterns evocative of acute emotional reaction. In Chapter VI, the execution of the cabinet ministers, water, as Earl Rovit writes, is "the objective correlative of the emotion": rain, wet dead leaves, and the puddle of water in which the typhoid-ridden minister sits as he is shot. The hanging of Sam Cardinella (Chapter XVII), on the other hand, has no pervasive objective correlative. It relies for the most part upon impersonal reportage of minutiae: the corridor in which the condemned are hanged is "high and narrow with tiers of cells on either side." Except for the subjective notation that the five condemned men are "very frightened," Hemingway limits himself once more to defining by describing. One man holds his head in his hands; another lies "flat on his cot with a blanket wrapped around his head"; and "they were carrying Sam Cardinella." Somehow, none of the details about the prison or the prisoners finally shatters composure—they fascinate rather than appall. The shudder of revulsion is prompted by fleeting glances at the officials present at the scene. When Sam's sphincter control fails, the guards "were both disgusted." One of them wonders whether a chair will help and is told by "a man in a derby hat" that he had "better get one." The "refinement" of the guards and the officiousness of the "derby hat" contract the reader's peristalsis. But it is the priest's "Be a man, my son," murmured just before he "skipped back onto the scaffolding," that releases the flood of nausea and defines the quality of the experience.

Occasionally, voice rather than vision elicits that effect, a tonality sometimes serving instead of actual speech. Thus, hard-boiled American diction accents Hemingway's grisly report, his first, of a bullfight.[7] Chapter II, about the "kid" who fights five bulls, tells of a matador "rammed wham against the wall," gored but rising "like crazy drunk" and trying "to slug the men carrying him away." The "kid," so tired he "couldn't hardly lift his arm," kills his last bull; as "the crowd hollered," he sat "down in the sand and puked." Lively verbs, slangy modifiers, and bad grammar overlay the exposition with the felt presence of one deeply moved by his experience. Conversely, the dramatic monologues in Chapters IV and V about "potting" Germans stir emotion by denying it. Now the voice is British: [8] "an absolutely perfect barricade . . . simply priceless . . . absolutely topping"; and "We were frightfully put out when . . . we had to fall back." The clichés of understatement dramatize ironically the actual savagery of the speaker who comments that the German soldier, shot as he climbed the garden wall, "looked awfully surprised." So too do those who follow: "We shot them. They all came just like that."

In the last of the vignettes, Hemingway experiments with direct and paraphrased quotation. Again, the voice is impeccably British, but the speaker is King George of Greece. Working in his garden—the Queen "clipping a rose bush"—he is regally and insufferably unaware of his country's tragic plight: "We have good whiskey anyway . . . Of course the great thing in this sort of affair is not to be shot oneself." Harmless in themselves, the king's affectations of speech and attitude symbolize in the context of his country's recent defeat and current internal strife a disastrous lack of national as well as personal identity. At the close of the "jolly" interview, the reporter notes, "Like all Greeks he wanted to go to America." The explicitly contemptuous tone of the paraphrased quotation summarizes Hemingway's view of a collapsed world. If he is more outspoken here than elsewhere in the vignettes, it is because he discerns in the futile figure of the decadent king, as Charles Fenton writes, "the ultimate irony of a contemporary experience." [9]

Such were the "simplest things" Hemingway drew upon as he tried to learn to write. The materials of fiction saturate the vignettes of *in our time*, but Hemingway was not yet ready to dip into them. Analysis of motive and character, consideration of the implications of commitment and accommodation

—these lay just ahead. *in our time* concentrated on rendering surfaces so perspicuous that the subsurface seemed exposed. Though his revelation was of a barbarous world, Hemingway's motive in description was aesthetic more than ethical. He was, "like Goya," as Edmund Wilson observed in the first American review of *in our time*, "concerned first of all with making a fine picture." [10] But as in Goya's paintings and lithographs, the moral force often surpasses the aesthetic intention.

5

Nick Adams,
Master Apprentice

In his final dispatch to *The Toronto Daily Star* about the Greco-Turkish War, cabled late in 1922, Hemingway wrote that "the Thracian evacuation . . . was already beginning to seem unreal. That is the boon of our memories." [1] Ten years later, at the outset of *Death in the Afternoon* as he tells of the fate of the picador's horse, Hemingway recalls how the Greeks, when they abandoned Smyrna, "broke the legs of their baggage and transport animals and shoved them off the quay into the shallow water" [2]. With only minor variations, Hemingway is quoting from his own introduction to the second edition of *In Our Time* (1930). The "boon" of memory had failed to erase. When he alludes to the scene again in *Death in the Afternoon*, the Old Lady reminds him that he is repeating himself. "I know it and I'm sorry," he answers. "Stop interrupting. I won't write about them again. I promise" [135]. A few years later, however, in "The Snows of Kilimanjaro," Harry remembers in his delirium having seen in Constantinople "things he could never think of." And when he gathered his materials for *The First Forty-Nine Stories* in 1938, Hemingway reproduced his introduction as the story "On the Quai at Smyrna." The image of dead Greek babies on the

pier, pack animals in the shallow water, and minarets sticking up in the rain clung stubbornly to Hemingway's imagination. "That was the only time in my life," he says in "On the
Quai at Smyrna," "I got so I dreamed about things." Sixteen
years had passed since he had cabled his final dispatch; still
the "boon" of memory lingered to haunt the man and the artist.

"If he wrote it he could get rid of it. He had gotten rid of
many things by writing them." What sounds like Hemingway
reciting his own sacrament of exorcism is, in fact, Nick Adams's reflection in "Fathers and Sons," the last of the published Nick Adams stories.[2] Thinking back upon his boyhood,
Nick, now thirty-eight and a writer, realizes that "even remembering the earliest times before things had gone badly
was not good remembering" [589]. But he cannot stop the
flow. His initiation into sex with an Indian girl and his father's suicide flood his thoughts as he drives through the
countryside, oblivious of his young son sleeping beside him.
When the boy awakens, his first questions are about Indians
and his grandfather.

At the age of thirty-eight, Nick has erected a substantial if
conventional system of defense. He has married, become a father, and launched a career. Comparison with the garden variety of middle-class American men of his generation ends
there,[3] for Nick never masters the art of holding off the past
so that he can hold on in the present. He cannot at will
thrust aside the memory of his father's death. Even as he assures himself that he can, a vision of the undertaker's "handsome job" leaps before him. Nor can he shun knowing that
Trudy, the Indian girl, "did first what no one has ever done
better."

Nick Adams and Hemingway are not identical twins but
they are intimately related. They share like—sometimes exact
—experiences [4] and recall obsessively whatever has scraped
their sensibilities. They grow rather tougher as they mature
and learn how to guard against the furies. But they can never
quell them. Both the character and his creator are at last

master apprentices, skilled in the trade of living, knowing in its complex minutiae, but not quite able to accomplish the job of survival professionally. Nonetheless, Nick served Hemingway by allowing him distance from the disabling force of his traumatic memories and by shielding him (and us) from the devastating truth that writing it does not really get rid of it. Nick Adams is, in one sense, the first scapegoat led to the abattoir to assure Hemingway's survival.[5] Apart from his biographical function, Nick has his own dimension. In the twelve stories in which he is identified by name, as well as in at least a half-dozen others in which he is recognizable though nameless, the outlines of a *Bildungsroman* may be discerned or, as several critics have titled the scattered sequence, of "The Education of Nick Adams." If *in our time* first defines the world, the Nick Adams stories first define a way to live in it. Most of the stories are narrated externally but the center of consciousness is always Nick. Usually, as might be expected of an apprentice, his role is that of spectator, but behind the physical passivity there is continuous psychic activity as Nick absorbs and assesses experience, clinging to what protects, trying to shuck what threatens.

Nick's father and the Indians appear in the opening story as they do in the last, "Fathers and Sons," forming a frame whose emblem might read 'In the beginning was the end.' What happens in "Indian Camp" is prototypic of the disasters etched on Nick's consciousness during the more than twenty-five years depicted in these stories. "Indian Camp" starts as an idyl (or a rite of passage), father and young son journeying by canoe to an Indian settlement in the forest. In one of the cabins, the boy watches his physician father perform a Caesarean delivery on a squaw—using a jackknife, fishing gut, and no anesthetic. In the bunk above, her husband, driven frantic by her screams, slits his throat.

The boy does not return from the forest "idyl" initiated into manhood. A caul of innocence protects him from more than partially comprehending the tragedy he has witnessed. His questions to his father are sensitive but, predictably, childlike, curious rather than searching: "Do ladies always have such a hard time having babies?" "Is dying hard, Daddy?" His father's answers are wisely brief, honest, and comforting. Yet the hideous introduction to birth, suffering, and death demands a surer solace, one Nick finds in childish fancy: "he felt quite sure that he would never die." Comfort drawn from others and self-indulgent flights from reality mark the early stages of apprenticeship for several of Hemingway's characters. A more substantial resource for both apprentice and exemplar appears for the first time in "Indian Camp." At the end of the story, sandwiched between his questions to his father and his fantasy of immortality is a brief paragraph of sheer sensation: "The sun was coming up over the hills. A bass jumped, making a circle in the water. Nick trailed his hand in the water. It felt warm in the sharp chill of the morning" [193]. Unconscious of feelings he will comprehend years later, Nick already plucks from nature a sense of renewal and reassurance. There are a few "good" places, Nick will learn, where reality is tolerable even though fantasies of immortality must be abandoned.

For his sensitivity to nature, Nick is indebted to his father, Dr. Henry Adams, a debt he acknowledges in some detail in "Fathers and Sons." As Nick later realizes, not all his debts to his father deserve gratitude. In the stories of boyhood, however, the reader perceives more clearly than Nick Dr. Adams's complexity. In "Indian Camp," for example, the reader recoils from Dr. Adams's callous indifference to the squaw's agony and his schoolboy exultation in his own skill. Whether Nick recognizes these crudities is unstated. What is certain is, as he says in "Fathers and Sons," that he "loved him very much for a long time." And he preferred to be with him rather than with his mother, who, as he remembers in "Now I Lay Me," was "always cleaning things out," and had once charred, while burning household debris, her husband's prized boyhood collection of arrowheads and stone axes. Nick is not witness to his father's partly deserved humiliation in "The Doctor and the Doctor's Wife" as an arrogant Indian hired hand forces him to back down from a fight. Nor does he hear his mother's priggish Christian Scientist's defense of the Indian. But when his father, leaving for a walk, tells Nick his mother wants him, the boy firmly responds, "I want to go with you . . . I know where there's black squirrels." And off they go as the story ends. The genius and intent buried in the tale surface in these final moments when Nick first appears and speaks his only words in the entire story. To that point, each parent's shortcomings have been sharply outlined for the reader. Nick has not even been present and, one suddenly realizes, need not have been, for, like any perceptive child, he has already on like occasions watched, absorbed, and formed his preference. When called upon to choose, he does so unhesitatingly.

In "Fathers and Sons," Nick becomes more explicit about Dr. Adams's influence. His father's fine eyes, his skills in fishing and hunting, and his companionship—all had delighted the boy. But some things diminished delight, a strain of cruelty, for example, and—to a boy's unformed sense—a harsh, vindictive, and frightening attitude toward sex. In "Ten Indians," shrewdly crafted structure and dialogue underline Dr. Adams's mild but perceptible sadism. In his early adolescence, Nick has just returned from a July 4 picnic, feeling "hollow and happy inside himself" because neighbors have teased him about having a "girl," Prudence Mitchell, an Indian. In the Adams kitchen, Nick is animated, his father reserved, his questions about Nick's day framed to elicit no more than brief answers, his gaze fixed upon the boy. The craft here is stunning as Hemingway repeats "His father sat watching him," suggesting the subtle pressure on the boy to ask about his father's activities—and he does. Cunningly evasive, Dr. Adams gradually lets Nick know that he has seen Prudence and another boy "threshing around" in the woods. The information out, Dr. Adams leaves for a few moments and Nick weeps. A sharp and bitter irony—perhaps unconscious on the father's part but certainly not on Hemingway's—coats Dr. Adams's words as he returns. Pointing to a pie, he asks, "Have some more?" But what Nick has heard is already enough. Still the father persists with vinegary innuendo, "You better have another piece," as Nick leaves for his room.

Face buried in his pillow, Nick thinks, "If I feel this way my heart must be broken." For those few moments it is—the pain intensified by Dr. Adams's cautery. But Nick is still very young and such pains pass swiftly (and quite soon Prudence, or Trudy as she is named in "Fathers and Sons," will complete his sexual initiation). What is particularly interesting in "Ten Indians" is that once more, as in "Indian Camp," nature is the emollient. A cool wind through the screen helps him to forget Prudence and to fall asleep. When he wakes, it is to hear "the wind and the hemlock" and "the waves of the lake," and Nick listens contentedly to these for a long while "before he remembered that his heart was broken." [6]

Dr. Adams, then, mingled burden with blessing. With him and because of him, Nick first learns of the natural cruelty of the universe, the conscious perversity of man, and, as a countermeasure, the partial release of "sinking into nature." Not an exemplary hero (his tutelage marred by a narrow Victorian morality), Dr. Adams functioned as Nick's sole preceptor until the boy was fifteen. After that, as Nick recalls in "Fathers and Sons," his father "shared nothing with him." Indeed, Nick symbolically discards his father when he suffers a whipping rather than don Dr. Adams's underwear. He "hated the smell of him," of all his family except one sister, and he walks alone in the dark to the Indian camp to rid himself of the smell.

The end of parental influence frees Nick for the next stage in the *Bildungsroman*, his initial encounter with society. As in boyhood, Nick is again more acted upon than active. In his adventures along the road, he is perplexed and unsettled by the ugliness of experience, barely able to cope with the profaneness of the world. One motif in the stories of this period is flight, a direct disengagement. Another motif, however, marks an advance in his education—the appearance of characters who play variations on the role of exemplary hero. A particularly shabby lot they are too in these stories, but they thrust Nick beyond the near horizon of Dr. Adams's shrunken vision and instruct him variously in techniques of survival he must learn to master.

In each of the stories about Nick's vagabondage, events move swiftly and their import is resolutely withheld. In "The Battler," Nick is thrown off a speeding train, first welcomed, then threatened by a punch-drunk ex-fighter, saved by the fighter's guardian, an almost too courteous Negro, and goes on his way. In "The Light of the World," one of Hemingway's noisiest stories, a nameless seventeen-year-old, probably Nick, lingers with an older friend at a railroad waiting room in northern Michigan. The room is crowded with five whores and ten men, four of them silent Indians. The "action" is all talk, loud, vulgar, and comic: the whores and several of the men crudely bait a homosexual cook; and two of the whores raucously debate which of them has been the true love of a famous prizefighter. Nick is briefly attracted to the fattest of the tarts but is led away by his friend. In "The Killers," Nick vainly tries to save another boxer, this one the intended target of two comically prototyped but grimly real Chicago gunmen. Although Nick warns the boxer, he cannot persuade him to escape. His stoic passivity unnerves Nick, who decides to get out of town.

Each of the characters Nick encounters has been hurt by society and discarded as dross. Ad Francis in "The Battler" had been a lightweight champion until he married the girl who managed him and had, for publicity purposes, passed as his sister. Howls of public outrage wrecked their marriage and, along with too many beatings in the ring, sped his fall. "He just went crazy," his friend Bugs explains to Nick. "He was busting people all the time after she went away and they put him in jail" [235]. Now the two men just "move around," Bugs, as Philip Young suggests, a less than innocent Nigger Jim,[7] alternately blackjacking his charge and maternally coddling him. Whatever Ad's former status, he is now crazy and dangerous. Hardly an exemplary hero, he exemplifies the fate of those—even champions—who try to battle the world. Ad is a warning in the guise of a physically disfigured, mentally distorted wreck that a "separate peace" is not always self-willed. These outcasts squatting near a swamp beside the railroad track have no choice and little more than tattered fragments of dignity. For Nick, who has taken to the road to learn what middle-class life had failed to teach, the lesson is appalling, the shock so acute that, as Young observes, he does not even realize until he has left the two men and walked some distance along the track that he carries in his hand a sandwich Bugs had given him.

Another boxer and former champion, Steve Ketchel, figures prominently in "The Light of the World," even though he never appears. It is he, however, who kindles the spirit of spiritual love in a profane story which is, incidentally, one of Hemingway's best and least appreciated. "I am the light of the world," Jesus says (John, 8:2) to the scribes and Pharisees after refusing to condemn the woman taken in adultery.[8] Ketchel is described as "the finest and most beautiful man that ever lived," is "like a god," loved "like you love God," and, finally, is killed. The parallel is obvious but the deeper relevance of the title concerns those who follow in the way and "shall not walk in darkness, but shall have the light of life." Few of the characters packed in the country depot enjoy that inner illumination, shadowed as they are by cold, insensate carnality.

Yet Nick, the first-person narrator here rather than the more frequent central consciousness, is acutely conscious of subtle as well as gross distinctions. He observes, for example, that the loud-mouthed spokesman for the cult of virility is himself whey-faced, his hands thin and as white as those of the cook he taunts as a "sister." Most important, he selects at the outset from the thousand plus pounds of available whores' flesh the only creature present on whom the light has truly shone. Understandably, Alice's size first commands Nick's attention—"the biggest whore I ever saw in my life and the

biggest woman." But as soon as she speaks ("Oh, my Christ,"
she laughs in her opening line when the cook calls her a "big
disgusting mountain of flesh"), her voice wins Nick, a voice
described thereafter as "nice," "low," "really pretty," and
"sweet lovely." Nick sharply discriminates Alice's voice from
the "high stagey way" Peroxide, another whore, talks when
she tells of her adoration of Ketchel and their allegedly profound love affair. The assembled connoisseurs of lust are saddened and embarrassed by Peroxide's melodramatic narration. Not until she finishes does Nick realize that Alice's bulk,
shaken by laughter early in the story, is now racked by sobs.
Anger rather than sentimentality has moved Alice, an anger
rooted in her knowledge that Peroxide's tale is fantasy, that
she alone in the room had known Ketchel, that he had said,
"You're a lovely piece, Alice," and that it makes no difference
whether anyone believes her.

Peroxide's world—not unlike that of the "manly" lumber-
jack and the "queer" cook—consists largely of false dreams
translated into self-deluding memories. Not a single phrase in
Peroxide's account, as Alice hints, might not have been found
in newspapers. Alice, on the other hand, refuses to gloss her
world or to idealize it with abstractions. She proves her relationship with Ketchel by citing a single concrete memory of
what he said about her, the kind of memory that adheres
within the spirit. Whoredom is Alice's domain, and because
she makes no apology for it, she graces her coarseness with
dignity. "I'm clean and you know it and men like me, even
though I'm big, and you know it," she says, "and I never lie
and you know it" [488]. When Alice finished, as Nick observes, her face lost its "hurt look" and became "the prettiest
face I ever saw." The transfiguration is complete.

The honest whore is a commonplace in Hemingway's fiction and has been on some occasions justly ridiculed as sentimental. Though Alice is an honest whore, she is neither commonplace nor sentimental. For the most part, she is tough
enough to "grin and bear it" along with Hemingway's most
disciplined exemplary heroes. And like them, she acknowl-

edges feeling but scorns the cant that needlessly embellishes it. Nick's father would never have approved of Alice but, far more than he, she is an exemplar of sensibility, courage, and integrity. In the aberrant world of crazy fighters, whores, and homosexuals, Nick learns, a "code" exists that enables decency. For Dr. Adams, as for the bartender who appears briefly at the beginning of the story, no such niceties exist. "All you punks stink," the bartender says as he boots Nick and his friend out. What happens in "The Light of the World" proves that not all do. Characteristically, however, Hemingway avoids the "wow" in his ending. A glimmer rather than incandescence lights Nick on his way, for as he and his friend leave, the cook is still flirting with them.

Hemingway's most frequently analyzed and anthologized story, "The Killers," [9] brings Nick's adolescence to a bruising close. A comic spirit informs "The Killers" as it does "The Light of the World" but dwells here in the precincts of death rather than life. The stereotyped whores, lumberjacks, and wooden Indians at the rail depot are harmless enough, but the movie-style Chicago gangsters Al and Max (complete with derbies, chest-buttoned black overcoats, silk scarves, and gloves, which they wear while eating) pop out of the imaginary screen intent upon actual murder. As ridiculous and unreal as Kafka's expressionistic "undertakers" in *The Trial*, their purpose is as serious and sinister. Along the length of this razor's edge between the comic and the tragic Nick is painfully stretched.

Nick's reactions to Ole Andreson's imminent death contrast sharply, as several critics have shown, with those of the other characters. Sam, the Negro short-order cook, simply shuts himself off from the reality and advises Nick to do the same. George, the counterman, acknowledges the horror and even sends Nick to warn Ole, but later urges Nick not to think about what has happened. Ole, disciplined in the "code," faces the wall and stoically resigns himself to the inevitable. Nick's effort to persuade Ole to save himself is a rare shift from his wonted role as passive observer. Though he fails,

Nick's short journey from the diner to the boarding house marks an important milestone in his educational progress. The diner is not Nick's first sight of the world but through Ole he has his first full glimpse of how a man lives and dies in it. Awed and dizzied by the sight, Nick must turn away. "I can't stand to think about him waiting in the room," he says later to George, "and knowing he's going to get it" [387]. Almost a cliché of terror, Nick's words reveal how language fails to sound his nameless dread. Again, his refuge is flight: "I'm going to get out of this town."

As with even more conventional modes of primary and secondary education, Nick's curriculum informs him about the world without adequately preparing him to adjust to it. The end of innocence always arrives too suddenly, sometimes destructively for the hypersensitive. Despite some useful instruction, Nick emerges from his adolescence unable to protect himself, still too tender to avoid psychic contusion. War damages his body as well as his spirit, scarring the tissues of both forever. Healing inward wounds takes even longer, for Nick at least to his thirty-eighth year, the farthest Hemingway leads him. By the end of the war, the third stage of the *Bildungsroman*, Nick will have learned nearly all he must know about living with pain. He will even have the protection of a calloused inner skin. But he will also have the dubious "boon" of memory to penetrate that hardened surface, to keep him vulnerable, always an apprentice.

The beginnings are sketched in the vignettes of *in our time:* first, as the young soldier cringes in a trench during the bombardment of Fossalta and prays for deliverance, not from sin but from shellfire; then, wounded, as he declares his "separate peace." "Now I Lay Me," a technically disappointing story, [10] elaborates Nick's wartime fears and compensations. Narrating in the first person, Nick tells of convalescing after his wounds, chiefly of how he averts sleep. Nowhere else in his fiction is Hemingway so explicit about the insomniac. All his heroes suffer this syndrome of anxiety; only Nick makes palpable that it is not a matter of being unable to sleep but a willed determination not to. In sleep, control lapses and "bad" places pock the landscape of the mind. At the instant of his wound, Nick (like Frederic Henry in A Farewell to Arms) had felt his soul leave his body. Since then, the threshold of sleep seems an abyss of terror, a place where self is lost forever. Insomnia is a small price to pay for the privilege of selecting and controlling memory, directing it away from the "bad" place, the abyss.

For Nick—and probably for Hemingway's other heroes as well—insomnia is not only a symptom of psychic illness but also a form of therapy, another "opium of the people." Listening to silkworms feeding on mulberry leaves, remembering places where one dug for bait to fish trout streams (even imaginary streams will do)—these dam or divert memory and avoid the equally terrible emptiness of lying "cold awake." When these fail, prayer distracts or even a banal conversation with a fellow soldier about girls and marriage. Insomnia, then, helps to deaden the ache; it can neither kill the cause nor even wholly block out every infiltrating strand of terror. In each of Nick's selected memories lies hidden a charged fragment of agony that threatens to blast his soul into the abyss he dreads. His recollection of trout-fishing is marred by unsought and unwanted details, like the memory of a salamander pitiably grasping the fishhook Nick baited him on, or finding no worms in the swamp and having to cut up a trout as bait. Similarly, prayer evokes the image of his mother burning Dr. Adams's relics; and even the girls he conjures from the past finally blur and "all became rather the same." Nevertheless, Nick fares reasonably well. Certainly he is better prepared for reality than the other soldier, who firmly believes that marriage will "fix up everything." And, by discriminating among his reveries (fishing, for example, is better than girls—the streams are always new), Nick has begun to learn how to choose in order to buttress his psychic defenses.

What happens when those defenses are overrun—when sleep or delirium triumph over the limited control of insomnia—is distressingly clear in "A Way You'll Never Be."

Succumbing to delirium during a post-convalescent visit to his former battalion, Nick relives in a long internal mono- logue scenes he has struggled to repress. Seeing too many helmets full of brains has weakened his control. One vision especially obsesses and unnerves him. Clear and separable, its parts persist in flowing illogically and irrationally into one another, denying expectation, shattering composure. There is an image of a long, low yellow house, a low stable, and a canal outside Fossalta; and there is a related image of a river that "runs wider and stiller than it should." The house seems simultaneously to belong where the canal is and where the river is: "If it didn't get so damned mixed up he could follow it all right. That was why he noticed everything in such de- tail to keep it all straight . . ." [507]. But the bits defy Nick's efforts to order them and the effort exhausts him emotionally. He admits that he has been "certified as nutty" and "reformed out of the war." Whether he has been released or has escaped from the hospital is conjectural, as is evidence to support his claim that his self-control is gradually returning.

Unsettling, disjointed, and vague, "A Way You'll Never Be" is technically one of Hemingway's weakest stories, almost as if the pain of remembering had dislocated his artistic centers of control. Hysteria is clearly the mode, but the modality spills over and stains the narrative method. The external point of view fails here to create that "second self" so effective in stories like "Indian Camp," "The Killers," and "The Light of the World." The tension apparently intended by contrasting the impersonal description of Nick's journey to his battalion with the hallucinatory stream of delirious consciousness fails to hold taut.

If, however, the style falls even more slack than in "Now I Lay Me," the distortions of Nick's fantasy sustain unremitting interest. Why, the reader asks along with Nick, should "he wake, soaking wet, more frightened than he had ever been in a bombardment . . ." because of a "long yellow house and the different width of the river" [507]? For the clues, as Philip Young has convincingly demonstrated,[11] the reader must turn to other stories as well: the vignette in *in our time* that finds Nick at Fossalta under bombardment; and, nearly twenty years later, *Across the River and Into the Trees*, as Colonel Richard Cantwell, in the third chapter, surveys that same area to determine the precise spot where he too had been wounded (as had Frederic Henry in *A Farewell to Arms* and Hemingway in fact). What Cantwell sees is a bend and a change in the width of the river, the river bank where he was hit, and, across the river, a house rebuilt from rubble.

When Nick returns home after the war, he enjoys alone a respite in northern Michigan. In the second part of "Big Two-Hearted River," the reader will recall from earlier discussion, [12] Nick avoids fishing the sunless swamp where "the fishing would be tragic." As he stands on the river bank looking downstream, Nick notices that "the river narrowed" as it entered the swamp. Most of the discrete, incongruous bits that shape Nick's mad collage suddenly fall together. The physical similarities between the Piave River in northern Italy and the Big Two-Hearted River in northern Michigan merge into the mainstream of Nick's anguish. Each river is a tributary along which he traveled toward the "tragic adventure" of his war wound. "Big Two-Hearted River," it should be added, was written almost ten years earlier than "A Way You'll Never Be." As Philip Young writes, "it is in such a way that Hemingway's work extends backward and forward, is enigmatic and then clearer, and is integrated, and bound tight about a core of shock." [13]

Within the chronology of fictional events, Nick has regained some controls by the time he returns to Seney, Michigan. Now in the last stage of his training, he has become a "master apprentice," putting to use all he has wrenched from his violent education. He turns to nature not merely as a retreat but as a "clean, well-lighted place," a "good" place, an arena in which he can discipline his emotions ("It was all back of him") and test his skill against "the big ones." At first glance, the precise, minute descriptions of hiking, camping, cooking, and fly-rod fishing seem mindless, and the ceaseless, unmodulated rhythms of simple declarative sentences monotonous. Yet both the mindlessness and the monotony waken the reader to an underlying tension, a recognition that so long as Nick can regularize (even mechanize) his actions, he can govern his fears. Each step toward the climax of fishing is ritualistically prepared, "a series of little ceremonies," as Malcolm Cowley has noted, that ". . . might be regarded as an incantation, a spell to banish evil spirits." [14]

Even ritual is not infallible. Any surge of emotion, however pleasurable, threatens Nick's equilibrium. When he hooks an enormous trout, the thrill is too much and, "feeling a little sick," he rests: "He did not want to rush his sensations any." More than his senses, Nick must control his thinking. At the close of his first day in camp, his mind begins to work, but he is able to "choke it off because he was tired enough." What Nick is "choking off" and what lies "back of him" remain unstated but no longer unknown to readers familiar with Nick's history.

"Big Two-Hearted River" opens in the burned-out town of Seney alluded to in the early poem, "Along with Youth." [15] Desolate, barren, the ghostly place re-creates for the reader (and surely for Nick) the devastation of war limned in *in our time* and elaborated in "A Way You'll Never Be." Yet when he crawls into his tent that night, Nick is happy because he has been too busy to remember. Things had had to be done and were done: "He had made his camp. He was settled. Nothing could touch him. It was a good place to camp. He was there, in the good place" [313]. Toward the end of the story, when he considers fishing downstream where the biggest trout lurk in the swamp, Nick sees the difference in the width of the river. This time, his response is so swift and automatic that he need not try to choke off thought. Summarily, he rejects the project and climbs from the river bank to high ground and the safety of his camp site. "There were plenty of days coming," the story closes, "when he could fish the swamp." That he will ever do so is unlikely. More knowing now than ever before, Nick avoids whatever threatens his de-

fenses. Years later, in "Fathers and Sons," he responds almost
identically when a memory of his father's suicide usurps his
imagination. Tempted to write about it to "get rid of it," he
shies from the temptation: "But it was still too early for that.
There were still too many people." Suicide was another
"tragic adventure" and Nick has already had a surfeit of tragedy.[16]

Little more remains to tell about the dynamics of Nick's defense mechanism. Beyond "Big Two-Hearted River," Nick's
postwar adventures are scant. In the sharply drawn "Soldier's
Home," the hero's name is Krebs, his home Oklahoma, his
wartime experiences less traumatic than Nick's. But Krebs's
return to Midwestern life bears a certain likeness to what
Nick might have encountered in Illinois. Dying was a truth
Krebs had learned to live with and it had left him "cool and
clear inside himself." But as John Peale Bishop has observed,
"The Midwest had never known what it was to die every day
it lived," [17] and its townsfolk were responsive only to melodramatic exaggerations of wartime experience. As Krebs lies
to meet the expectations of society, his own self-respect
drains away, leaving him blank and barren, desiring neither
factitious nor authentic experience: "He did not want any
consequences. He did not want any consequences ever again"
[245]. Rejecting faith, parental love, and sex, Krebs complai-
santly promises anything "to keep his life from being complicated."

Krebs is Nick's "double," an extreme version of the apprentice who abandons the trade of life, yields to *nada* to assure
that his life will run smoothly, and accepts oblivion without
dignity. Poor, battered Ad Francis in "The Battler" has more
vitality than Krebs. For Nick, as for most of Hemingway's apprentices, Krebs's way is inadequate. Risking "consequences"
they acknowledge as a given. Both the apprentice and the exemplary hero try to channel them to their own advantage,
but they learn how to abide with loss too. Krebs's refuge is
self-deception. He is given to lengthy introspection, for example, about girls, protesting too much that he does not need

one, that the effort is not worth it. At last, he settles for his kid sister's companionship and continues to think about not thinking about girls. However, Nick, like most apprentices, is learning to gamble on the slim chance that desire may be transformed into love. Either way, the end product is loneliness, but that too is part of the "separate peace."

Nick's early sex education is limited to an efficient introduction to pleasure with an Indian girl. Before he goes to war, Alice, the prostitute in "The Light of the World," broadens his perspective of love. When Nick returns to Michigan after the war, Hemingway narrates in companion stories the break-up of an affair with a girl named Marjorie. In the earlier story, "The End of Something," Nick rows Marjorie past a landscape romantically associated with their love. Rejecting her gentle, affectionate reminders, he tells her, "It isn't fun any more." Yet when she leaves, Nick feels neither joy nor release, only that "everything was gone to hell inside of me." A superbly crafted story, "The Three-Day Blow" studies Nick as he tries to fill—with light conversation and heavy drinking—the emptiness gnawing within since his romance ended. Nick's lovesickness proves rather mild, though, for he recovers rapidly when a friend prescribes that he stop thinking about it. The strong wind off the lake helps—as it had in his boyhood ("Ten Indians")—blow remorse out of his mind and Nick feels happy again: "There was always a way out."

None of the published Nick Adams stories suggests that Nick Adams is ready to endure a more serious encounter with love. But during the war, while Nick recovers from his wounds in a hospital in Milan, Hemingway exposes him to a character who is—the prim, sensitive Italian major, the exemplary hero of "In Another Country," one of Hemingway's finest stories. Nick's loneliness and fears are real and understandable, for he is, in many ways, "in another country." A wounded American officer in the Italian army, he is isolated by nationality and rank. Even his medals set him apart, since others know he received them less for valor than for being American. Unlike the brave "hunting hawks," Nick admits to himself his fear of death and dreads leaving the hospital (which is also "another country") to return to battle.

The Major's other country, as Nick discovers, is one Nick has explored only superficially. About his own death the Major is unconcerned, and he entertains no illusions about his recovery either. Bravery and therapeutic machines he dismisses as nonsense, preferring the discipline of good grammar and good manners. The tragedy he must play out centers on the death of another, his young wife, unexpectedly dead of pneumonia. Her loss deprives his life of meaning because, as Earl Rovit points out, his "commitment to love and his shock at his wife's death have placed him 'in another country' than the one he has prepared to defend. That other country is nothing less than the human condition itself, for the human will is always vulnerable to destruction." [18] Briefly, the Major loses his composure, angrily insisting to Nick that a man must not marry: "If he is to lose everything, he should not place himself in a position to lose that . . . He should find things he cannot lose" [369]. Three days after he has wept and confessed, "I am utterly unable to resign myself," the Major, once more composed and dignified, resumes his worthless machine therapy.

"In Another Country" is more than another paradigm of courage. The Major's complex of responses ranges from a negativism like Krebs's to the stoicism of the "code" and beyond it to a humanity that embraces love as a wondrous as well as a fatal reality. As narrator, Nick admits nothing of the Major's impact upon him. Its power emerges, as in "The Light of the World," in the significant details Nick records. What the reader perceives is what Nick learns—that displayed feelings need not signify weakness and that bravery is not measured only on the battlefield. Above all, Nick must recognize that the admonition to "find things he cannot lose" is one the Major has not himself paid heed to. Spat out in the agony of loss, the Major's words are nevertheless a critique of the limitations of the "code," for the Major knows that settling for what cannot be lost excludes love. Few of Hemingway's exemplary heroes risk or reveal so much as the Major. That he does so and with such dignity and courage makes him Nick's single most important mentor.

Paradoxically, Hemingway gives Nick little chance to apply what he has learned from the Major, reserving that honor for Frederic Henry in *A Farewell to Arms*. Though Nick does wed, his wife is conspicuously absent from each of three stories about marriage. The details of marital life are too skimpy for generalization, but it is easier to think of Nick and his wife as the disenchanted couples in "Out of Season," "Cat in the Rain," or "A Canary for One" than as the Major and his young wife. "Cross-Country Snow," a trivial story otherwise, has relevance because it indicates at the outset of marriage Nick's preference for skiing and male companionship to the prospect of returning to the United States because his wife is pregnant.[19] "Fathers and Sons" pays his wife no tribute with its rhapsody about an Indian girl's matchless sexual prowess. Leslie Fiedler suggests that Nick's Trudy and Edgar Allan Poe's Annabel Lee are "projections both of a refusal to surrender the innocence of childhood."[20] In a story filled with harsh memories, Trudy may symbolize an idyl Nick has selected to protect himself from the past. A more likely and simpler thesis is that Nick is recalling accurately his most satisfactory sexual encounter, a variety of experience having little to do with innocence. Moreover, most of the night-blooming memories planted in Nick's childhood and adolescence have proliferated into a rank garden, not a "woodland Eden." It is not innocence that Nick yearns after but relief from memories of experience. Obviously, his marriage has not afforded him that respite.

Marriage has, however, made Nick a father, and even as he remembers Dr. Adams in "Fathers and Sons," his own son sits beside him. As he tells the boy about his grandfather's "wonderful eyes" and prowess as hunter and fisherman, and promises him a shotgun when he reaches the age of twelve, the reader senses a cycle ending and beginning anew. Like Nick, the boy faces death early. In "A Day's Wait," confused by the difference between Fahrenheit and centigrade thermometers, Schatz (as the boy is called) believes he is about to die. Unlike Nick in "Indian Camp," he does not take refuge in a fantasy of immortality but secludes himself in his room, refusing entry to all. A Lilliputian model of an exemplary hero, he "looks straight ahead" and, as Nick observes, is "evidently holding tight onto himself about something." All he asks his father is, "About what time do you think I'm going to die?" Only when Nick explains the error does the boy slowly relinquish his adult pose and return to childhood. By the next day, he cries, Nick tells us, "very easily at things of little importance."

What lies ahead for Nick's boy is unknown and unwritten.[21] One hopes his wounds would be slighter, his memories less terrifying, his maturity more solidly rewarding than his father's. With a master apprentice as his father, he would learn very early to discard such expectations as absurd and sentimental.

6

The Journalist, the Poet, the Satirist, and the Dramatist

Although the core of Hemingway's artistic genius is his fiction, he wrote much else. Beyond the genres suggested by the title of this section, Hemingway wrote a substantial body of non-fiction: full-length accounts of bullfighting (*Death in the Afternoon*) and hunting (*Green Hills of Africa*), a memoir of his early years in Paris (*A Moveable Feast*), scattered pieces of art and literary criticism, and thousands of letters (most of them unpublished).[1] The three non-fiction books will be discussed in their proper places. About his criticism, some observations have already been made in the section on style; others will appear elsewhere throughout this book. Of the genres discussed in this chapter, journalism is the most considerable, in volume and quality.

Something of the poet, satirist, and dramatist pervades all of Hemingway's writing, but as he attempts each genre itself, Hemingway proves himself inept. None of these attempts is aesthetically satisfying; the sustaining interest is thematic and biographical. Most of them are early work; only *The Fifth Column* (1939) and the two poems to Mary Hemingway (written in 1944, published in 1965) were written after 1926. To label them "early Hemingway," does not imply apology or invite compassion, for these were the years when he wrote his dispatches to *The Toronto Daily Star*, the vignettes of *in our time*, the stories of *In Our Time*, and *The Sun Also Rises*. They must stand or fall for what they are and, as the account which follows will show, the best of them totter.

THE JOURNALIST

Conceivably, a handful of readers exist who know Hemingway only incidentally as a novelist, their exposure having been limited to the reportorial pieces he wrote in the thirties and forties for *Esquire, Ken,* and *Collier's;* for *True, Look,* and *Life* in the fifties. Unfortunately, these articles occasionally lack the freshness and resonance of his apprentice news work in the twenties. By the time he was established as a writer of fiction, Hemingway made explicit his differentiation between art and "newspaper stuff." Writing to a bibliographer in the early thirties, he protested against the inclusion of his journalistic work as having "nothing to do with the other writing which is entirely apart." [2] The news writing, he argued, was "timely rather than permanent," all part of learning the trade, and "no one has any right to dig this stuff up and use it against the stuff you have written to write the best you can."

Though Hemingway was shrewd in trying to limit the canon, his concern about his journalism was excessive, especially about what he wrote during the twenties for *The Toronto Daily Star* and *Weekly*. During those years of apprenticeship, "his craft was the craft of fiction," as William White, the editor of *By-Line* notes, "not factual reporting." [3] He was encountering for the first time the places, the people, and the attitudes that would infuse his vision of the world and inspire him to elaborate the terms of his "separate peace." And he was disciplining his language to express both.

Sham, injustice, and cruelty are major targets of his anger, vessels of his anguish. Among the bohemians in Paris, there is the incapable lady painter with "a face like a pink enameled ham," her masterpiece "a red mince pie descending the stairs." She is but one among a host of poseurs and loafers who populate postwar Europe and upset "that premier seat of the emotions, the stomach." War profiteers idling in Switzerland along with "utterly charming young men" and the middle-aged women "with a flashing of platinum rings on plump fingers" they amuse in "cuckoo-clock style" hotels—each of these is captured with the eye of the poet and the sensibility of the moralist. The pompous, xenophobic German, the monstrously ineffectual kings of Greece, Rumania, Spain, and Italy are deflated; Mussolini, "the biggest bluff in Europe," is reported as comic but dangerous—as all who "registered Dictator" would be for Hemingway throughout his life.[4] The deepest vein of hurt and compassion is tapped in the reports about the Greco-Turkish War. One of the "fruits of the Turks' return to Europe" is the evacuation from Thrace toward Macedonia, abundant with materials he would use again in his fiction. This passage—later altered to become part of *in our time*—is typical:

> It is a silent procession. Nobody even grunts. It is all they can do to keep moving. Their brilliant peasant costumes are soaked and draggled. Chickens dangle by their feet from the carts. Calves nuzzle at the draught cattle wherever a jam halts the stream. An old man marches bent under a young pig, a scythe and a gun, with a chicken tied to his scythe. A husband spreads a blanket over a woman in labor in one of the carts to keep off the driving rain. She is the only person making a sound. Her little daughter looks at her in horror and begins to cry. And the procession keeps moving. [51]

Not all of Hemingway's reportage is grim. The excitement and purity of the outdoors lighten the shadows. There is a setting for fishing rainbow trout in a "pool where the moselle colored water sweeps into a dark swirl and expanse that is blue-brown with depth and fifty feet across"; and a description of a big tuna as "silver and slate blue, and when he shoots up into the air beside the boat it is like a blinding flash of quicksilver"; and a detailed account of his first bull-fight and a consciousness that it is not a sport, but a "very great tragedy. The tragedy is the death of the bull . . . It is a tragedy, and it symbolizes the struggle between man and the beasts."

The early journalism, then, served as the crucible of Hemingway's art. Some of these dispatches would reappear—hardened and tempered—as the vignettes of *in our time*. The explicit commentary and most of the adjectives would by then have been cut.[5] Necessary for the reporter, they were surplus for the artist. Bits and fragments from the dispatches recur in both the short stories and the novels, transmuted but recognizable. Journalism is not art, but as Hemingway practiced it in his formative years, it can hardly be said to have had "nothing to do with the other writing which is entirely apart."

The same is true, though to a lesser extent, of Hemingway's journalism after his fame as an artist was secure. The germ of *The Old Man and the Sea* lay in "On the Blue Water: A Gulf Stream Letter," a fishing article he wrote for *Esquire* in 1936. A year later, Hemingway began to send graphic dispatches from Spain, writing sometimes in a hotel room in Madrid as shells burst in the square below, and as well from the battle fronts of the Ebro delta. Part of what he reported from Madrid entered a few short stories [6] and his play, *The Fifth Column*. One of his best short stories, "Old Man at the Bridge," was originally cabled from Barcelona as a news story.

But the worth of Hemingway's later journalism cannot be measured by how many cables he turned into fiction. Judged on merit, his reporting is—apart from other considerations—alive and immediate. He wrote (when he was not writing about himself) about whatever interested him—war, politics, outdoor sports, domesticity—and whatever he reported revealed nearly as much about himself as about his subject. He is always visible, whether playful or vehement, unassuming or arrogant.

War is what Hemingway continued to report best. He writes about the agony of the Civil War in Spain—"a strange new kind of war where you learn just as much as you are able to believe"—with the same sensitive and acute vision, poignant sorrow, and compassion that etched his dispatches from Thrace more than fifteen years earlier. One report, "The Flight of Refugees," sent from Barcelona in 1938, seems almost a reprise of that early piece—roads clogged with carts, peasant, and soldiers, a newborn babe clutched in its mother's arms. Only the weather differs, a day "so lovely that it seemed ridiculous that anyone should ever die." On a gray June morning sixteen years later, Hemingway stood aboard a landing craft threading its way on D-day through sea-staked mines ("They were the ugly, neutral gray-yellow color that almost everything is in war") toward the French beach. His account of chaos in "Voyage to Victory" is never chaotic. It is, rather, surrealistic in its shocking juxtaposition of the almost comic floundering of vessels and tanks and the terrible actuality of men dying. Landing craft drift about, vainly seeking a control ship to tell them where to land; tanks crouch stupidly on the beach "like big yellow toads" until, hit, they burst into flames; waves of men reach the beach and are immediately shot down, lying where they fall and "looking like so many heavily laden bundles"; and as the guns of a destroyer wreck a pillbox, Hemingway sees "a piece of German about three feet long with an arm on it sail high up into the air . . . It reminded me of a scene in Petrouchka" [354–55].

The overwhelming force of Hemingway's war reports derives from his skill in selecting relevant details, ordering them for dramatic effect, and discovering the precise images to sustain his emotional thrust. Though his passion is full and deep, it seems always controlled, his eloquence restrained, barely audible. When, on the other hand, Hemingway acts as a political analyst and war strategist—as he does in a series of reports about the Far East for the newspaper *PM* in 1941—he is noisily knowing. One need not deny him insight and a good measure of foresight in these pieces. But his pontificating tone grates: "Japan has built up a reserve supply of gasoline and oil to last her air force and Navy for one year of war. If the U.S.A. and Great Britain shut off her gasoline and oil she would be forced to remove south toward oil at once or else begin exhausting her war reserve" [321–22].

Or: "The Generalissimo [Chiang] is a military leader who goes through the motions of being a statesman. This is important. Hitler is a statesman who employs military force. Mussolini is a statesman who is unable to employ military force" [327]. Or: "Any one who says that the troops of the Central Government armies are not a magnificently disciplined, well trained, well officered and excellently armed defensive force has never seen them at the front" [330]. In less than six months in Asia, Hemingway learned much about the "big" issues, but little about the humility with which he might more persuasively have reported and interpreted them.

When he drops his podium posture and gets behind a duck blind or boards the *Pilar*, he is a more engaging and a more interesting writer. From the thirties through the fifties he continued to describe fishing and hunting with unabated excitement in the pursuit and undiminished skill in recording it. Philip Young writes that reading these reports makes suddenly clear "that taking the lives of fish and animals was for Hemingway an essentially aesthetic experience entirely comparable to those aroused by the experience of great painting or music." [7] Perhaps so, but one suspects also that Hemingway's lifelong interest in the killing of beasts and men has other import as well. Of that, more later.[8] One sullen demurrer about the outdoor articles might be entered here, however, in behalf of those readers who have a less than insatiable appetite for such cultist delights as tackle specifications or instructions on how to avoid having marlin and tuna hit by sharks (a skill Hemingway claims but which, curiously, his old fisherman, Santiago, never mastered).

But Hemingway is generally companionable in his adventure reports and, in a few rather surprising pieces, he reveals a delightful ability to enjoy horseplay and even to make fun of himself. His experience with a navy petty officer who tries to protect Hemingway's privacy and literary reputation in Havana; his dream of Senator Joe McCarthy and his aides; and a dream of himself affianced to a lioness—all are good-natured and hilarious.[9]

Compared with his early reporting, Hemingway's journalism from the thirties on is rather more diverse in subject matter and tone. Only the remarkable discipline of observation and language remains constant. The later work was, in many ways, a luxury. Having served a hungry journalistic apprenticeship to literature, he could now let the journals cater to his appetites. They did so readily enough (his name or picture guaranteed sales), paying him extravagantly to go where he wished and to talk about whatever he liked or disliked. Yet Hemingway was never really easy about the "easy money" he earned as a freewheeling journalist. Though he was usually ready to drop an article to work on a book, he remained defensive, and, as late as 1956, he wrote from Havana that journalism "is not whoring when done honestly and with exact reporting" [472]. It is well that Hemingway insisted on separating the journalist from the artist—our literature is richer because he discriminated. But his readers may discover in his journalism (apart from the simple pleasure of its readability) still another, perhaps unexpected, way to understand the artist and the man.

THE POET

A biographical note in *Poetry: A Magazine of Verse* for January 1923 describes Hemingway as "a young Chicago poet now abroad, who will soon issue his first book of verse." The book was *Three Stories and Ten Poems*, published six months later and containing four additional poems besides those *Poetry* printed under the heading "Wanderings." The poems, as

Edmund Wilson wrote of them later that year, "are not particularly important," but they do reveal that Hemingway swam in the main poetic current of the time and that poetry, like journalism, exercised his developing skill in discerning the poignant and recording it poignantly. His first published poem (apart from a half dozen that appeared in his high-school magazine), "Ultimately," is emblematic of what he was after in theme and style:

> He tried to spit out the truth;
> Dry-mouthed at first,
> He drooled and slobbered in the end;
> Truth dribbling his chin.[10]

The source, as Philip Young suggests, is probably Stephen Crane's short poems, a channel that led Hemingway to the imagism Ezra Pound had espoused a decade earlier before abandoning it to Miss Lowell's "Amygism." Hemingway's "Ten Poems" somewhat distortedly mirror Pound's insistence upon "direct treatment of the 'thing' whether subjective or objective," a plea for freshness, economy, and precision of image and organic rather than metronomic rhythm.[11] Except for a nod toward Vachel Lindsay in "Riparto d'Assalto"— "Drummed their boots on the camion floor./Hob-nailed boots on the camion floor"—Hemingway's rhythms are functional and unobtrusive. He attacks his material (predictably, war, sex, death, and cant) with a Kiplingesque directness, his focus narrow but sharp. Yet only two of the poems approach success. The military imagery of "Mitraigliatrice"—the only sustained image in his early poetry—pictures in seven lines the artist's battle with language and thought:

> The mills of the gods grind slowly
> But the mill
> Chatters in mechanical staccato.
> Ugly short infantry of the mind,
> Advancing over difficult terrain.
> Making this Corona
> Their mitrailleuse.

The typewriter ("Corona") is the machine gun (Italian in the title, French in the final line) controlled by the poet's fingers, the "ugly short infantry." But the no-man's-land of the mind is "difficult terrain" to conquer; the combat with words and ideas must go on. The images are hard and clear, the rhythm effectively adjusted to theme and image.

"Along with Youth" affectingly records the end of adolescence, cataloguing the artifacts of a boy's room:

> A porcupine skin
> Stiff with bad tanning,
> It must have ended somewhere.
> Stuffed horned owl
> Pompous
> Yellow-eyed;
> . . .
> Drawers of boys letters
> And the line of love
> They must have ended somewhere.

Despite a clumsy explicitness that dissipates the effect of the refrain: "Yesterday's tribute is gone/Along with youth," the poem regains force in the closing lines:

> And the canoe that went to pieces on the beach
> The year of the big storm
> When the hotel burned down
> At Seney, Michigan,

as storm and fire become metaphoric destroyers of innocence, the commonplace in Hemingway's world.

None of the other "Ten Poems" shows even this moderate originality. The sexual sea imagery of "Oily Weather" is embarrassingly obvious: "The screw churns a throb" and "the sea rolls with love/ . . . Undulating its great loving belly." The torment of war is sung prosaically in "Captives" and "Champs d'Honneur." "Chapter Heading," reprinted in Best Poems of 1923 (obviously not a vintage year), is a banal diatribe upon religious hypocrisy; "T. Roosevelt" tries with meager success to dispose of the man and the legend. "Oklahoma" has potential as a sermon about appearance and reality but depends too heavily upon transparent gimmickry, a parenthetical antithesis at the end of each stanza to underscore its irony:

> *Pull an arrow out:*
> *If you break it*
> *The wound closes.*
> *Salt is good too*
> *And wood ashes.*
> *Pounding it throbs in the night—*
> *(or is it the gonorrhea)*

"Montparnasse," a poem about suicides among expatriates, also leans for inadequate support upon the parenthetic aside.

Of the other poems Hemingway published during the twenties, none deserves serious attention. "Neo-Thomist Poem" is a one-liner Ezra Pound published in *The Exile:* "The Lord is my shepherd, I shall not/want him for long." [12] A generous critic might call the poem clever. Sincerity and raw force distinguish some of the Gertrude Stein-inspired lines in "They All Made Peace—What is Peace?" an attack upon the urbane diplomats who arranged a settlement of the Greco-Turkish War at Lausanne:

> *All of the turks are gentlemen and Ismet Pasha is a*
> *Little deaf. But the Armenians. How about the*
> *Armenians?*
> *Well, the Armenians.*
> *Lord Curzon likes young boys.*
> *So does Chicherin.*
> *So does Mustapha Kemal. He is good looking too. His eyes*
> *Are too close together but he makes war. That is the way he is.*
> *. . .*
> *Mrs. Child has flat breasts and Mr. Child is an idealist and wrote*
> *Harding's campaign speeches and calls Senator Beveridge Al.*
> *You know me Al.*
> *Lincoln Steffens is with Child . . .*[13]

For the rest, the fourth-rate satirist took over from the third-rate poet. In "The Soul of Spain," Hemingway once more affected, as he called it, the "manner of Gertrude Stein" to write one of several "rather obscene" (his term) poems published in *Der Querschnitt*. Here, he is not an angry young man but a naughty and rather silly little boy:

> . . .
> *Democracy is the shit.*
> *Relativity is the shit.*
> *Dictators are the shit.*
> *Mencken is the shit.*
> . . .
> *They say Ezra is the shit.*
> *But Ezra is nice.*
> *Come let us build a monument to Ezra.*
> . . .
> *We have done a monument to Ezra.*
> *A monument is a monument.*
> *After all it is the spirit of the thing that counts.*

Equally tasteless but not so funny is "The Lady Poet with Footnotes," an attack upon Amy Lowell's girth and sex habits.

Though about forty poems remain unpublished, there is no reason to assume they show improvement.[14] In fact, no further discussion of Hemingway's poetry would be necessary were it not for the posthumous publication of two long poems Hemingway wrote during World War II.[15] What is tonally different from his early poetry is a sense of desperation and urgency, a deeper consciousness of the sum of experience as a bitter residue of profound hurt and loss.

"To Mary in London," the shorter (about one hundred and ten lines), less ambitious, and less engaging of the two, was written in May 1944 while he recovered from head injuries suffered in an auto crash during a blackout. A headache persists, "a friendly and true headache/And I do not like him to know that he bores me." The headache is bearable, but the emptiness is not, especially the feeling that he is no longer his own man: "The battle will be another man's battle/And we will be only baggage." Combat flying affords some release, but nostalgia for the sub-chasing exploits aboard the *Pilar* gnaws: "Killing I know and believe in./Or do not believe in/ But practice./Practice make perfect make practice make perfect make practice." Hope lies, however, beyond the somber ambiguities implicit in the parody of Gertrude Stein. The only real possibilities are language and love. The poem opens with Hemingway "Trying to make with a phrase and a sentence/ Something no bomber can reach"; near the close, he awaits the arrival of Mary "To cure all loneliness/and bring the things/We left behind upon the boat." Like the adventure of combat, the adventure of love makes the present bearable. "I'm all right and would not change/ For any ever time," Hemingway cheerily apostrophizes Wolfie (Winston Guest, second in command aboard the *Pilar*) at the end. But the gallant, if self-conscious, show of bravado seems incongruent with the homesick man conscious of lost grandeur and of the unwanted changes a "censor" has made, "Not in the copy but in me."

Although a work of unmistakable feeling, "To Mary in London" holds interest chiefly for the honesty of its portraiture and the sense it imparts of tired but resolute courage.

"Second Poem to Mary" numbers nearly two hundred lines and was begun, as Mary Hemingway relates, later in 1944 during the battle of Huertgen Forest and completed at the Ritz Hotel in Paris when he was on leave from the Fourth Division. Technically his most ambitious poem, it is also the most revealing of the tensions ever in conflict in his writing. Abhorrence of violence and the void, for example, is sustained and explicit, but intertwined with loathing is a profound admiration for those who face death courageously (and scorn for those who evade the confrontation), and even a fascination with the sacrament of death itself. Similarly, despite his sardonic handling of Catholicism, his quasi-liturgical form shows Hemingway as much moved as repelled by its ritual. In "Second Poem to Mary," the tensions yield no resolution, not even the meager hope Mary's arrival promises in "To

Mary in London." A car crash in a London blackout had failed to rouse the memory of 1918 so graphically as the holocaust of Huertgen Forest.

Throughout Hemingway's fiction, alternate images of apprentice and exemplary hero document his inward strife. In "Second Poem to Mary," the figures appear once more, the exemplary hero in the guise of confessor or catechist, the apprentice as an aspirant barnacled to doomed ideals. Two voices sound throughout the poem as well. The exemplar's voice is assured, his tone ironic, his questions barbed, his demands harsh. The apprentice is alternately angry, suppliant, and hysterical. By the end of the poem, the figures appear to blend; the voices too are indistinguishable, but the timbre is that of the exemplar.

The poem begins as the apprentice, having thrice denied "that old whore Death," takes her to wife. The bitter nuptial ends with the confessor's injunction: "You are alone at the time and the time now is always. Always was a word you used in promises. It is valueless." The apprentice rejects the vision of *nada*, but admits that one suffers without "any possibility of changing the result or the outcome." But what remains, he insists, is to "look at one another with infinite love and compassion," and to face terror with courage and with "the ability to maneuver and fight." But the confessor insists that it is not Love that abides but Hate, the "dark sister" of Death, and urges the apprentice to pray:

> Pray to all of nothing
> Pray to all of nil
> Throw away your own true love
> Walking up a hill.

Dully now, the apprentice repeats the ritual of his nuptial with Death, mocking religion as a way out, yearning for an "If" (not Kipling's) that answers condition with hope, but knowing that it cannot be. As the poem ends, the mood reflects a calm of resignation and control.

"Second Poem to Mary" has a few passages of undeniable

power. Depressed in mood, it is animated by an acerb edginess. As a lyric of anxiety, its emotive force is palpable. Its essential weakness is an ill-controlled blending of the lyric and the satiric, the latter an intrusion of what Ezra Pound decades earlier had called the "wise-guy," intent on bluntness and coarse, heavy-handed humor. Nevertheless, it is Hemingway's best poem—in a sense, his only poem. That it was motivated by the immediacy of violence and death links it more closely to the vignettes of *in our time* than to his early poetry. The control and economy of *in our time* are barely discernible here, but the comprehensive sense of disaster remains intact. Yet there is change too, in that Hemingway seems even more frenzied as he plumbs the depths of terror. Where economy of language once served, here even plethora seems too little. As if obsessed to tell it all again lest some dark truth remain unspoken, Hemingway bursts with words. "Second Poem to Mary" is thus perhaps more notable as a portrait of the man than as a poem. Either way, it memorializes the fatality of war, the war within a man as well as that about him.

THE SATIRIST

In Our Time was published October 5, 1925. By then, Hemingway had finished the first draft of *The Sun Also Rises*, writing, he admitted, "too fast and each day to the point of exhaustion." [16] To "cool out" before starting his revision, he spent a week in November writing *The Torrents of Spring* and mailed it off promptly to Horace Liveright, his publisher, who, with matching speed, rejected it. [17] Liveright had little choice since *The Torrents of Spring* minced his best-selling star performer, Sherwood Anderson. Released from further obligation to Liveright, Hemingway sent the manuscript to Scribner's, who published it, unaltered, in May 1926. A week earlier, Hemingway had written Anderson from Madrid explaining that the book was intended as an inoffensive joke, but also as a sincere indictment of Anderson's literary misde-

meanors, especially those in his latest novel, *Dark Laughter.*
Among themselves, Hemingway insisted, writers ought not
to pull punches.[18]

No purpose is served here by weighing Hemingway's arrogance or ingratitude against his critical acumen or his independent spirit. One tips the balance according to his own
scale of values. What matters is the quality of the work. Most
contemporary reviewers agreed that Hemingway had justly
exposed the conspicuous excesses of Anderson's naïve fancy
and self-conscious primitivism. Some took delight, as did
Allen Tate, in its "deftly tempered ribaldry" and "economically realized humor of disproportion." [19] Anderson, in his
Memoirs, after taking exception to Hemingway's self-styled
"all right letter" as "the most completely patronizing letter
ever written," called *The Torrents of Spring* "a parodistic
book which might have been humorous if Max Beerbohm
condensed it to twelve pages." His point is well taken, though
not so apposite as Harry Hansen's that ". . . parody is a
gift of the gods. Few are blessed with it. It missed
Hemingway." [20]

The sources of Hemingway's failure are easy enough to locate. Fundamentally, he cannot settle upon a sustained tone.
Instead, he drifts within the satiric framework from the controlled mannerisms of parody to the loose distortions of burlesque to the mallet blows of caricature. Doing so, he violates
the injunction his epigrapher, Henry Fielding, put upon him
that "a comic writer should of all others be the least excused
for deviating from nature . . . the only source of the true Ridiculous . . . is affectation." Anderson provided abundant natural evidence of the Ridiculous: stereotypic portraits of free-
spirited, amorous Negroes and stiff-backed intellectuals in
Dark Laughter; sexual ritualism in *Many Marriages* (where a
man parades naked before his daughter to free her of her
mother's frigidity); and the vague, sentimental introspection
that afflicts all his characters.

Where the ground is sodden, the satirist must be light-
footed. Occasionally, Hemingway's agility is creditable. The

Negroes become Indians, their dark laughter war whoops, and they run a private club above a stable for "town" Indians (no whites allowed, "woods" Indians tolerated). One of the Indians even affects the cultivated speech of an Oxonian. Two waitresses vie for honors as beanery bluestockings, and a naked squaw brings to flood tide the spring torrents dormant in the breast of red and white man alike.[21] And always there is the question of what it all means: "The three of them walking, walking, walking. Where were they going? Where could they go? What was there left?"

All of which bears the hallmark of parody. Anderson's subjects and style are pushed just far enough beyond their natural boundaries to suggest the essential lack of naturalness that makes them ridiculous. Unfortunately, these high spots are rare. More often, the pastiche unwittingly and witlessly sets the dunce cap on the wrong head. Yogi Johnson and Scripps O'Neil may be intended as burlesques of Anderson's characters but they inhabit Hemingway's country (northern Michigan) and, excepting their tendency to think and talk too much, frequently sound like the most wooden of Hemingway's exemplary heroes. At one point—the most serious reversal of tone in the entire work—Yogi Johnson eloquently denounces Sherwood Anderson's and Willa Cather's (in *One of Ours*) notions of war, killing, nightmares, and discipline. Yogi argues at considerable length that war, like football (Yogi, like Hemingway, played on the line), is "stimulating, exciting" but "intensely unpleasant" and, he adds, "Nobody had any damn business to write about it . . . that didn't at least know about it from hearsay. Literature has too strong an effect on people's minds" [63]. In all this, Hemingway foreshadows the dark themes of much of his later writing.[22] But in the madcap context of *The Torrents of Spring*, it is all much too deadly earnest Hemingway. One can but sympathize with the two Indians (also exemplary, tight-lipped, and wounded) who determine to join the Salvation Army after hearing Yogi's outburst.

With his waitresses, too, Hemingway overplays his hand.

The silences of the naked squaw are more telling than most of Mandy's literary anecdotes. The comic outlines of Diane Scripps's reading as an index of her personality are deftly established at the outset. Thereafter, Hemingway simply catalogues names and titles whenever she appears. This expands the possibilities of bludgeoning assorted contemporaries with his Indian club—H. L. Mencken, William Lyon Phelps, the Van Dorens, Ruth Suckow, and others—but it shrinks the relevance and softens the impact of his parody.

One critic has suggested that all of Hemingway's writing belongs to the old tradition of burlesque, and that his hardboiled attacks on euphemism and gentility—like Fielding's and Cervantes's—strip away the deadwood of imagination to compel a redefinition of experience in direct, forthright language. Certainly, Hemingway's motives in satirizing Anderson's work were grounded in a similar thesis. Insofar as *The Torrents of Spring* declares his independence of Anderson (and possibly of Gertrude Stein),[23] the book merits passing notice. And also, perhaps, for a few moments of good fun and for one moving, though misplaced, outburst by Yogi Johnson. But as a contribution to the literature of satire, it falls noiselessly among Dr. Johnson's crab apples.

THE DRAMATIST

Hemingway published only two dramatic works, "Today is Friday" (1926), an unproduced one-acter, and *The Fifth Column* (1940), a full-length play that ran for two months on Broadway as a Theater Guild production. "If you write a play," Hemingway once said, "you have to stick around and fix it up. . . . After I've written, I want to go home and take a shower."[24] The only alterations in "Today is Friday" were a few changes in punctuation made when Hemingway added it as one of the "stories" collected in *Men Without Women*. He exercised himself even less with *The Fifth Column*, turning over to another the thankless task of adaptation while he

went on writing *For Whom the Bell Tolls.* With both plays
Hemingway wisely left bad enough alone.

In the most awkward way, "Today is Friday" anticipates
the characters and action of "The Killers," published a year
later. The setting of "Today is Friday" is a bar instead of a
restaurant, though the owner, George, has the same name; in
both the dialogue is tough and laconic, appropriate to the
soldiers of the play and the gangsters of the story. A killing,
imminent in "The Killers," has already taken place in "Today
is Friday." One soldier, mindless, regards the dead man
coldly, indifferently, leering that he "knew" the man's girl-
friend earlier and mocking the "gang" that deserted him. A
second thinks the victim as he died "was pretty good in
there," and the third, shaken, pale, merely keeps repeating
that he feels "like hell." George ignores the event altogether:
"I wasn't out there. It's a thing I haven't taken any interest
in."

The unfleshed outlines of "The Killers" are easily discernible, especially that of Nick Adams in the sketch of the third
soldier. But when we know that Friday is the day of Jesus'
crucifixion, that George is a Jewish wine merchant, and that
the soldiers are Roman centurions, language, characters, and
theme suddenly sink into caricature. The clichés that become
remarkably pertinent in "The Killers" stubbornly remain in
"Today is Friday" as stereotypic as the dialogue is absurdly
anachronistic. The problem is not one of irreverence but of ir-
relevance. Worst of all, feeling "like hell"—so moving when
Nick or Jake Barnes says it—is, in this inadequately motivated blackout skit, woefully insufficient. That "Today is Friday," as Sheridan Baker notes, represents "Hemingway's first
use of Christianity as a symbology for brave Man crucified by
the world," [25] helps to place the four-page play in a larger,
possibly more usable context. Beyond that dispensation,
"Today is Friday" is better left to heaven.

In his preface to *The First Forty-Nine Stories,* in which
The Fifth Column is collected, Hemingway tells of writing
the play in the fall and winter of 1937 while he lived at the

Hotel Florida in Madrid. More than thirty high-explosive shells hit the hotel, he wrote, "So if it is not a good play perhaps that is what is the matter with it. If it is a good play, perhaps those thirty shells helped write it" [v]. Shelling neither saved the play nor destroyed it, though action (which includes shell explosions as well as shooting) is its strongest asset.[26] The demolition team that flattens the play is its characters, built-in fifth columnists. They betray Hemingway's serious and legitimate purpose—to document the horror of the Civil War without making superheroes of the Loyalists he supports or supervillains of the rebels.

A few of the local gentry come off better than the protagonists and function more significantly in the ideological context. Antonio, for example, the Spanish officer in charge of the Loyalist counter-espionage activities, cleanly and tersely defines the impartiality of death and the code of dying well: not slobbering and crawling like a politician—" I have never seen a politician die well." But like young Fascists; the real ones know how: "They are mistaken, but they have much style." So do the priests, however much Antonio, as a lifelong socialist, opposes them: "To die? Priests? Terrific . . . just simple priests. I don't mean Bishops" [43]. Other minor characters are less persuasive. The self-seeking hotel manager and Anita, the idealized whore-in-residence (both of whose dialects, incidentally, sound more like ruptured American Indian than fractured English), as well as Max, the selfless, broken-faced agent—all are too broadly drawn for comic or tragic effect.

Philip Rawlings and Dorothy Bridges, the protagonists, lay waste whatever is not already barren. Their relationship is intended to highlight a dual motif—a longing for a past that might have allowed their affair to survive, and an acceptance (at least on Philip's part) that, in parlous times, one must go it alone "with others who go there for the same reason." It is not the motifs that are improbable. Hemingway had successfully exploited them for more than a decade, even before adding the note of commitment to social action. Rather it is

Philip and Dorothy who render the probable impossible. Between her former lover's charge that she is a "bored Vassar bitch" and Philip's semi-indictment of her as "a very handsome commodity," brave but uneducated, useless, and a fool, Philip's verdict is not only kinder but more accurate. Dorothy is neither bored nor bitchy, just unbelievably dense. That she, a trained correspondent, could live in the Hotel Florida so long as she has—considerably longer than the five days of the play—exquisitely unaware that Philip is more than a drunken lecher wasting his life, passes belief. Action erupts everywhere about her—the death of an agent in Philip's room, for example, elicits from her a shocked "Who shot him?" followed by silence after Philip's irrelevant answer. Never more than feebly does she reach after insight. Dorothy's name, Hemingway wrote in his preface, "might also have been Nostalgia." True, but to value the past, one ought first know and assess the present.

Philip Rawlings does. "We're in for fifty years of undeclared wars," he says, "and I've signed up for the duration" [95]. He enters that battle burdened with the familiar appurtenances of the apprentice hero: an insomniac, he has the "horrors" at night but refuses to talk about them, he is superstitious, and he cannot watch the actual process of torturing prisoners. Despite these limitations, Rawlings copes extremely well. His exploits behind the lines and beneath the sheets would shame most of Hemingway's exemplary heroes. So too, for a self-styled, tight-lipped fellow, would his rhetoric: "I'd like to never kill another son-of-a-bitch, I don't care who or for what, as long as I live. I'd like to never have to lie. I'd like to know who I'm with when I wake up. I'd like to wake up in the same place every morning for a week straight. I'd like to marry a girl named Bridges that you don't know. But don't mind if I use the name because I like to say it. And I'd like to marry her because she's got the longest, smoothest, straightest legs in the world, and I don't have to listen to her when she talks if it doesn't make too good sense. But I'd like to see what the kids would look like" [44].

If Dorothy fails to convince because she lacks dimension, Philip Rawlings is unbelievable because his is stretched to contain his boundless versatility. Individually, these two are incredible; together they are also incompatible. Not only does their love affair seem a travesty but it distorts the focus of the play whose true center is the terrible reality of the war. Having Philip forsake his love merely substitutes for distortion diffusion and, at last, chaos. But that, after all, is the aim of the fifth columnist.

7

The Sun Also Rises

Hemingway began writing *The Sun Also Rises* on July 21, 1925, his twenty-sixth birthday, and finished a self-acknowledged bad first draft little more than a month later. "I had to rewrite it completely," he recalled years later,[1] but before he did so, he disposed of *The Torrents of Spring* in the fall and went off to ski in the Austrian Voralberg. Then, for five months, he labored at revision, and mailed to Scribner's on April 26 the completed manuscript. Before the novel was published, Hemingway cut from galleys an entire first chapter about Brett Ashley and Mike Campbell, and the early parts of a second chapter in which Jake Barnes tells about his life in Paris, his work, and his friends. That the novel omits all this material and begins perfectly with the now famous sentence, "Robert Cohn was once middleweight boxing champion of Princeton," is an unacknowledged debt Hemingway owed to F. Scott Fitzgerald.[2] Not until five weeks after Hemingway had shipped off his manuscript did he show a carbon copy to Fitzgerald, who urged him to delete those wordy opening passages of "elephantine facetiousness." Later, from Paris, Hemingway wrote that he had dropped them and that the novel, now in final proof, read well. "I hope to hell you like it," he added, "and I think that maybe you will."[3] Fitzgerald did like it, though "with certain qualifications" about Brett and Jake.[4]

The literary crowd in Montparnasse and along the Left Bank liked it too, partially for the wrong reasons since many were reading it as if it were fact rather than fiction. To some extent they were justified, for Hemingway had modeled his fictional characters on identifiably real people. Most of Hemingway's contemporaries readily ferreted out the clues hidden in his *roman à clef:* that Brett Ashley was in fact Lady Duff-Twysden, an English voluptuary; Pedro Romero, the brilliant young matador Cayetano Ordóñez (nicknamed Niño de la Palma); Robert Cohn, the editor of an avant-garde little magazine, *Broom*, Harold Loeb; and Bill Gorton, the journalist and later Hollywood scenarist, Donald Ogden Stewart.[5] For today's reader, what endures is the symbolic rather than the actual identity of the gay but shattered creatures whose fragmented lives Hemingway re-formed in the crucible of his imagination. Even Jake Barnes, the most readily identifiable (he was called Hem and Ernie in the first draft), is Hemingway only insofar as any writer must intrude some distance into his writing. Jake's wound was not Hemingway's any more than Nick Adams's was.[6] A writer's "invention," Hemingway once remarked, "should produce a truer account than anything factual can be."

in our time describes a world of terror and the Nick Adams stories of *In Our Time* tell the terror of learning to live with the terrible. In *The Sun Also Rises,* Hemingway refused to shade his vision from the harsh glare of truths he had already perceived. The sun that rises and sets on Jake Barnes and his friends is neither benign nor bountiful; its heat is sterile, its light cold. But though the world is the same as he had previously described it and the shock of encounter similarly traumatic, Hemingway's first novel records with a trenchancy of style and theme beyond what he had yet managed, perhaps beyond what he would ever again master in the novel form. As in the short stories, the plot is minimal, the "wow" suppressed. But the action is swift and continuous, thrust forward by internal narration that makes Jake Barnes actor as well as witness.

Though dramatically vivid and immediate, first-person narration poses risks.[7] Is the narrator's version of reality trustworthy or has he distorted to advance his own sense of life? In *The Sun Also Rises*, the danger is singular because Jake's wound might easily tempt him to cynicism or self-pity. Neither suborns his scrupulous objectivity in reporting. As Jake's wound sets him apart from those whose restive lives he must report, it compels him to establish some distance from himself as well. Only so can he learn to live with both the wound and the world. To help control and discipline his emotions, he strives for the detachment objective recording allows. This does not mean, however, that what Jake reports is mere data. When he retreats to San Sebastian after the fiesta, he details literally and without comment what he does: unpack, stack books, lay out shaving things, hang up clothes, bundle laundry; eat lunch, wrap a swimming suit and comb in a towel, walk to a cabin, undress, don a swimming suit, and walk across the sand to the beach. The reader must infer the emotional relevance of these orderly, routine gestures that follow immediately upon the devastating chaos of the fiesta. Like Nick Adams fishing at Big Two-Hearted River, Jake needs and welcomes the retarded pace and the mechanical gestures that afford him an at least temporary release. Because the details themselves and the rhythm of the sentences which contain them suggest the depth of Jake's feeling, he need not search other words to state it explicitly.

When, on occasion, the emotional strain is too great, Hemingway shifts the setting to the privacy of Jake's bedroom (as in Chapters IV and XIV) and lets him release his subjective feelings through an interior monologue. These rare but unforgettable passages of introspection in no way diminish Jake's reliability as a narrator. Rather, they provide a necessary, humanizing glimpse into the heart of his darkness (where also resides the thematic center of the novel) and accent his awesome task of adjustment.

Well-crafted despite its superficially rambling disjointedness, the structural pattern of the three parts of *The Sun Also*

Rises is also thematically sure and true. As the characters wander purposelessly in their Parisian wasteland—their altar a bar, their grail a glass of absinthe—the boredom, hysteria, and agony mirror the chaotic past of the war experience and the cynical or hedonistic masks that later disguise disfigured or mutilated dreams and illusions. What sustains the characters is the possibility of restoration implicit in the fiesta and its climactic bullfight. In the second part of the novel, then, the characters move resolutely and eagerly toward Spain. Trysts and squabbles heighten tension and strengthen characterization, but all lines converge in the bull ring.

There, in the ritualistic confrontation between Pedro Romero and the bull—man and nature—seems to lie the chance to revivify dead ideals and sterile hopes, to establish a unity of love, life, and death. Using "no trick and no mystifications . . . no brusqueness," Romero works his big bull with such finesse as to give a "sudden ache inside. The crowd did not want it ever to be finished." At the kill, Romero becomes "one with the bull," and for that brief moment the action of the novel suspends, its link with time severed. By the next day, the pure passion has been spent. Brett has gone off with Romero, and Jake, drinking one absinthe after another, repeats again and again, "I feel like hell." The moment of truth clatters absurdly to the rubbled streets of post-fiesta reality.

The single brief chapter of the third part opens with "In the morning it was all over," and closes with Jake's flat rejection of Brett's nostalgia for the impossible. At the outset of the novel, Brett and Jake leave their friends at the bar and ride off together in a Parisian taxi whose driver has been given no direction other than "to drive around." They talk of love, Brett of its misery, Jake of his refusal to think about it. Again, as the novel closes, they enter a taxi, this time to ride aimlessly through the streets of Madrid, once more hopelessly.

Structurally, then, *The Sun Also Rises* echoes the hollow ache of Ecclesiastes: "The thing that hath been, it is that which shall be . . . and there is no new thing under the sun."

Hemingway's dialogue resonates the same chords. A single example will do. In Chapter XVII of Book Two, having just called Jake a pimp and knocked him down, Cohn tries to apologize, insisting he had lost his head but did not want to lose his best friend. Thrice during the ensuing dialogue, Jake answers either "That's all right" or "It's all right." As Jake leaves, Cohn asks how he feels; again his answer is, "I'm all right." The full impact of Jake's repetitive statement has been consciously delayed until its final expression. Then, the cumulative force of the incremental repetition hits hard. For Jake is not altogether "all right." He is emotionally and physically crippled and, in Cohn's vulgar sense, he is a pimp. But, unlike Cohn, he has learned to control his inward and overt response to the tragedy of his experience. He means what he says, but the meaning is more complex than his statement suggests.

As Hemingway's subtleties of perspective, structure, and dialogue communicate underlying thematic motifs, so too does his treatment of setting. What his characters are is often suggested by their response to where they are. Some, like Brett Ashley and Mike Campbell, are barely conscious of their physical environment. For them, Paris, Pamplona, and Madrid all have bars and beds, sufficient landscape for the uprooted. Robert Cohn, on the other hand, yearns for distant places—the South America of W. H. Hudson's *The Purple Land*. Meanwhile, he ignores the possibilities of his immediate locale. He has, as Jake says, an "incapacity to enjoy Paris"; he refuses the opportunity to fish in the mountains with Jake; and he is essentially unmoved by the excitement of Pamplona.

For Jake Barnes, however, place helps him nearly as much as people to define the disease of his time and to discover the remedies that ease pain. Unlike Brett and Cohn, Jake's consciousness of environment is neither abstract nor generalized. Like Henry James's Paris in *The Ambassadors*, which, as Stephen Spender wrote, is the "*thing* . . . the object which we hold on to and see from every angle," metropolis and fishing village alike become Jake's objective correlatives for his inner world. At night, Paris is for Jake motion without meaning, pain without purpose, a labyrinth of dark streets and lighted bars, of whores on duty and of zinc bars and dance floors where Brett and her crowd dissipate time and self. It is on a spring night in Paris that Jake meets Georgette, the pretty tart with bad teeth, who voices what Jake feels about the City of Light: "Everybody's sick. I'm sick too." By day, though, Paris is wholly different: "It was a fine morning. The horse-chestnut trees in the Luxembourg gardens were in bloom. There was the pleasant early-morning feeling of a hot day. I read the papers with the coffee and then smoked a cigarette. The flower-women were coming up from the market and arranging their daily stock. Students went by going up to the law school, or down to the Sorbonne. The Boulevard was busy with trams and people going to work. All along people were going to work. It felt pleasant to be going to work" [35–36].

Disorder is not chaos, and the directed busyness—the commitment to work—of the city restores Jake from "feeling like hell." Work is one way to discover purpose. There are others too, and again Jake's response to his environment cues the reader to Hemingway's intention. En route to Spain with Bill Gorton and Robert Cohn, Jake is ever alert to the countryside: "For a while the country was much as it had been; then, climbing all the time, we crossed the top of a Col, the road winding back and forth on itself, and then it was really Spain. There were long brown mountains and a few pines and far-off forests of beech-trees on some of the mountainsides. The road went along the summit of the Col and then dropped down, and the driver had to honk, and slow up, and turn out to avoid running into two donkeys that were sleeping in the road. We came down out of the mountains and through an oak forest, and there were white cattle grazing in the forest. Down below there were grassy plains and clear streams, and then we crossed a gloomy little village, and started to climb again. We climbed up and up and crossed

another high Col and turned along it, and the road ran down
to the right, and we saw a whole new range of mountains off
to the south, all brown and baked-looking and furrowed in
strange shapes" [93].

Panoramic and close-up views alternately command Jake's
attention. An unmistakable exhilaration suffuses the prose, a
sense of anticipation, of imminent discovery of the new and
the beautiful as distant mountains and oak forests yield to the
immediacy of sleeping donkeys and white cattle. Yet the
prose is relaxed, the sentences elongated by a leisurely flow
of coordinated clauses that coil like the road itself. Jake is at
ease, or, better, at one with the natural world, even if briefly.
Bill Gorton too has absorbed the landscape and he and Jake
need only nod silently to share their pleasure. Robert Cohn
sleeps throughout the journey. To learn how to *live in it,*
Tony Tanner has written, "it is essential first of all to learn
how to *look at it.*" By charting their sensory and emotional
responses to their environment, Hemingway explores the geography of his characters' minds, their sensibilities, and their
value systems.

The antics of most of the characters in *The Sun Also Rises*
seem to fulfill the exhortation of the ancient preacher of Ecclesiastes ("Then I commended mirth, because a man hath no
better thing under the sun, than to eat, and to drink, and to
be merry." Jake Barnes's complex role as narrator precludes
so neat a formula, for though he eats and drinks, Jake is not
merry—and he has little cause to be. His wound demands a
gamut of psychic adjustment even Nick Adams never had to
run. However threatening the spiritual impotence menacing
Nick, he never had to confront the incontrovertible fact that
an act of physical love lay beyond possibility. And from what
we know of Nick, he lacks the emotional stamina to cope
with Jake's reality. Most of Nick's psychic energy has been
expended in learning the intricacies of the "code" and the
"separate peace." At last he understands them without wholly

embodying them—the eternal apprentice, isolated, incapable of the human intimacy he desires but dreads. Jake's single advantage over Nick here is that he knows the outlines of both the "code" and the "separate peace" at the outset. His apprenticeship consists of translating knowing into being, of risking involvement, even of loving a woman he cannot make love to. Each of the characters in *The Sun Also Rises* has suffered a wound, but Jake's alone *physically* manifests the pervasive impotence and sterility of the expatriate cult. If Jake is the symbolic core of futility, he is also one of the few characters whose psychic and spiritual resources enable maturation. And if, as Malcolm Cowley and Philip Young have suggested, Jake is Hemingway's Fisher King without T. S. Eliot's hint of rejuvenation, he is also an apprentice slowly and painfully absorbing the lessons he must master to achieve rank as an exemplary hero. "All I wanted to know was how to live in it," Jake tells himself just before the fiesta. The impersonal pronoun does not refer to Jake's wound: it symbolizes rather the dread *nada* that envelops his world. As king of the wastelanders—admired by all the men, hopelessly loved by and in love with one of the women—Jake is uniquely positioned not only to report on their response to *nada* but also to learn from those responses. Although Jake rarely explicitly generalizes or judges (he mocks his abstractions as "bilge"), he does, like any apprentice hero, discard or save chunks of possibility. However covert or disguised, Jake's responses do reinforce a sense of life as worth living and even, within narrow boundaries, as coherent and ordered.

Jake's internal monologue at the beginning of Chapter XIV in Book Two is a rambling but revelatory discourse, the most nearly direct statement of his values in the novel. That it comes just before the fiesta is significant, for Jake must consolidate his resources before the ordeal that lies ahead. That he is drunk, tense, and sleepless, is equally important, for his musings are thus intuitive, reflections of feeling rather than reason. "All I wanted to know was how to live in it" is a cry from the heart. To answer it, neither self-pity nor rational clichés will serve. What Jake offers himself is a self-study course in emotional pragmatism: "No idea of retribution or punishment. Just exchange of values. You gave up something and got something else. Or you worked for something. You paid some way for everything that was any good. Either you paid by learning about them, or by experience, or by taking chances, or by money. Enjoying living was learning to get your money's worth and knowing when you had it. You could get your money's worth. The world was a good place to buy in" [148].

Even when drunk, Jake allows that his "philosophy" may become "as silly as all the other fine philosophies" he has had. In fact, it does not. Whatever its shortcomings, Jake's philosophy helps him to escape the stagnation afflicting most of his fellows. Jake's values, in turn, may not strike all readers as worth having. They do not, for example, include commitment to nation, job, wife and kids, norms established early in the novel by his bland fellow American journalists, Woolsey and Krum. Nor do they embrace the clubby religiosity of the Lourdes-bound pilgrims from Dayton, Ohio, whom Jake meets on the train. Like them, Jake is a Roman Catholic.[8] It is, he insists, a "grand religion" and his regret that he is a "rotten Catholic" is genuine. But he is a "rotten Catholic" because the "grace under pressure" he seeks has its fountainhead in man rather than God. Jake's focus is on the temporal —people and events—not the supernatural. For Jake, as for most of Hemingway's heroes, redemption or damnation is the result of action, not faith, of a decision based upon pragmatic, not traditional, principles. And it is always an intensely personal, private decision whose governance lies beyond the administrative power of established authority. In this at least, Jake is, like Shaw's St. Joan, a protestant Catholic.

"Perhaps as you went along you did learn something," Jake reflects in his monologue. Just to *go along*, however, demands unceasing struggle with minute dilemmas whose resolution may win an "exchange of values" payable in grace and redemption. What shall he make, for example, of the implications of his friends' drinking? Mike is a bad drunk, Brett and Bill Gorton good drunks; Robert Cohn is never drunk. When drunk, Mike taunts Robert Cohn. "I like to see him hurt Cohn," Jake thinks. "I wished he would not do it, though, because afterwards it made me disgusted at myself" [148–49]. Of such observation and reflection, Jake fashions his pragmatic morality—what is immoral is "things that made you disgusted afterward." Each encounter with the world thus engages Jake in an act of creative revaluation. Freed from the formalism of "other-directed" choice, he is compelled to discover with pain his own system and discipline himself in its mode.

Hemingway's treatment of the orthodoxy he rejects is neither cavalier nor simplistic. If the Knights of Columbus en route to Lourdes are comic Catholics, Jake is not. Similarly, if Woolsey and Krum are genteel versions of Babbitt, Robert Cohn is not. Critics might have reached accord about him long ago had Hemingway portrayed Cohn simply and categorically as a man to be hated or laughed at or admired. The trouble is—as Jake and Bill Gorton realize—that Cohn is "nice" and "awful." Most critics settle upon the awful, sharing Carlos Baker's contempt for his "emotionalism . . . essential cowardice . . . miserable fawning dependence . . . self-pity . . . basic rudeness and egotism." 9 Some, however, defend Cohn as "the only normal character in the book," 10 a modest, sensitive, intelligent young man whose romantic naïveté becomes a virtue when contrasted with the sophistication of the "neurotic hedonists" around him. And one critic (rather off by himself) argues that Cohn is neither a villain nor a hero, but a "humorous character" who should be taken no more seriously than Jake, Brett, or Mike. All of them, he insists, are targets of Hemingway's satiric indictment of sentimentality and self-pity.11

Robert Cohn eludes the neat classification critics try to impose. As the most civilized bourgeois personality in the novel, he embodies all the attendant traits of that breed, the "nice" and the "awful"—to which, unhappily, it must be added that Cohn has, as his most sympathetic critic, Jake, observes, "a wonderful quality of bringing out the worst in anybody." Jake tries the hardest to be fair and his relationship with Cohn is, therefore, subtly complex and ambivalent, a compound of affection, compassion, anger, and scorn. But even Jake is not above sharing with Mike and Bill Gorton gratuitous anti-Semitic remarks, such as noting Cohn's "hard, Jewish, stubborn streak," or commenting that his nose had been improved by being flattened, or that Cohn's expression when he first sees Brett resembles that of "his compatriot . . . when he saw the promised land . . . that look of eager and deserving expectation" [22].[12] Toward Cohn's more conspicuously orthodox bourgeois traits, Jake is even more ironically negative and nasty: "He was fairly happy, except that, like many people living in Europe, he would rather have been in America . . ." [5]. "I am sure that he had never been in love in his life" [8]—this, despite Cohn's marriage and several affairs.

Jake's antagonism is tempered by more than mercy, for much of Cohn's apparent innocence and idealism appeals to him. Like Jake, Cohn wants something more enduring than a bargain in the flesh mart and is also repelled by the physical and spiritual decadence of moral spendthrifts. But Cohn irritatingly persists in rationalizing reality into an ideal. Failing that, he tries to alter fact by force. He leaves the novel as he entered it, a sensitive, embittered *boy* trying ineffectually to punch the face of an indifferent world. What may appeal about an undergraduate's self-indulgent, masochistic romanticism may appall in a man in his mid-thirties (and Cohn, as Jake pointedly observes in their final encounter, is still wearing the kind of polo shirt he had worn at Princeton).

Cohn is, as Earl Rovit has suggested, Jake's *double*, "the secret sharer who suffers cruel and comical ignominy in order to demonstrate to Jake the dangers inherent in 'letting go' and falling into the pit of self-deception." [13] When, in Chapter XIII, Jake explains to Bill Gorton how steers are used to quiet the bulls and are often gored for their trouble, Bill

comments, "Must be swell being a steer." The bitterly relevant irony, though unintended, cannot be lost on Jake, who
nevertheless lets it pass without comment. Later on, when the
others gather to watch the bulls enter the corral, a steer is
gored, retreats against a wall, and is shunned by the other
animals. Unaware that the sentence is an apt self-description,
Cohn ventures, "It's no life being a steer." With characteristic
viciousness, Mike Campbell clarifies the ironic resemblance,
suggesting mockingly that Cohn ought to enjoy being a steer:
"They never say anything and they're always hanging about
so." The physical or psychic correspondences that link Jake
and Robert Cohn to the steer and to one another are painfully, inescapably clear. What discriminates the two men is
Jake's ability to suffer the torment of reality without whining.
For Cohn as for Jake—and for nearly all the other characters
—the sun has risen and set, changing little. How one adjusts
and adapts to that fact measures maturity.

Because Cohn remains spoiled, pouting, self-deluded, he
can neither understand nor enjoy the rare moments of pleasure experience allows. Sex with Brett (as with his mistress,
Frances Clyne) holds for Cohn the same significance as boxing had at college—pride in victory rather than delight in the
event itself. Cohn aspires to the grand, quixotic gesture (saving the honor of a most unlikely maid or starting life afresh in
South America) but—through evasion or indifference—misses
the excitement of immediate, real adventure (the fishing trip
and the bullfight). Above all, he is, despite his bursts of violence, passive and weak-willed. He wed "the first girl who
was nice to him," and lost her to a miniaturist while he pon-
dered leaving her. Each of his mistresses sweeps *him* off his
feet. Frances, Jake observes, "was very forceful, and Cohn
never had a chance of not being taken in hand" [5]. Brett
leads him to a tryst in San Sebastian hoping it will be "good"
for him. Even Cohn's prized morality is spurious, for he
grossly neglects one mistress as he dogs another; then, failing
with Brett, he will probably (as Jake hints) return to Frances
in Paris.

Although Jake's threshold of pain is no higher than Cohn's, his self-control is more rigorous; at least in public he is never daunted. Moreover, his insights are more acute, his tolerance more ample, and his resolution more mature. Opening the novel with these two men leads the reader, as Philip Young has written, to an understanding of Jake's situation with Brett. But it is also an astute way to abrade Jake's evolving sense of "how to live in it" against Cohn's decent but rigid vision. What is wrong about Cohn's sense of experience is his refusal to reconcile the illusory with the real. Certainly, he is not alone in confusing the two; but more than any other person in the novel, he refuses to see what he is doing.

Even Mike Campbell, "undischarged bankrupt" and archetype of waste, is rather more appealing than Cohn because his cynically amused self-portrait is both frank and accurate. So too, for a different reason, is Bill Gorton, Jake's hard-drinking, good-natured fishing companion. Bill's defense of stuffed dogs ("Simple exchange of values. You give them money. They give you a stuffed dog" [72]) implicitly argues for settling upon an imitation of life instead of the real thing —an imitation assures at least some pleasure and minimal pain. But Gorton *knows* the dogs are fake; Cohn would wish them real and act as if they were.

Despite their relative appeal, Mike and Bill are at last fugitives from reality too, their values as suspect as Cohn's. Choosing between the values of the scions of orthodoxy and of the minions of the "lost generation" is not, then, altogether simple. And by quoting Gertrude Stein's comment, "You are all a lost generation," as the epigraph to *The Sun Also Rises*, Hemingway further muddies the issue. Is the epigraph to be taken as literal or ironic? Writing to Maxwell Perkins in 1926, Hemingway commented that Stein's utterance was sheer bombast; to Carlos Baker he said in 1951: "I thought we were beat-up . . . Lost, no . . . We were a very solid generation though without education (some of us). But you could always get it." [14] And in *A Moveable Feast*, Hemingway recalls his irritation with Miss Stein at the time she first used the expression: ". . . the hell with her lost-generation talk and all the dirty, easy labels." [15]

Should one, then, regard Mike Campbell, or Brett and her Parisian coterie, or even Robert Cohn as representatives of "a very solid generation"? Or, aware that Hemingway had also written to Perkins that he had "a great deal of fondness and admiration for the earth, and not a hell of a lot for my generation," [16] should the reader regard Jake's friends as exemplars of decadence? Whatever "intentional" clues one seeks in Hemingway's correspondence or conversation baffle or confound—his glosses are too often at odds with his text. For the truths of *The Sun Also Rises*—about the age and about man—the reader must return to Hemingway's art, not to his commentary or his ill-chosen (or at least badly explicated) epigraphs. Within the aesthetic frame of the novel, Hemingway's theme is far more clearly demonstrated. The reader recognizes that Mike Campbell and Robert Cohn, extremes of their antithetic modes, inevitably attract and repel Jake. That they have shared the woman he loves intensifies his pain but also quickens his determination to find ways other than theirs to relieve it without sacrificing his integrity.

The five-day fishing holiday at Burguete proves to be one of the most satisfying. Once more, Jake's response to his environment suggests that one of the best ways, as well as places, to "live in it" is out-of-doors. As he leaves behind the "brown, heat-baked mountains" and enters the "rolling green plain, with dark mountains beyond it," Jake is more relaxed than at any other time or place in the novel. None of Brett's homosexual "chaps" are here to disgust him. Neither must he endure the agony of embracing Brett, or the nightly insomniac terror of a darkened bedroom. As with Nick Adams in "Big Two-Hearted River," nature's purge is real: Jake sleeps well; he is sensually alert to and satisfied by the landscape and trout-fishing he lovingly details; and his consciousness of time dims. In better control of himself than Nick, Jake enjoys company despite the risk that conversation may revive the dormant past. In fact, Bill Gorton does occasionally jar the serenity, but the idyllic mood survives the shock. Bill's inadvertent reference to impotence turns to banter about Henry James's so-called "wound," and his tentative probes into Jake's feelings for Brett and his Catholicism are genially turned aside. Little of apparent significance occurs during the five days: Jake, Bill, and Harris, the affable Englishman, climb, fish, eat, drink, jest, and read. But, like Nick Adams in "The Three-Day Blow," Jake seems to find that Eden without Eve is not only possible but preferable.

What happens at Burguete is not, however, merely a celebration of nature and its healing force, despite Hemingway's statement to Perkins that *The Sun Also Rises* is a "damn tragedy with the earth abiding forever as the hero." As Mark Spilka has noted, "there are no joyous hymns to the seasons . . . no celebrations of fertility and change." [17] To what purpose, one must ask, does the earth abide; what makes it heroic? The center of the "damn tragedy" is man—Jake Barnes —and though the earth affords him a necessary and helpful respite, it provides no resolution. Mike Campbell's letter and Robert Cohn's telegram announcing the arrival of bankrupts and bourgeois at Pamplona recall Jake to time and a harsher reality.

For Nick Adams, there were always other days when he could fish the swamp. In *The Sun Also Rises,* Hemingway thrusts his protagonist into the dark place as part of his ritual of initiation as an exemplary hero. At first glance, the fiesta at Pamplona may seem an unlikely setting. It is, as Spilka writes, "an extension of Burguete for Barnes: gayer and more festive on the surface, but essentially more serious." [18] In the clash of events and personalities at Pamplona, Jake endures the most shattering test of his apprenticeship to life, love, and death. At Burguete, he seems almost to have learned to live with his hurt, to have mastered the lesson taught him in Paris by another veteran of life, Count Mippopopolous: "It is because I have lived very much that I can now enjoy everything so well . . . You must get to know the values" [60]. Jake too has lived much, knows the values, and tries to abide by them. But the purity of his passion for them is stained at Pamplona by his continuing passion for Brett.

If Brett is merely, as Robert Cohn suggests, a Circe who turns men to swine, Jake must be numbered among those who foolishly fall under her spell. Before the fiesta ends, he panders for her with Romero and, by risking the young man's career, squanders his reputation with Montoya, the hotelkeeper and fellow *aficionado*—a poor exchange of values, surely. Yet, without denying Brett's destructive force, a more generous view of her is both justifiable and necessary. Only so does the full sense of Jake's plight and his ultimate resolution of it become clear. War and peace have scarred Brett too: her first love and her ex-husband have been destroyed by war, one actually, the other psychically. What she tendered in womanly love brought as payment frustration, anguish, and humiliation. The terrible consequence is that, despite her promiscuity, Brett's sexual identity is psychically more tenuous than Jake's. Incongruously mannish in attire and manner, determined to swill with the "chaps" as an equal, she uses sex aggressively but vainly to restore her womanhood.

From the outset she knows that she will at last settle for the bankrupt Mike Campbell: "He's my sort of thing." Yet she clings desperately to illusion: going off with Cohn because "it would be good for him" is less random nymphomania than hysterical romantic idealism. A similar motive sends her away from Romero. At worst, Brett's whimsical morality grows as boring and offensive as Cohn's. But it has a nobler side too, a dogged honesty and—despite Brett's pagan irreligiousness [19] —a Christian humanity. Sending Romero away is, of course, Brett's best moment. Its grandeur, however, resides not merely in her moral refusal to spoil Romero but also in her tacit acceptance of her fate. Letting Romero go seals her doom; henceforth, she will always be one of the "chaps," never a woman.

Brett is not, like Catherine Barkley in *A Farewell to Arms,* Maria in *For Whom the Bell Tolls,* or Renata in *Across the River and Into the Trees,* a prototypic mistress—soft, yielding, long-haired. But neither is she a prototypic bitch like Frances Clyne or Margot Macomber or Dorothy Hollis (*To Have and Have Not*). Critics debate whether Brett's relationship with Jake is, for her, truly love or just tenderness or self-pity or, as Jake once remarks, a desire for something she cannot have.[20] Something of each is probably true, but perhaps more persuasive than any of these is Brett's just sense that Jake, more than any of the others, profoundly comprehends and shares her anguish, her desire, and her terror. Because he does, Jake's growth from apprenticeship to exemplary hero must be measured by his ability to disengage himself from Brett. Cleaving to one another, they symbolize the vanity of human wishes; worse, they drain one another's psychic strength. Being near Brett, in Jake's own words, is "getting something for nothing." But, he adds, "that only delayed the presentation of the bill" [148]. Until after the fiesta, Jake cannot face the reckoning.

Pedro Romero's behavior and a swift succession of almost Greek ironies help to prepare him. Romero is not the only exemplary hero in *The Sun Also Rises*. Jake has learned from Montoya and Count Mippopopolous too. Montoya's passion and integrity are conspicuous—for their restraint as well as for their omnipresence. "We never talked for very long at a time," Jake notes of his conversations with Montoya about bullfighting. "It was simply the pleasure of discovering what we each felt" [132]. Yet Montoya is too like Jake to serve him fairly. He too is a spectator rather than a participant in what he loves most, and he can do nothing to prevent its corruption. Silence is all he can muster in face of Brett's imminent seduction of Romero.

Count Mippopopolous, on the other hand, has directly engaged in life and pain—to the tune of seven wars, four revolutions, and a couple of arrow wounds—as well as the pleasures of food, wine, and women. Precisely what the values are he boasts of, Hemingway never states. Brett denies him any, which leaves him "dead" and therefore "one of us." In a sense she is right, for Mippopopolous's discipline and courage belong to his past; he has become a connoisseur and a bon vivant. But if a certain flabbiness has weakened him, he can still testify vigorously and truly, "I am always in love." And that is what his values are about—the grace and vexation of living. Such instruction has not been wasted on Jake.

But it is Romero who symbolizes the truly elect, the wholly exemplary hero—brave, skilled, modest, uncompromising in his dedication to his art. Pulped but undaunted by Cohn the night before,[21] Romero celebrates in the bull ring a solemn ritual of life against death, man against nature. What Jake, Brett, and the mob feel is Romero's private commitment to his sense of joy and responsibility. Unlike Cohn, he looks neither to Brett nor to the crowd for approval: "Because he did not look up to ask if it pleased he did it all for himself inside, and it strengthened him, and yet he did it for her too. But he did not do it for her at any loss to himself" [216]. All views of experience are privative, but risking life endows subjectivity with a special moral seriousness and manly dignity. Jake's ideal—a simple harmony of God, man, and nature; life, love, and death—is Romero's reality. About him, Jake speaks unequivocally: "Pedro Romero had the greatness."

But the price of greatness comes high and the exchange rate is rarely favorable. Grim ironies of incident (their implication unstated, their poignancy inescapable) undercut Jake's hope of amelioration by vicarious participation. What begins as a promise of cathartic ritual ends as a paralyzingly tragic parody. Thus, moments before Romero thrills the crowd, the aging, fistula-plagued matador Belmonte—once as stirring in the arena as Romero, now a silent harbinger of Romero's future—draws catcalls for his cautious handling of the bulls. Earlier in the morning during the street running of the bulls, a young farmer had been gored to death—the ultimate exchange of values, life for death—by the same bull Romero slays that afternoon. Finally, the bull's ear, symbol of virility and power, finds its way to Brett's night drawer, ironically wrapped in Jake's handkerchief.[22] That night, as Book Two ends, Brett goes away with Romero, and Jake, blind drunk, repeats "I feel like hell."

With that binge, Jake Barnes ends his apprenticeship. The third book, as noted earlier, is brief, a deliberately anticlimactic vignette of futility. In it, however, Jake gains his maturity. Once more, he draws strength from a respite out-of-doors—swimming in the Bay of Biscay and talking with bicycle racers at San Sebastian, and sleeping. A telegram from Brett wrecks his peace; as he is on his way to join her in Madrid, his insomnia returns. The clue to Jake's imminent resolution lies, as Rovit points out, in his description of the railroad station in Madrid as "the end of the line. All trains finish there. They don't go on anywhere" [239–40].

Jake listens sympathetically to Brett's barely controlled narration of her renunciation. But he is also remote, his questions and answers about her affair with Romero laconic or, more precisely, monosyllabic. Exemplary heroes avoid talking about pleasure and pain; they simply enjoy or endure. For the first time, Jake controls a situation with Brett. In an earlier reflection about their relationship, Jake mused that getting something for nothing only "delayed the presentation of the bill. The bill always came. That was one of the swell things you could count on" [148]. As they leave the hotel in Madrid, the owner takes no money. "The bill," Jake observes, "had been paid."

Not quite. For Jake to accept his "freedom" so stoically would fall just short of truth. At lunch with Brett, he drinks enough to bear the pain, but not to kill it. Earlier in the novel, he needed a fuller dose: "Under the wine I lost the disgusted feeling and was happy. It seemed they were all such nice people" [146]. Now Jake stays sober enough in their last taxi ride to counter Brett's "Oh, Jake, we could have had such a damned good time together" with "Isn't it pretty to think so." The ironic force of *pretty*—a determined rejection of the last shred of illusion—is Jake's payment in full for his bill of manhood.

In the Hollywood movie version of *The Sun Also Rises,* the bitter pill of Jake's reply to Brett is coated with a sugary "There must be a way for us." That there is none is symbolically made explicit in the novel as the taxi suddenly brakes, pressing Brett against Jake—and a policeman raises his baton before them. "You gave up something and you got something else," Jake had said. Nothing can restore what has maimed him physically. But psychically, he has bartered reasonably well. He has traded off false hope and empty illusion and salvaged integrity, discipline, and control. Scarcely a "simple exchange of values," it might, in a marketplace where moral bankruptcy destroys most traders, be accounted a margin of profit.

8

A Farewell to Arms

Early in 1928, Hemingway had written about sixty thousand words of a second novel, a kind of "modern Tom Jones" set in Oak Park, Illinois, to be narrated omnisciently rather than in what he had begun to call the "bloody first person." [1] Illness and injury (a skylight had fallen on his head!) had slowed his writing during the winter months. By spring, no longer absorbed in a project about which he later admitted he knew too little, he cast about for something better. He had already published in *in our time* a sketch of his war wound, and in "A Very Short Story" recounted an abortive love affair carried on during his convalescence. Now Hemingway began another short story about love and war. By fall, his new manuscript had swelled to six hundred pages; a year later (after serialization in *Scribner's Magazine*) it was published as *A Farewell to Arms.* [2]

As in *The Sun Also Rises*, Hemingway blends fact and fantasy. Frederic's knee wound is analogous to Hemingway's, but not the head injury. Moreover, though Hemingway knew about the retreat from Caporetto, he played no part in it or in any act of desertion. Still further, his love for his own wartime nurse, Agnes von Kurowsky, was never consummated. [3] Also as in *The Sun Also Rises*, the subject matter is love, violence, and death, the narrative mode internal, the "bloody first person" after all. Curiously, despite its wartime setting, *A Farewell to Arms* seems more remote from actual experience, more romantic in conception and fulfillment. In part, this results from a strong infusion of lyricism into the usually brittle, metallic style. A more considerable reason is the idyllic love story, so compelling in its idealism that one may momentarily forget that *A Farewell to Arms* is a war novel. But if among the trysts in hospital beds and Alpine ski resorts Hemingway occasionally strays toward a sentimentality that never threatens *The Sun Also Rises*, he does not linger overlong in that precinct. Love and war are at last welded inseparably and tragically in this story he once called his *Romeo and Juliet*.[4] The flux is death: *A Farewell to Arms* is Hemingway's first full-scale treatment of mortality.

Except for the goring of a local Pamplonan during the running of the bulls, death in *The Sun Also Rises* is limited to the formalized ritual of the bull arena. There, death is inevitable but man has a chance to control the outcome. War affords no such opportunity, as Frederic Henry—like Nick Adams before him—must learn. Both men, when wounded, share for an instant the feel of death. Nick identifies it in "Now I Lay Me" as feeling his soul "go out of me and go off and then come back." Frederic's encounter is more acutely disquieting, for it shatters an innocent faith in his own immortality, a conviction that neither the war nor death had anything to do with him: "It seemed no more dangerous to me myself than war in the movies" [38]. When the shell explodes, however, he too knows terror: "I went out swiftly, all of myself, and I knew I was dead and that it had all been a mistake to think you just died. Then I floated, and instead of going on I felt myself slide back. I breathed and I was back" [57]. The screams of a dying comrade beside him and, soon thereafter in an ambulance, the hemorrhaging corpse that drips down on him from a stretcher above, scar Frederic's consciousness with a reality that sunders all illusion. For as long as he is able afterwards, Frederic clings, like Nick, to stability through detachment. But Frederic's experience is richer, more complex, and at last more devastating because it embraces love as well as war.

And it is in this exploration of the mortality inherent in the life-giving process of love that Hemingway probes deeper than he had either in *The Sun Also Rises* or in the Nick Adams stories. Sterility haunts Jack Barnes's wasteland, fear the shadowy recesses of Nick Adams's world. Luckier in a sense than either, Frederic is also more vulnerable and pays a steeper price for his brief residence in Eden, for death stalks there as confident and ominous as on the battlefield. Thus, Frederic must twice bid farewell to arms, first as a soldier, finally as a lover.[5] With that last goodbye, he will have learned what Hemingway had not taught so thoroughly or so painfully before—that neither in war nor in love can man expect victory. Yet the novel does not end in total negation. Like Jake and Nick, Frederic is an apprentice who must master the paradox that life can be full even though empty. And he must learn too that courage and compassion animate humanity even when uncontrollable forces threaten to quench the last glimmer of hope.

The themes Hemingway voices in *A Farewell to Arms* extend rather than alter his ideology. Technically, he experiments, modifying what is already familiar in his style. Here, for example, he first uses time as a structural and thematic device. And a more complex system of images and symbols amplifies meaning, playing one against another strain of lyricism and brutality. Occasionally, the strain is too much, the imagery overwrought, the tonality slightly eccentric. But if *A Farewell to Arms* lacks the integrated perfection of craft *The Sun Also Rises* attains, it is not without its compensations. Structural pattern is subtly interwoven with theme; characters, both minor and major, spring alive in vivid settings; and, in scenes like the retreat from Caporetto, the lovers' night journey to Switzerland, and their hours together in Milan, Hemingway provides some of the best prose ever written about love or war.

The plot is, as usual, slight and straightforward, its basic outline almost sentimentally trite: a young American serving in the Italian ambulance corps falls in love with an English volunteer nurse. He is wounded, she attends him at the hospital, and there they consummate their love. He returns to the front, deserts during a massive retreat, and escapes to Switzerland. Their idyl ends when she dies in childbirth. So presented, A *Farewell to Arms* seems little more than a likely script for a soggy film, which Hollywood twice made of it.[6] But though certain limitations inhere in the plot (the melodramatic ending, for example), Hemingway's narrative genius nearly transcends them.

What is perhaps most remarkable is the absolute trust Frederic inspires in his reliability as narrator. Never again in a novel would Hemingway maintain the precisely appropriate distance between himself and a hero so like him. A perfect apprentice, Frederic blends admirably the familiar traits of the hurt, uprooted young man who must, like Nick Adams and Jake Barnes, learn "how to live in it." He is, however, in certain ways better suited to fictional purpose than either of them. For one thing, he knows at the outset just enough less about life than Jake and just enough more than Nick to serve as an ideal subject for a *Bildungsroman*. Furthermore, he is, despite his wound, physically whole and psychically strong enough to endure his trials of love and war. And finally, though Frederic, like Jake, is the chief actor and remains ever at the center of all actions, he has the signal advantage of seeming also to report as if after a time lapse. The effect is not of returning to the past but of experience as part of an eternal present in which the logic of sequence or causality matters little, the persistence of emotion matters much.

Through this latter stratagem particularly, Hemingway weaves the multiple strands of structure, scene, and symbol into a unified thematic design. In the foreshortened opening chapter of about six hundred words, for example, Hemingway simultaneously thrusts time back to 1916, a year before the crucial events of the novel, yet foreshadows doom. In that chapter, only nature, troops, and the machinery of war fill the landscape. No character appears, and even the narrator is effaced as "we" instead of "I." All is recorded with rigorous objectivity, the risk of "pathetic fallacy" avoided by locating significance in what Frederic sees, not what he thinks. And what he sees and reports in this chapter, despite the air of detachment, patterns what follows—the emotional tone, the thematic line, and, most important, the relationship between fictional event and universal experience.

In large measure, Hemingway achieves his effect by correspondences. Each of the five paragraphs of the opening chapter, for example, is roughly proportional in length to each of the five books of the novel, and the pace anticipates the cadence of the novel as a whole. The slow, measured rhythm of the third paragraph (each sentence long, the last more than eighty words), as troops advance toward the front, ironically anticipates the retreat from Caporetto detailed in Book III. A more profound irony appears as the paragraph ends, for the soldiers, carrying cartridge boxes under their capes, march "as though they were six months gone with child." As the birth-death motif is tragically resolved in Book V, the shortest of all, so is it in the two brief understated sentences of the final paragraph of the first chapter: "At the start of the winter came the permanent rain and with the rain came the cholera. But it was checked and in the end only seven thousand died of it in the army" [4].

Other correspondences exist too, symbolic as well as structural. Most occur in nature. Like the body of the novel itself, Chapter 1 begins in a dry summer and ends in wintry rain. Scattered throughout the chapter are hints of birth: "The plain was rich with crops . . . the nights were cool and there was not the feeling of a storm coming." And of death: "The trunks of the trees too were dusty and the leaves fell early that year . . . the dust rising and leaves, stirred by the breeze, falling and the soldiers marching and afterward the road bare and white except for the leaves." Always too there is the rain, the rain Catherine is later afraid of "because sometimes I see me dead in it" [131], the rain that drenches the muddy retreat from Caporetto, and the rain that falls in Lausanne when Catherine dies. All this is prefigured in the opening chapter: "All the country *wet* and brown and *dead* with autumn . . . the troops were muddy and *wet* in their capes; their rifles were *wet* . . ." (italics added). Until at last comes the "permanent rain" and death.

When correspondences are too neatly manipulated —either by the author or by his critics—their force withers. Some of Hemingway's critics have labored more consciously than he to discover such nuance.[7] At his best, as he is here, Hemingway never sacrifices art to artifice. The correspondences cited above are, as they should be, suggestive rather than insistent. Rain does not always equate with death in the novel (a "cheerful" rain falls on the lovers in Switzerland); and the dry country does not always denote desolation (Abruzzi, the good place where the priest lives, is dry). What Hemingway projects in the opening chapter is a macrocosmic metaphor that arches the entire novel, ironically reducing the scale of the fictional events to microcosmic proportion.

At the center of that small world stands Hemingway's representative man, an apprentice learning to endure the tragic conditions of life, questing some foundation to support a belief beyond *nada*. Like most apprentices in Hemingway's fiction, Frederic Henry absorbs what others teach, then acts at last on his own resolve. His situation is again different, however, for he has no wholly exemplary male figure before him, no one like Pedro Romero who has "the greatness." Besides, at the outset, Frederic's self-image is so atrophied as to prohibit any exercise of will. He has, in fact, drifted into his role, apparently unaware of motive or purpose. At least he offers no explanation of why he has abandoned his studies in architecture, or even—barring a vague notion about defeat—why he has volunteered to serve in the Italian ambulance corps. About family, he refers casually to a letter from his grandfather "containing family news, patriotic encouragement, a draft for two hundred dollars, and a few clippings" [141], and cynically to a stepfather whom Catherine need never meet. When first observed among others, he is sitting with his friend Rinaldi at the window of the officers' whorehouse drinking and staring at the snow outside. That evening at mess, he is conspicuously silent as his comrades debate whether he should spend his leave amid the fleshpots of the big cities or, as the priest urges, in the clear, dry countryside of Abruzzi.

Frederic's intention, he tries weeks later to explain to the disappointed priest, had been to take his holiday at the priest's home in the Abruzzi, "where the roads were frozen and hard as iron, where it was clear cold and dry . . ." [13]. Yet he had somehow—without wholly understanding why—yielded to the pleasures of the cities, "to the smoke of cafés . . . nights in bed, drunk . . . and the strange excitement of waking and not knowing who it was with you . . . and the world all unreal in the dark . . . sure that this was all and all and all and not caring" [13]. Although he tries to rationalize that one never gets to do what he chooses, Henry admits to himself that the priest "had always known what I did not know and what, when I learned it, I was always able to forget. But I did not know that then, although I learned it later" [14].

This early scene is crucial to understanding the process of Frederic's "education." The long interior monologue quoted in part above defines at once his emptiness, his pained consciousness of it, and his awareness that another way of life does exist. Though he is at the outset a hollow man, knowing that he is and despairing of it mark his first step forward.[8] It is a step, however, not a stride, for Frederic still knows more than he feels about the value of life. And he cannot yet choose between the priest's way and Rinaldi's. Both of these sympathetically drawn and persuasive theorists are with him at critical moments until he is ready to act on his own during the retreat from Caporetto in Book III. Frederic's mentors are apparently polarized, the young priest an apostle of the sacred and the pure, Rinaldi of the pragmatic and the profane. Yet they share compassion and—what prevents them from becoming exemplary heroes—a need to articulate their own loneliness and desperation.

At first, Rinaldi is gay and self-assured. When he visits the wounded Frederic at the field hospital, he boasts lightly of his expertise in sex and surgery, the realities that sustain him through chaos. Toward Frederic's involvement with the priest and Catherine, his mockery is mild but insistent: "You are really an Italian. All fire and smoke but nothing inside" [69]. He warns Frederic against a serious affair with Catherine, "your lovely cool goddess," pointing out that the only difference between a good girl and a woman is that with a girl the end is pain. At their next meeting, however, after Frederic returns to the front, the gentle libertine has transformed into a harsh, embittered cynic whose banter is labored, his anger genuine, his self-discipline shorn. Convinced that he has syphilis, Rinaldi is frightened, almost hysterical, arguing as "the snake of reason" against all love and in defense of the inevitability of *nada:* "You're dry and you're empty and there's nothing else . . . Not a damned thing" [180].

Much of what Rinaldi epitomizes compels Frederic's interest and sympathy, not only Rinaldi's hedonism but also his skill at his work. Yet, in his moods of despair, Rinaldi too closely resembles Frederic to teach him all he must know. True, Rinaldi's mode of life makes explicit what Frederic had not been able to explain to the priest, that the night (i.e., sensuality) is always better "unless the day was very clean and cold" (i.e., disciplined, orderly, and significant—like surgery). But as Frederic already knows and feels, Rinaldi's assumption that one learns only that all ends in disease is, however valid, too confining, especially when bounded by the precincts of a whorehouse.

The saintly young priest serves Frederic better, clarifying the choices he must at last make on his own. Unembarrassed by those who ridicule his limpid faith, the priest reminds Frederic that in his province "it is understood that a man may love God. It is not a dirty joke" [74]. To more urgent purpose, he dismisses Frederic's nights as incidents of passion and lust, not of love. "When you love you wish to do things for. You wish to sacrifice for. You wish to serve" [75]. To all this, Frederic remains ostensibly impassive, insisting that he is happy though he loves neither God nor man nor woman. Yet, when the priest leaves, Frederic lies awake for a long while thinking of the clean, orderly world that is the priest's country, a world where caring about others is natural.

At their final meeting—immediately after Rinaldi's outburst—the priest too has changed, become more subdued, less certain of his ground, less persuasive. Significantly, it is Frederic who carries the conversation now, his thoughts a curiously contradictory mixture of what he has absorbed from the priest and Rinaldi as well as from his actual experience in love and war. Early in the novel, he had argued with his drivers about their defeatism, insisting that no matter how bad or stupid war is, defeat is worse. With the priest now, Frederic momentarily shifts ground and, sounding more saintly than his companion, ventures that "it is in defeat that we become Christian . . . like our Lord . . . We are all gentler now because we are beaten" [184]. A moment later he retracts, saying that he cannot believe in defeat, even if it is better. When the priest presses him about what he does believe in, Frederic evades the query with a quip, responding —as Rinaldi might have—"In sleep." Out of such a paralysis of psychic resolve, Frederic must discover a means to move toward choice.

Dramatically effective and entirely credible, Frederic's exchanges with Rinaldi and the priest constitute an important part of his early education in the theory of life. Other characters—like the drivers under his command—perform lesser but relevant service. Some function—like the journalists and tourists in *The Sun Also Rises*—only as empty-spirited outsiders akin to H. G. Wells's Mr. Britling, whose middle-class insights Frederic scorns. Ettore Moretti, the "legitimate" hero who bores everyone he meets, is one; Mr. Myers, who profits from rigged horse races, another. Miss Van Campen, in charge of the nurses at the hospital in Milan, judges people by their social status; Helen Ferguson, Catherine's friend, is better than most, but she cleaves to moral platitudes. And there are singers like Simmons who talk much about their art but always fail in performance; or doctors who discuss, delay, then botch their task. (Whereas others, like Dr. Valentini, consult no one and perform brilliantly. As Rinaldi says, "I don't think, I operate.") From the outsiders, Frederic learns what he does not want. That aspect of education is comparatively painless.

A more subtle effect is wrought through the nameless British major who appears briefly at the beginning of Chapter 21, shortly before Frederic returns to the front. Majestically detached, he surveys all battle fronts, then sweeps the war aside with two resoundingly grim conclusions: "It was all balls"; "We were all cooked." But, he adds reassuringly, ". . . we were all right as long as we did not know it . . . The thing was not to recognize it" [139]. The major serves as Frederic's "double," rendering ridiculous the stance of aloofness. To pretend cheery indifference to doom or, worse, to refuse to recognize it, shrinks tragedy to farce. That Frederic is not wholly unaware of what the major signifies is evident in his ironic understatement after their encounter: "There was a great contrast between his world pessimism and personal cheeriness." Yet, later in the same chapter, when Catherine tells him she is pregnant, Frederic reacts to love and life as the major had to war and death. He feels "trapped biologically," but adds that he feels "cheerful" as well. Before his education is complete, Frederic will learn to discriminate his terms more carefully. At this moment, however, his response is ugly in its self-pitying immaturity. What he says in effect is that despite the prospect of life born of love, he remains cheerful. He is, in fact, still nearer his "double" than he realizes, still incapable of that feeling for another he must discover before he can end his agony of indecision.

No one prepares him for that experience so patiently, so lovingly, so selflessly (or, some would add, so incredibly) as Catherine Barkley. Compared with the long-haired heroines who succeed her in Hemingway's fiction, Catherine is almost realistic. But beside Brett Ashley, she seems archetypally ideal, the quintessence of adolescent and middle-aged male desire. Since Hemingway's women either caress or castrate, most critics indict them at either extreme.[9] One might argue in reply that, like Hemingway's heroes, Catherine is the creation of a romantic imagination and is bounded only by its limits. Even so, though she strains against the outer edges, she never bursts through to absurdity. At the outset of the novel, her psychic tension should reassure the most clinical of realists that she is authentic; her death leaves unaffected only those already dead in life.

Hemingway's heroines, Carlos Baker has written, "are meant to show a symbolic or ritualistic function in the service of the artist and the service of man." [10] Less the cool, English goddess Rinaldi labels her than a passionate priestess, Catherine ministers to Frederic's needs with near-total disregard of her own. Rarely does she allow her own fears to surface, and when they do—about feeling like a whore or seeing herself dead in the rain—she finds strength to suppress them lest they cause Frederic concern. The Abruzzi priest told Frederic that love involves sacrifice and service. When Catherine comes to Frederic's bed in the hospital, she incarnates in deed and word the priest's thesis. "I want what you want," she says. "There isn't any me any more. Just what you want" [110].

Catherine is more substantial than these vulnerable lines suggest. Her docility is a reaction, perhaps an overreaction, to the death of her first lover in an affair left unconsummated because she thought (her words recall Brett Ashley's when she leaves Pedro Romero) "it would be bad for him." Again in love, she determines not to err in the same way. If she is too susceptible and thus too available, her terms are nonetheless more humane than Frederic's, her insights more penetrating. Her intensity when they first meet, for example, persuades the cavalier Frederic that she is "probably a little crazy." For him, she is a meaningless diversion from a meaningless war. That she seems crazy adds zest to the game, and as a game (chess, bridge) he images their relationship. Cheating is allowed (" 'Yes,' I lied. 'I love you' ") and, since no stakes are indicated, no one—certainly not he—loses.

With cunning skill, Hemingway exposes Frederic's failure of sensibility by having Catherine swiftly perceive and label each gambit of his inner consciousness:

> "This is a rotten game we play, isn't it?"
> "What game?"
> "You're a nice boy," she said. "And you play it as well as you know how. But it's a rotten game."
> "Do you always know what people think?"
> "Not always. But I do with you. You don't have to pretend you love me . . ."
> "But I do love you."
> "Please let's not lie when we don't have to. I had a very fine little show and I'm all right now. You see I'm not mad and I'm not gone off. It's only a little sometimes." [32]

It is a shrewd, sensitive woman, not an abstract paragon of submissiveness who conducts Frederic's first lesson on the higher levels of the art of love. And it is a puzzled young apprentice who later can make no reply to Rinaldi's teasing comment, "Thank God I did not become involved with the British."

Frederic's narcissistic dream of easy conquest lasts but a day longer. Lying in his room the next afternoon, he links with his reverie about personal immortality a fantasy of lying naked beside Catherine in a hotel and loving "all night in the hot night in Milan." [11] When she is unable to see him the next evening, he leaves feeling "lonely and hollow," conscious that he has treated her "very lightly." Except for a hasty farewell the next morning as he leaves for the front, Frederic sees Catherine again only after he has been wounded. As she enters the hospital room, he knows for the first time that he is in love: "Everything turned over inside of me . . . [95]. God knows I had not wanted to fall in love with her. I had not

wanted to fall in love with anyone. But God knows I had . . ."
[97].[12]

During his long summer of convalescence and continuing
education, Frederic shows few signs of loving Catherine so
much as needing her. His concern for her is prosaic, the
product of his mind rather than his heart. Though he admits
to himself preferring not to marry, he frets about the risks of
their affair and thus offers her marriage. Nothing he does or
says matches her fine abandon, her delight in creating a
"home" for him in his hospital room, her ceaseless desire to
please him. For her, formalities have no relevance. Marriages
are made official by church or state; her only religion is her
lover, her only society themselves: ". . . there's only us two
and in the world there's all the rest of them. If anything comes
between us we're gone and then they have us" [146]. Nor is
she unaware that the world will ravage them. She allows that
"all sorts of dreadful things" will happen to them. And she
knows too that courage will not ease pain, that only cowards
die but once. "The brave dies perhaps two thousand deaths if
he's intelligent," she tells Frederic, and adds—in the language
of the "code"—"He simply doesn't mention them" [146].

Catherine's words ironically comment on those the British
major had uttered to Frederic a few hours earlier. By choosing not to *recognize*, the major had no need to confront the
realities Catherine faces and transcends. Such insight and
courage as Catherine owns is not yet Frederic's either. Unable
to commit himself as she has, he halfheartedly attempts to
cloak their love with a safe, social respectability he despises
in others. His motive seems less to serve her than himself, to
lessen the risk of losing her and sinking once more to *nada*.
His fears loom again when he is about to return to the front.
As they prepare to leave their hotel room in Milan, Frederic
hears an auto horn sound below and recalls Andrew Marvell's
lines, "But at my back I always hear / Time's winged chariot
hurrying near." Other than foreshadowing events in the narrative and perhaps deliberately conjuring the image of

T. S. Eliot's *The Waste Land*,[13] the couplet has relevance to Frederic's immediate state. At once he asks where she will have their child, what arrangements she will make. Innocuous in themselves, the queries follow too hard on his admission of feeling "biologically trapped" not to betray his self-interest, his dread that the baby may cost him his refuge. Once more, Catherine must placate and relieve him of responsibility. She will have the baby in the best place she can find and in the best way she can. Above all, she insists, he must not worry; she will always provide a home for him.

Not until the raw details of the retreat from Caporetto bite into his imagination does Frederic begin to behave like a man truly in love. Still impelled more by events and personalities than by his own psychic impetus, he reacts to experience for the first time out of profound feelings for a self other than his own. Failing at his assigned task (salvaging three ambulances from the advancing enemy), he succeeds at a more formidable level. Nearly all that occurs during the retreat recapitulates what he has known of love and war. Only hours before the retreat begins, a young patriot rehearses Frederic's earlier views about defeat, denying that all has been "in vain." Now it is Frederic who remains silent, his inner thoughts recorded in the famous passage about the "obscenity" of abstractions like *hallow*, *glory*, and *honor*. The facts of the retreat bear out his disgust with "things that were glorious [but] had no glory and the sacrifices were like the stockyards at Chicago if nothing was done with the meat except to bury it" [191]. The glories of the retreat are mud-clogged roads jammed (as they were in Greece) with hapless peasants; [14] the hallowed are the frantic deserters; and the honorable are the brutal, callous battle police. Frederic must himself shoot a deserter, see one of his own drivers killed by his fellow Italians, and face the threat of his own death.

Frederic's leap into the Tagliamento River is undeniably an act of survival. Yet more than merely that, it affirms life by accepting its risks. As others passively stand by, awaiting execution, Frederic rebels against the nothingness of destruction; he breathes, as it were, as when he was wounded. His immersion in the river becomes then, as many have noted, a purificatory rite, cleansing him after his trial by chaos. On the train to Stresa and Catherine, Frederic officially declares his farewell to arms by refusing to read the newspapers: "I was going to forget the war. I had made a separate peace" [252].

It would be too much to argue that Frederic's love for Catherine alone motivates his desertion. But it is pertinent to observe that his attitude toward her undergoes a decisive change during the retreat. Though war is the central matter of Book III, the retreat itself is framed by references to love, both sacred and profane. The initial action in the retreat is the evacuation of the whorehouse; Book III ends as Frederic ponders where he may stay forever with Catherine. Counterpoint is sustained throughout by the byplay between two frightened young virgins and the coarse but friendly drivers who have given them a ride. But the dominant theme is sounded lyrically in a dream Frederic has immediately after reassuring himself that the drivers will not harm the girls.

In an extraordinarily perceptive essay about this dream sequence in Chapter 28, Charles R. Anderson demonstrates how ingeniously Hemingway informs his writing with warmth and spirituality.[15] Most important, however, is that during this dream Frederic for the first time manifests a sincere desire to serve his love rather than himself. The dream ranges from an initial eroticism ("In bed I lay me down my head. Bed and board. Stiff as a board in bed") to a sleep-spoken outburst of husbandly tenderness and concern: " 'Goodnight, Catherine,' I said out loud . . . 'If it's too uncomfortable, darling, lie on the other side . . . I'll get you some cold water. In a little while it will be morning and then it won't be so bad. I'm sorry he makes you so uncomfortable. Try to go to sleep, sweet' " [204].

Literary allusions texture the passage, heightening Frederic's metamorphosis. "In bed I lay me down my head," derivative from the familiar child's prayer, sets a tone of humility developed by a reference to Tennyson's lullaby from

The Princess—"Blow, blow, ye western wind"—with its contextual hint that the gentle spring wind will restore his love. Subtlest of all is Hemingway's use of the anonymous sixteenth-century lyric, "The Lover in Winter Plaineth for the Spring": "O Western wind, when wilt thou blow/ That the small rain down can rain?/ Christ, that my love were in my arms/ And I in my bed again." Of these lines, Frederic dreams only the last two, but the entire dream is imbued with the force of the other two lines. Rain drenches Frederic's dream as it does the real world outside. It is the "small rain" of spring and revitalization he wishes for: "that my sweet Catherine down might rain"; but "it blew and it wasn't the small rain but the big rain down that rained . . . Every one was caught in it and the small rain would not quiet it" [204].

A vision of idyllic romance and a prophecy of doom are thus eloquently fused in this remarkable passage. That doom will prevail is presaged when, as Frederic wakes, the first word he hears is an obscenity from his driver's lips. The real world must triumph, as Frederic has now all but learned. At this moment, however, the fullest relevance of the dream lies in its adumbration of Frederic's humanity. Awake, he is again defensive and tough, but, as Anderson writes, "the dream is not lost, merely locked in the hero's heart." As Book III ends, Frederic reflects upon the war without rancor: "Anger was washed away in the river along with any obligation" [241]. He thinks briefly about Rinaldi and the priest but determines that "that life was over." Instead of *nada*, Frederic has chosen —albeit still within the passive structure of a dream—to accept, as his only obligation, service to the woman he loves. When, a few days later, he jumps into the river, dream translates into reality, passivity to active commitment.

With swift, telling strokes, Hemingway sketches the inexorable dénouement. The lovers' reunion at Stresa, their exciting flight to Switzerland, and their idyllic winter in Montreux (the clear, cold place Frederic had always yearned to be)— all sustain the illusion of a "separate peace." With Catherine at Stresa, Frederic thinks, "all other things were unreal." But they are not. War, for example, worms again into his consciousness. Despite Catherine's reassurance that it was, after all, only the Italian army, Frederic feels guilt about his desertion. Rinaldi's syphilis worries him, and the priest's welfare, and the way the war goes. To stop thinking, he turns to a familiar antidote of the apprentice, whiskey—"That was the sensible way." Nor are his thoughts about love more reassuring. At last aware of its goodness, Frederic cannot fend off dread of what happens when two stand "alone against the others." His inward response is somber: "If people bring so much courage to this world the world has to kill them to break them, so of course it kills them. The world breaks every one and afterward many are strong at the broken places. But those that will not break it kills. It kills the very good and the very gentle and the very brave impartially. If you are none of these you can be sure it will kill you too but there will be no special hurry" [258–59].

Not merely "impartially," Frederic discovers, but gratuitously. It is not the logic of the narrative that dictates Catherine's death, but the gratuitous irrationality and indifference of the universe. "It's just a dirty trick" are Catherine's last words. No one ever has time, as Frederic reflects, to learn the rules, and the penalty for an infraction in the game of life— not at all as in chess or bridge—is death. Prayer is vain too, though in desperation he tries it. As Frederic's parable of the ants, the fire, and the water suggests, even were God to act, nothing would change. Being steamed by an indifferent God is no better than being burned by an angry one.

When Frederic admits that kissing Catherine's dead lips "was like saying goodbye to a statue," he is done with illusion. That stage of his apprenticeship ends as he walks out into the rain. Were there no more than this dark enlightenment, *A Farewell to Arms* would linger in memory only as a fierce, Hardyesque study in naturalism and *nada*.[16] Much else remains as well—the unabashed joy and fun of physical love; the simple fortitude and determination of the lovers; and the stubborn quest for enduring even if private values. All are subsumed in that other stage of Frederic's apprenticeship which relates to his emergent humanity. It is the ancient and worldly Count Greffi who helps Frederic to recognize that he need not choose between Rinaldi's secularity and the priest's orthodoxy. Both blend into "a religious feeling," as Greffi calls it, that embodies sacred and profane love.[17] To love as Catherine loves and dies—in the full sense of belonging to another and wanting to serve—is the only possible triumph. Rinaldi too knows this when he admits to Frederic, "Even with remorse you will have a better time" [176]. Frederic does have a better time after he falls in love with Catherine. But more important within the dramatic and ideological framework of the novel, by his intense commitment to that love, he becomes a better man.

9

Death in the Afternoon
AND
Green Hills of Africa

With *Death in the Afternoon* (1932) and *Green Hills of Africa* (1935) Hemingway joined the large company of famous Americans for whom a published record of their travel experiences seems almost a condition of existence. Some have adopted the posture of a frontiersman, like Mark Twain a bluff, mocking, not-so-innocent abroad. Others, like Henry James, assumed roles as semi-expatriates, sympathetic but critical observers of international manners and morals. Hemingway incorporates something of each attitude, adding a dollop of conventional Baedekerisms about picturesque side streets in Spain and tribal customs in Africa. But in *Death in the Afternoon* and *Green Hills of Africa,* his first full-length ventures into nonfiction, curiosity about the customs of the country runs a poor second to Hemingway's preoccupation with the territory of his own mind.

Writing about his travels was not new for Hemingway; he had already reported as a journalist in Europe and the Near East. His first two novels also sketch country landscapes and urban scenes, as well as contrast Europeans and Americans.

In the earlier work, Hemingway engaged attention through carefully selected, precisely indicated detail and won sympathy with quiet lyricism or understated outrage. Here he is a much less comfortable traveling companion. Too often he is overbearing and condescending, too aware of himself as an exemplary guide to life as well as to the land. Robert Stephens has written of Hemingway's quest for new places where he might live by frontier values of the American West.[1] Interpreted so, Hemingway emerged in *Death in the Afternoon* as an advocate of the bullfighter as a frontier hero and in *Green Hills of Africa* as a hero in his own right, the intrepid hunter. Yet for all his frontier assurance and bouts of brag, it should be noted, Hemingway remains edgy, an anxiety-ridden, pessimistic, death-obsessed frontiersman, apparently more affected by *The Decline of the West* than by the *Leatherstocking Tales*.

The irremediable flaw in both of Hemingway's works is their self-consciousness. Without a Nick Adams or a Frederic Henry to screen him from his own ego, Hemingway swiftly lapses into self-indulgence. For that, his critics harshly censured him. Max Eastman, for example, titled his review of the earlier book "Bull in the Afternoon" and damned Hemingway's "juvenile romantic gushing and sentimentalizing of simple facts."[2] About *Green Hills of Africa*, John Chamberlain wrote that it is "all attitude—all Byronic posturing,"[3] an image Carl Van Vechten (who otherwise liked the book) also used to complain about Hemingway's tiresome habit of "talking or writing tough" whenever he reflects or argues.[4] But despite the just demurrers of the critics, there is about both books an inescapable excitement that attends an inner journey, even when it pretends to be otherwise.

Death in the Afternoon is loosely structured, its myriad details about bullfighting—until the closing chapters—strangely without discernible pattern and, worse, often redundant to the point of tedium—sometimes beyond the point. Both its diction and syntax are unexpectedly cavalier, more erratic than one might have expected after the honed precision of the earlier fiction. And Hemingway's ranging observations about life, death, and literature are, in *Death in the Afternoon*, random and casual, sometimes linked directly to the bullfight, but just as commonly extemporized or—rather too coyly—intruded into dialogue with the sharp-tongued Old Lady who appears on occasion as an *aficionado* in training. But if the craft is desultory, despair is so ingrained in *Death in the Afternoon* that it creates a unity of its own. Ostensibly, Hemingway's subject is bullfighting. The "real thing," however, the simplest and the most fundamental, is death, and Hemingway writes of it as Goya painted it in *Los Desastros de la Guerra*, without "any shutting of the eyes" [*DA*, 3].

Lest the Old Lady or the reader doubt the despondency inherent in Hemingway's world view, he interlards his exposition at one point with a set piece (part essay, part story) whose title and substance shroud not just the bullring but all mankind. "A Natural History of the Dead," Hemingway mockingly assures the Old Lady, is "the Whittier's *Snow-Bound* of our time," certain to meet her demand that he leave off bulls for a while and provide something "amusing, instructive, and conversational." At the outset of the piece, Hemingway ironically queries: "With a disposition to wonder and adore, can any branch of Natural History be studied without increasing that faith, love and hope which we also, every one of us, need in our journey through the wilderness of life? Let us therefore see what inspiration we may derive from the dead" [134].

In quick succession, Hemingway summons devastating, Goyaesque visions: broken-legged mules in the waters at Smyrna again, fragmented bodies of women blown up in a munitions explosion outside Milan ("it being amazing that the human body should be blown into pieces which exploded along no anatomical lines . . ."), and the stages of rot among corpses. Shifting from exposition to narration, he tells of a young army officer's outrage at a surgeon who delays treating a hopelessly wounded man whose head "was broken as a flower-pot may be broken." When the officer goes beyond insult to threat, the surgeon throws iodine into his eyes, then orders his aides to wash the officer's eyes with alcohol and water. As the officer screams, "Ayee . . . You have blinded me," the doctor says, "Hold him tight . . . He is in much pain. Hold him very tight" [144].

The surgeon already knows what the officer must learn, that holding tight is almost all a man can salvage. In Spanish, "holding tight" might translate as *pundonor,* meaning also pride, honor, and courage. More than most other people, Hemingway argues, Spaniards (especially Castilians) cherish this trait because, more than most others, they take the hardheaded, practical view that life, being much shorter than death, must be lived with dignity. One way to do so is to rebel against death—by killing: "Killing cleanly and in a way which gives you aesthetic pleasure and pride has always been one of the greatest enjoyments of the human race . . . One of its greatest pleasures . . . is the feeling of rebellion against death which comes from its administering . . . [But] when a man is still in rebellion against death he has pleasure in taking to himself one of the Godlike attributes; that of giving it" [232–33].[5]

Thus does Hemingway try to explain the rationale of bullfighting. It is not killing, he insists, as the English kill—for sport—or as the French, for money, but killing to give man respite from his own tragedy by imposing it upon the bull. It is not a slaughter, because the matador's pride and honor demand (for he is an exemplary hero) that he run the risk of death while administering it. If he does, yet has the skill to kill a brave bull bravely, then he and the audience know and feel the full significance of "holding tight" and—for an instant—the catharsis of triumph over death. The victory is, however, temporary, for bullfighting "is an art that deals with death and death wipes it out" [99].

A thesis born of desperation may be expected to generate shock and repugnance. Hemingway makes no effort to salve tender spirits; indeed, he mourns the decline of interest in killing. For the modern bullfighter, he protests, the "moment of truth"—the sword thrust that unites man and beast—is of secondary interest, a necessary but regrettable anticlimax to his balletic virtuosity with cape and *muleta*. Even Hemingway's favorite matadors are aesthetes rather than "rebels." Though Belmonte, El Gallo, Villalta, and Maera are all exemplary heroes, men of exquisite grace and considerable courage and pride, they bring to the final act of the tragedy skill rather than "a spiritual enjoyment of the moment of killing" [232]. Shorn of its basic reason for existence, Hemingway laments, bullfighting has become decadent.[6] Not so decadent, he is quick to add, that a superb performance by a matador may not provide a catharsis otherwise unavailable, even in Christianity. Admitting that, from a Christian point of view, the cruelty and risk of the bullfight are indefensible, the act of pride implicit in the kill a sin, Hemingway proceeds to discard the Christian position. In its stead he offers a pagan sense of virtue that cherishes pride and a pragmatic morality that judges by how one feels after an act. By such standards, the bullfight is wholly moral: ". . . I feel very fine while it is going on and have a feeling of life and death and mortality and immortality, and after it is over I feel very sad but very fine" [4].

Some of the trappings of Hemingway's theory are unintentionally funny: a brave bull keeps its mouth shut during the fray; he never bellows or bluffs. Hemingway is not above pedantic sophistry, as when he insists that the picador's horse is the comic character in the tragedy, abused but too parodic to cause suffering in the spectator. Nor does he wholly convince us that the Spanish audience shares his sense of tragedy or ritual. But beyond the straining and the excesses, *Death in the Afternoon* imparts a passion and an agony, a forlorn sense of defiance born of terror and a loathing of death. It is, at last, the work of a chastened, depressed writer.[7]

Green Hills of Africa, published three years later, lacks the sense of tragedy that informs *Death in the Afternoon.* Although *Green Hills of Africa* begins and ends with killing, its mood is insistently joyous and affirmative—rather too much so. For Hemingway, Africa is not a "dark" continent but a new Eden whose natives live in harmony with nature, a frontier land where man and machines have not yet exploited the earth. It is a "wonderful country . . . a country to wake from, happy to have had the dream . . ." [218]. It is a country in which the mystique of killing described in *Death in the Afternoon* as a mode of rebellion against death apparently yields to one less desperate but—except perhaps for hunters—even more distasteful. Now killing becomes an innocent adventure governed by the rules of the "code" and a lively spirit of healthy competition. "I did not mind killing anything, any animal, if I killed it cleanly," Hemingway writes. "They all had to die . . . and I had no guilty feelings at all" [*GHA*, 272].[8]

None of the people or events in *Green Hills of Africa* is fictitious, Hemingway assures us in his Foreword, his intention being "to write an absolutely true book . . . [to] compete with a work of the imagination." Although the outcome of that competition is debatable, the analogy is fairly made. *Green Hills of Africa* is structured like a novel, each of its four parts a variation on the central theme of the hunter. "Pursuit" is the key word in the heading of each section: pursuit discussed, remembered, experienced as failure, and, at last, as happiness. If only because the "plot" reaches its climax in fulfillment, *Green Hills of Africa* stands apart from *Death in the Afternoon*—and from most of Hemingway's other writing as well. Still further, the protagonist is similarly favored. Hemingway's happiness as an apprentice at the outset is disarmingly boyish: ". . . me sitting, the butt of my rifle on my foot . . . a flask of whiskey between my knees . . . feeling the cool wind of the night and smelling the good smell of Africa. I was altogether happy" [6]. Huck Finn at the game preserve. By the end of the book, Hemingway is happier still, for he wins his spurs as an exemplary hero. When he asks Pop, his white guide and mentor (already established as an exemplar),[9] why the tribesmen have grasped his thumb and pulled it while shaking hands, Pop explains, "It's on the order of blood brotherhood but a little less formal . . . You're getting to be a hell of a fellow" [293–94]. After such triumph, Hemingway's fictional heroes usually suffer. But in *Green Hills of Africa*, fact is kinder than fancy.

In nearly every way, Hemingway meets his own standards for exemplary behavior. He shoots well and kills cleanly. When he fails, he accepts the responsibility: "Every damned thing is your own fault if you're any good" [281]. Fully aware of his temperamental shortcomings, he is more than half delighted when his wife and Pop twit him about his vaunts as tracker, wing-shot, and writer. When he behaves rudely or is harsh—as when he berates his wife in front of the others—he knows remorse. Most of all, he struggles to purge himself of the competitive spirit that, until the very end, mars his full happiness. Though his rivalry with his fellow hunter Karl is friendly, Hemingway frankly dislikes being second best. When the horns of Karl's kudus show larger than his, Hemingway sulks all night long. But by the next morning the bitterness has passed: "It was all gone and I never had it again" [292]. Alone, he has mastered the lesson of the master. As Pop explains, "We have very primitive emotions . . . It's impossible not to be competitive. Spoils everything, though" [293]. A "very jolly breakfast" with Karl, Pop, and Hemingway's wife brings the "pursuit as happiness" to its exultant close. The naughty novice has metamorphosed to the Great White Hunter—Papa has supplanted Pop.

Artistically, *Green Hills of Africa* is a trivial work. Except for an occasional landscape caught with a quick, sure grasp of relevant detail, or an infrequent vignette of a native—the comic absurdity of "David Garrick," the shrewd dignity of M'Cola, the pathetic innocence of the Masai guide—little in the narrative commands interest. Even the hunting scenes soon pall. Nothing about the real Hemingway shooting sable or kudu matches the excitement of hunting beside the fictional Francis Macomber. In Hemingway's stories, as Ed-

mund Wilson writes, ". . . the emotional situations which ob-
sess him, are externalized and objectified; and the result is an
impersonal art that is severe and intense, deeply serious. But
as soon as he speaks in his own person, he seems to lose all
his capacity for self-criticism and is likely to become fatuous
or maudlin." [10] Wilson's strictures are just and delimit the
narrow, aesthetic boundaries of *Green Hills of Africa*. Yet
there is something more. However confident his stance, Hemingway so exaggerates his assurance as to leave it suspect.
And there is enough evidence in the book to suggest that the
sentimental lyricism about killing and bravura of code and
courage fail to disguise completely an unquiet spirit trying to
dispel omnipresent fear and thrust beyond despair to a sustaining hope.

To M'Cola, Hemingway's native tracker, the death of a
wounded hyena is a supremely comic spectacle, not unlike
the parody of death Hemingway had himself sensed in the
death of the picador's horse. But as Hemingway describes the
bizarre rite of a maddened creature circling, snapping at its
own entrails and devouring them, the comedy is black, "a
dirty joke" too obscene for laughter. The image of death as
fearsome and unclean distorts the otherwise bland façade of
Green Hills of Africa. Although death is generally adminis-
tered with aseptic neatness, once more, near the close of the
book, the hyena returns, this time to contaminate, not his
own death agonies, but those of a sable bull Hemingway has
"gut-shot." Not until "The Snows of Kilimanjaro" and "The
Short Happy Life of Francis Macomber," written a year
later, does Hemingway objectify as symbols of unclean death
the hyena and the "gut-shot" animal or work out for his hero
a system of atonement and retribution. In *Green Hills of Africa*, he nearly buries these foul jokes of mortality beneath the
innumerable hides and heads of beasts he has killed cleanly.
Yet the stench persists and the vision haunts: "But I felt rotten sick over this sable bull . . . I was a son of a bitch to
have gut-shot him. It came from overconfidence in being able
to do a thing and then omitting one of the steps in how it is

done" [272]. Hemingway's ostensible remedy in *Green Hills of Africa* is to work at killing until he perfects it—as a great bullfighter might perfect it—until knowledge, skill, and desire fuse into an indissoluble trinity of creative destruction. Only so can he shut off the smell and sight of the hyena. To settle for less would be to reduce ritual to butchery and to deserve the inward torment of inadequacy and fear.

In neither *Green Hills of Africa* nor *Death in the Afternoon,* then, is killing a mere celebration of the strenuous life. Fear and guilt are neurotically twisted in the entrails of Hemingway's hunter-killer complex. Always, despair and desolation hover about the moment of victory. And yet, in Hemingway's consciousness, a clean, unadorned kill somehow helps to atone for the compulsion to kill, and to provide some respite from, even a measure of control over, the elemental terrors of life and the inward doubts about one's own manhood and integrity.

Few writers would attempt to link killing and creativity. But in Hemingway's view, artist and sportsman are allied in method and purpose. The extensive discussions about writing and writers in these two books should therefore be read as relevant extensions of the salient points Hemingway makes about hunting and bullfighting. Thus, to attain the purest level of pr~ ~'~ "f0th dimension," there must be, Hemingway wri⟨ ⟩ *'lls of Africa,* no tricks or cheating, only tal⟨ ⟩ ⟨ ⟩ had"), discipline ("the discipline of Fla⟨ ⟩ ' survival.

To ⟨ ⟩ ...e and environment work against the artis⟨ ⟩ ...ly if he is an American. If he earns too much money, he risks betraying himself by writing slop; if he frets about critics' attacks, he may lose confidence and become—the diction is notable—"impotent." In both works, Hemingway's advice is identical. At the close of *Death in the Afternoon* he writes, "The great thing is to last and get your work done . . ." [278]; in *Green Hills of Africa,* "To work was the only thing, it was the one thing that always made you feel good . . ." [72]. Hemingway presses his thesis with

an urgency that suggests at once the inward gripe of conscience and a naïve petulance with the reality of too much
world and too little time. During an age of social, economic,
and political crisis, he seems determined to locate a clean,
well-lighted place where his own rigid rules of battle and
aesthetic decorum can be scrupulously observed. He wills
aside whatever is alien to his need: history, geography, even
humanity if it becomes necessary to "exchange the pleasant,
comforting stench of comrades for something you can never
feel in any other way than by yourself" [GHA, 148]. In the
longest sentence he ever wrote, Hemingway asserts that his-
torical events are but flotsam and jetsam that "float with no
significance against one single, lasting thing—the [Gulf]
stream" [GHA, 150]. And even when nature has been corrupted, as in America, by technology and greed,[11] it is possible, even necessary, to discover yet another good place
(Spain, Africa), a new frontier where a man may rediscover
and write once more about values that endure.

At the altar of a pure object, a pure style is the only proper
offering, and, for Hemingway, a clean sentence, like a clean
death, is at once an act of contrition and purification. Style
must be neither fussy nor blurred. The "bedside mysticism" of
Waldo Frank's *Virgin Spain*, for example, suffers ridicule in
Death in the Afternoon as "erectile writing . . . full of pretty
phallic images drawn in the manner of sentimental valen-
tines" [53]. Elsewhere, Hemingway more bluntly describes
such writing as "horseshit . . . any overmetaphysical tendency in speech" [DA, 95], or as "knowledge . . . wrapped
in the rhetoric like plums in a pudding" [GHA, 20]. Nor
should writing be, like Edgar Allan Poe's, merely "skillful,"
that is, "marvelously constructed, and . . . dead," like the virtuosity of a decadent bullfighter. Emerson, Hawthorne, and
Whittier are accused of writing like "exiled English colo-
nials," their style too derivative, their wisdom "small, dried."
Thomas Wolfe, on the other hand, is too torrential and needs
the shock of Siberia "to cut the overflow of words and give
him a sense of proportion" [GHA, 71]. "Wow" endings,

"characters," and solemnity as a substitute for seriousness are equally opprobrious, as are splendid but extraneous images and phrases: "Prose is architecture, not interior decoration, and the Baroque is over" [*DA*, 191]. If, however, the writer selects from his experience with honesty and discernment, his reader will *feel* the truth even if all has not been stated: "The dignity of movement of an ice-berg is due to only one-eighth of it being above water" [*DA*, 192].

Among the American writers who meet his standards are Mark Twain, Stephen Crane, Henry James, and William Faulkner; among the Europeans, Flaubert and Stendhal, Tolstoy and Dostoevsky, and James Joyce. Twain, of course, gets the highest praise: "All modern American literature comes from one book by Mark Twain called *Huckleberry Finn* . . . it's the best book we've had . . . There was nothing before. There has been nothing as good since" [*GHA*, 22]. Just why this is so, Hemingway fails to explain. Nor does he make clear in either book to what extent his other choices touch, exceed, or fall short of the mark. His reason probably lies beyond style. What the great novels of his chosen few share is the dramatization of some violent psychic dislocation to which the protagonist must adjust. Most of the heroes refuse to squint at fate, but rather face it boldly and without ruse (which would explain why Hemingway urges readers to stop in *Huckleberry Finn* where "Nigger Jim is stolen from the boys"). Thus do they become in their special ways analogous to great bullfighters and hunters, true models of the exemplary hero.

The early 1930's were for Hemingway years of outward defiance and inward doubt. To see himself and to be seen as an exemplary hero had become a profound psychological need, sufficiently powerful to displace his earlier concern with aesthetic discipline. As a result, the aesthetic standards he espouses most intensely, often belligerently in *Death in the Afternoon* and *Green Hills of Africa,* are lacking in those works. The metaphysical arguments are too often models of "erectile writing," the exalted descriptions of place and landscape conspicuous examples of the baroque. Both works respond more fully to Hemingway's psychic needs than to artistic demands. Yet they retain interest as stages in the evolution of an artist. "The essential American soul," D. H. Lawrence wrote," is hard, isolate, stoic, and a killer." It is as the author of these two books more than of any others that Hemingway deserves Lawrence's characterization. But the inner turbulence of *Death in the Afternoon* and *Green Hills of Africa* defies such neat classification. Each adjective cries out for a qualifier. And even a "killer" needs further distance from his prey than Hemingway allows himself before he can comprehend his compulsion to kill. Hemingway could never gain that distance when he wrote of himself as hero. Within a year, however, with the writing of "The Snows of Kilimanjaro" and "The Short Happy Life of Francis Macomber," he would explore the ground again, this time with the artistic discipline that had long ago earned him the praise and respect he coveted.

10

"The Snows of Kilimanjaro"
AND
"The Short Happy Life of Francis Macomber"

In February 1936, Scott Fitzgerald published in *Esquire* the first of three articles about his "crack-up." Though "all life is a process of breaking down," he began, two kinds of impact speed it toward disaster. External blows—the more dramatic —break a man quickly. But even more terrible is the inward stroke, the kind "you don't feel until it's too late to do anything about it, until you realize with finality that in some regard you will never be as good a man again." [1] Writing to friends about Fitzgerald's document of despair, Hemingway offered measured sympathy and abundant scorn. Fitzgerald's plight, he suggested, was the product of a mindless infatuation with youth and high life. Instead of disciplining his art, Fitzgerald was wasting his talent with an unmanly and senile whine.[2]

When "The Snows of Kilimanjaro" appeared in *Esquire* six months later, Hemingway clearly had not yet done with Fitzgerald. Harry, the dying writer, recalls "poor Scott Fitzgerald and his romantic awe" of the rich, an awe that blinded him to their being "dull and repetitious." [3] When Fitzgerald finally realized that the rich were not "a special glamorous race," Harry muses, that truth "wrecked him just as much as any other thing that wrecked him." [4]

Hemingway's cruel outburst—both in his letters and in his story—tells less about Fitzgerald than about himself. For too long now, Hemingway the artist had been an adventurer and he had apparently begun to brood about the waste of his own talent. Just after the publication of "The Snows of Kilimanjaro," Fitzgerald wrote a shrewd but not wholly precise comment that Hemingway was "as nervously broken down as I," but that Hemingway inclined toward "megalomania," Fitzgerald toward "melancholy." [5] Though Hemingway often preferred to bare his chest rather than his soul in public, in his fiction, melancholy prevails over bravado. This is especially true in "The Snows" and "Short Happy Life," tales saturated with guilt, self-doubt, and fear. Because Hemingway's ego prevented his writing such "awful things about himself" as Fitzgerald had written, he chose to reveal his anguish through the concealment of fiction rather than in open confession.

To avoid total identification with the hero of "The Snows," one of his most conspicuously autobiographical stories,[6] Hemingway altered his conventional mode ingeniously. Harry is an exemplary (but fallen) hero who has deliberately pledged allegiance to a corrupt society rather than risk declaring a "separate peace." Most of Hemingway's heroes search for a clean, quiet corner in Eden. Because Harry betrays that quest, Hemingway gains a necessary distance from him, and he can drive Harry into the "bad place," the miasmal swamp of real and imagined fears he allowed Nick Adams to avoid in Michigan. Now the setting is a hot African plain within sight of snow-capped Kilimanjaro, the hero a writer dying of gangrene and assessing in his final hours the wreckage of his life. "The marvelous thing is that it's painless," Harry says as the story opens. "That's how you know when it starts."

Though he is alluding to his gangrenous leg, the symbolic implications reach beyond. With as little pain, Harry (not unlike Dick Diver in *Tender Is the Night*) has slipped into moral and artistic decay, the consequence of an easy, undisciplined life.

In a series of flashbacks (some merely reflection, others induced by delirium) he conjures images of his first wife—the one he really loved, the one who left him—and of the many women who succeeded her, each wealthier than the last, none of them able to fill the emptiness in his psychic void. At first, Harry tries to charge his failure as an artist to Helen, his current wife, "this rich bitch, this kindly caretaker and destroyer of his talent" [158]. But though Helen is depressingly ordinary ("She was always thoughtful . . . On anything she knew about, or had read, or that she had ever heard" [157]), she has also suffered and, to her credit, tried for something longer-lasting than the anesthesia of liquor and lovers. Whatever her limitations, Harry at last admits to himself, he knew them when he traded his art for security: "He had destroyed his talent himself . . . by not using it, by betrayals of himself and what he believed . . ." [158]. Conscience and nostalgia fuse into a tortured strand of memory as Harry recalls unwritten and never-to-be-written stories, stories it had been his "duty to write of"—about love, violence, and death; about the beauty of Paris and the clean, cold simplicity of Austrian mountains; about the joys and terrors of his boyhood in Michigan; and, until he abandons the theme with his condescending reference to Fitzgerald, about the rich.

Strikingly juxtaposed to Harry's rotting leg is the symbol of a leopard whose "dried and frozen carcass" lies close to the summit of Kilimanjaro. "No one has explained," Hemingway writes in the epigraph, "what the leopard was seeking at that altitude." [7] Though critics differ in their interpretations of "The Snows," most agree that the leopard's death is clean, his failed search for the unattainable summit noble. Whatever spurred the leopard parallels the artist's drive. Harry had that drive, squandered it, and must pay the penalty of corruption: stench and unremitted, death-obsessed and—through the presence of vultures and a whimpering hyena—death-imaged remorse. To some extent, Harry's death further mocks his failure, for in his final delirium he sees from an airplane the top of Kilimanjaro, "wide as all the world, great, high, and unbelievably white in the sun." [8] Fondly clinging to a vision of himself as regaining his dissipated artistic and moral strength, "he knew that there was where he was going." In fact, he is in his last sleep, his rotting leg, the dressings down, hanging beside his bed.

"The Snows" yields more than a simplistic life message: a corrupt life breeds a corrupt death. In many ways disagreeably callous and self-indulgent, Harry somehow wins more sympathy and respect than the evidence may seem at first to warrant. Two methods produce this effect, the first dramatic and psychological, the second (and less successful) symbolic and philosophical. Hemingway locates the true center of the story in Harry's inward struggle to face himself as he is. With remorseless honesty, Harry strips away all pretense and discards every excuse for his failure as artist and man. Yet, as he does so, his delirious excursions into his past reveal too that he is a man of undeniable sensitivity, passionately alive to people, places, and experience. That he has been more than he is at once intensifies the dramatic force of his self-confrontation and increases our willingness to extend compassion. That at the last moment, after submitting momentarily to a death wish, he clings to a pure vision rather than succumb to despair or cynicism wins for Harry a narrow margin of victory. He has finally burned "the fat off his soul."

So long as Hemingway probes within the boundaries of Harry's tormented psyche, "The Snows" is a superb story, surely among his finest. That its structure is looser than usual is determined by Harry's physical condition and is admirably handled. Though Harry's delirium dissolves the orderly pattern of chronological time, the fragmented memories that course through his five internal monologues unmistakably mark the stages of his dark passage.[9] Even Hemingway's

symbols—more frequent than his norm—sometimes underscore Harry's inward struggle: the symbolic environmental
contrast between the pure, snow-peaked mountain where the
leopard dies a clean death and the hot plain where Harry
dies of rot.[10] The hyena is convincing, too, as a metaphor for
the pervasive atmosphere of death, entering precisely coinci-
dent with Harry's first awareness of his imminent death and
slipping lightly along the edge of "a sudden evil-smelling
emptiness."

Unfortunately, Hemingway on occasion solicits compassion
by trying to transmute Harry from the special case he is to
Man and Artist. As Man, he suffers the "huge, filthy" vultures,
suggestive of the mute, destructive force of nature. As Artist,
he suffers woman, whose voice curiously resembles the hyena's "strange, human, almost crying sound": beast (society)
and woman alike mourn too late the artist they harried in
life.[11] Finally, as Man and Artist, Harry seeks immortality
through his art. The symbolic correlative here is an allusion
in the opening epigraph to the western summit of Kilimanjaro
as "The House of God," a motif Hemingway recapitulates at
the end as Harry flies toward the gleaming peak.[12] These occasional intrusive efforts to explain and defend Harry (and
perhaps himself) with cosmic half-truths are labored and
fruitless. Harry is neither a particularly good man nor a great
artist, but he does die honest. From that clearly defined and
dramatically impressed image, Hemingway's portrait draws
its memorable force. The rest softens and diffuses but certainly does not destroy the image.

Published a month after "The Snows," "The Short Happy
Life of Francis Macomber" is a neater story, its virtues more
readily discernible, though perhaps less distinguished. Structurally compact, it frames the events of one day of shame by
plunging at the outset into the succeeding day of redemption
and retribution, flashing back, then returning to the present.
No symbols clutter either the surface or the subsurface—lion

and buffalo are precisely what they appear to be, hunter's prey. The range of characters is narrow and familiar, but the exemplary hero, the apprentice, and the bitch woman are drawn with painstaking care. Above all, "The Short Happy Life" is an exciting and absorbing adventure story in which all human conflicts are resolved by the actual drama of the hunt.

Like Harry in "The Snows," Francis Macomber enters the "bad place" and emerges a better man (though soon a dead one) after the experience. Macomber's problem is simpler, however, though its impact is felt just as deeply and its resolution is just as fatal. As he lies on his cot the night after he has fled, panicked, from the rush of a wounded lion, Macomber admits to himself that "more than shame he felt cold, hollow fear in him" [110]. Fear rather than guilt threatens Macomber's manhood, the same fear of death that binds him to the brotherhood of bullfighters, boxers, and soldiers who precede him as apprentices. As they learned the "code," so must Macomber, and, as for many of them, the cost of honor is prohibitive but worth paying.

The genius of Hemingway's story lies, then, less in its freshness of theme than in its firmly controlled, subtly ironic interplay of action and character. Carlos Baker has shown, for example, how cleverly Hemingway positions his characters in the automobile to illustrate the tensions among them.[13] During the lion hunt, Macomber sits in front at the outset, but on the ride back after the debacle, it is Wilson who occupies the front seat, Margot who withdraws her hand from Macomber's and leans forward to kiss Wilson on the mouth. When they pursue buffalo the next day, Margot rides "sitting far back in the seat," Macomber "sitting forward" to tell Wilson how his fears have gone. Finally, when Margot kills Macomber—violating the hunter's code by shooting from the car—she is alone in the back seat.

They are at first glance a sophisticated but disagreeable and unattractive lot. Francis and Margot Macomber "had a sound basis of union. Margot was too beautiful for Macomber to divorce her and Macomber had too much money for Margot ever to leave him" [121]. Robert Wilson, their English guide, has "a very red face and extremely cold blue eyes" and carries "a double size cot on safari to accommodate any windfalls he might receive." They earn from one another appropriate labels: Macomber is a "bloody coward" and a "poor sod," Margot a "bitch," and Wilson "an insolent bastard." And yet each is rather better than his deserved epithet and more complex. Margot turns away briefly to weep after Macomber runs away from the lion, understanding, as Wilson surmises, his anguish and humiliation. She has also tried, the omniscient narrator observes, to make their marriage work, and he adds, ". . . the way they were together now was no one person's fault" [133]. But though Hemingway adds dimension to Margot with these insights, it would be too much to assume, as some critics have, that she kills her husband accidentally or even accidentally-on-purpose.[14] To do so would be, among the other things, to dismiss Wilson as imperceptive and wrongheaded when he tells her, after Macomber's death, "That was a pretty thing to do . . . He *would* have left you too" [135].

Wilson's words cannot be ignored anywhere in the story, for if he is an "insolent bastard," he is also the spokesman for Hemingway's moral thesis. An admitted opportunist in everything but the hunting, he accepts his client's standards whenever feasible. But he holds fast (with the possible exception of chasing buffalo in a car) to his own code in killing: ". . . they could live up to [it] or get some one else to hunt them" [125]. Sleeping with Margot Macomber does not blemish Wilson's reputation as an exemplary hero, because the sexual demands of rich, neurotic women never impinge upon his rigidly honorable standards for the hunt, the real arena in which a man's worth is tested. There, no thinking is needed, only integrity, ability, and the memory of a line from Shakespeare's *Henry IV*—"a man can die but once; we owe God a death." [15]

What Macomber must learn about the "code," Wilson al-

ready knows. What Wilson does not quite know is how to an-
alyze this prize specimen of the "great American boy-men."
At thirty-five, Macomber is still an apprentice, vain but
doubtful about his manhood, battling desperately against his
wife's domination. But Macomber has also a vitality and intensity that at once repel and attract the efficient but blood-
less Englishman. Macomber's candor—even about his fear—
is disarming, his determination is appealing, and even his
outbursts of anger are youthful—sullen but plaintive. In
brief, he has from the outset the potential to become a man,
to fear neither living nor dying.[16] Though Wilson cuckolds
him, the Englishman serves nonetheless as an unwitting preceptor, inspiring him by example not to think or talk, only to
thrust himself "into action without opportunity for worrying
beforehand." Macomber's anger at Wilson and Margot speeds
him toward defining himself through action. Like the inward
radiance induced by the climax of a religious ceremony,[17]
Macomber's act of heroism purges his fear—not only of nature but of Margot—and inspires a faith in self that makes
even his death a kind of victory.

With "The Short Happy Life" and "The Snows," Hemingway arrived at a watershed in his career. A year earlier, in
Green Hills of Africa, he had already warned of the dangers
success lays upon an artist. In that book too he spoke as well
of the artist's need to reach toward a "fifth dimension" in his
craft, to burst the limits of traditional achievement. These African stories mark the adventurer's return to his early commitment to art. The experiments with symbolism and stream-
of-consciousness in "The Snows" hint at Hemingway's
determination to take technical risks beyond his already
proven skills.[18] But what is perhaps most remarkable in these
stories is how effectively for the most part he maintains adequate distance from characters whose obsessions reflect his
own. Macomber and Harry are just about Hemingway's age,
and their fears—Macomber's of death, Harry's of unfulfilled
promise—are Hemingway's fears. A lesser artist might have
sought a lower level of soft redemption. Hemingway follows

instead the inexorable ironic logic of the story, compelling each of his heroes to die at the moment of insight. Hemingway's debt to art paid, he may have benefited from the psychological relief of surviving his "double." At least the success of the stories buttressed him against the "crack-up" Scott Fitzgerald had perhaps too poignantly and painfully conjured in his imagination.

I I

To Have and Have Not

That Hemingway could write successful fiction indirectly protesting social and domestic malaise on the American scene he
had already proved before publishing, in 1937, his third
novel, *To Have and Have Not.* In several of his short stories
and especially in *The Sun Also Rises,* Hemingway's idle
spendthrifts, mismatched couples, hoboes, and whores serve
as tacit reminders of disorder and unrest. All appear once
more in *To Have and Have Not,* gathered now uniquely in
their homeland. Recognizable, even familiar, the "haves" and
"have-nots" of Hemingway's only American-based novel are
disturbingly, even distressingly, different from earlier portraits. For one thing, they are conspicuously types, sketchily
drawn, inadequately discriminated, barely felt. And they
squirm comfortlessly beneath the weight of a hitherto un-
voiced "message," Harry Morgan's dying words: "One man
alone ain't got . . . no bloody f——ing chance."

In his earlier fiction, Hemingway subordinated the theme
of protest, stressing rather the emergent consciousness of his
apprentice hero. For Nick Adams, Jake Barnes, and Frederic
Henry, the challenge is to see, to know, and to salvage a
"separate peace." Harry Morgan knows the score from the
outset. If he serves any apprenticeship, it is complete by the
end of the first chapter. By then, he has witnessed cold-

blooded murder and been grossly cheated. Once the social and moral niceties of contemporary un-civilization have been thus defined, Harry Morgan takes his own part. Three chapters later, he proves his own mastery as thief and killer. Ultimately, the world grinds Morgan down and destroys him without the largesse of a "separate peace"; but not before he unburdens himself of that oft-quoted final line. To which of many possible queries did Hemingway intend it as an answer: Has modern society wiped out any chance for a "separate peace"? Should a man who fails to conclude a "separate peace" declare a private war? If a man alone has no chance, should he join with other victims to crush his oppressors? Regrettably, no straightforward response may be offered, for among other crippling faults, *To Have and Have Not* is hobbled also by lame thinking.

Hemingway's interest in socio-political problems is clear, as his journalism attests. But his judgments are intuitive and emotional, derived more from personality than from principle —and often therefore contradictory or inconsistent. All dictators were anathema, but so too were all politicians. Though he foresaw tragedy in Spain and prophesied world conflict by 1938, he adopted an isolationist's stance and warned Americans to avoid a Roosevelt and elect as their leader "a man without ambition, a man who hates war and knows that no good ever comes of it." [1] Nevertheless, his sympathies at home and abroad were always with the tyrannized and the oppressed. And even as he filed his virile fishing and hunting stories with *Esquire* during the 1930's, he could not shut his ears to the thunder on the left. The confusion of sounds from within and without damaged Hemingway's artistic inner ear and contributed to the intellectual imbalance of *To Have and Have Not*.

What the literary dogmatists of the left demanded was that the artist commit himself to the class struggle, not to the private quest for such bourgeois luxuries as the "separate peace." The bloody textile strike of 1928 in Gastonia, North Carolina, that Richard Gordon is writing about in *To Have and Have*

Not, for example, had already become the subject of a half dozen novels, including Sherwood Anderson's *Beyond Desire.* Moreover, consistent with the literary policy articulated by Mike Gold and Granville Hicks in the Communist magazine, *New Masses,* many of the proletarian novelists followed a familiar creative pattern: draw the workers as good, the *bourgeoisie* as evil; and resolve the plot affirmatively, that is, trumpet the imminent fall of capitalism and the victory of the masses.[2]

The cliché-ridden excesses of these novels led some theorists of the left to admit that polemic heat often failed to generate literary light. Two among them, William Phillips and Philip Rahv, founded in 1934 a new journal, *Partisan Review,* which, while faithful to the principles of the Communist Party, rejected the use of art "as an instrument of political propaganda." To dramatize their determination to "resist every attempt to cripple our literature by narrow-minded, sectarian theories and practices," Rahv wrote a reasonably favorable review of a recently published collection of stories by a "bourgeois" writer—*Winner Take Nothing* by Ernest Hemingway. While insisting that Hemingway's "second-hand nihilism" and concern with effects rather than causes rendered his material useless to proletarian writers, Rahv adds that Hemingway's "supple precision and impersonality of method" might teach the proletarian writers "how to restrain themselves from intruding upon their material."[3]

From the mid-thirties until the publication of *For Whom the Bell Tolls,* the left esteemed Hemingway in part for his craft but more for the propaganda value of his extra-literary statements. In the fall of 1935, Hemingway appeared for the first time in the pages of *New Masses* with a brief essay called "Who Murdered the Vets?" While living at Key West, Hemingway came to know several of the unemployed war veterans working on a government road and bridge-building project. Later, of course, they would appear in *To Have and Have Not* as habitués of Freddy's Bar. When more than four hundred of them died during a hurricane, Hemingway raged against the federal government for failing to evacuate them in time. "Who left you there?" Hemingway demanded. "And what's the punishment for manslaughter now?" [4] In 1937, he wrote "Fascism is a Lie" for *New Masses* and delivered it as a speech before the radically oriented Second Writers' Congress. Yet Hemingway never rose higher than the rank of "fellow traveler," for he was unwilling to join the left in its announced intention "to defend the Soviet Union against capitalist aggression" or to work with them to develop and strengthen the revolutionary labor movement.[5]

Abstractly drawn to the idea of revolution, Hemingway recoiled at the implications. "They're beautiful," he wrote about revolutions in *Green Hills of Africa*. "Really. For quite a while. Then they go bad" [192]. What undermines Hemingway's political radicalism is his profound commitment to the individual. Wyndham Lewis missed the point when he wrote in 1934, "It is difficult to imagine a writer whose mind is more entirely closed to politics than is Hemingway's." [6] Like all other experience he knew and recorded, politics was for Hemingway intensely personal. He hated Fascism less for what it did to men than for what it did to a man, and he feared politicians because they had the power to deflect a man from his quest for love and peace. In Hemingway's world, loneliness and dignity are private and subjective, not collective or dialectical. When he tried to fuse private motives with social consciousness, he failed.

The most obvious technical flaw in *To Have and Have Not* is structural. Even Hemingway's most unabashed apologists yield on this point, adding nonetheless that he knew the novel was in trouble but lacked the time to rework or repair it. A more likely possibility is that Hemingway excised (without making substitutions) chunks of narrative that might have occasioned libel suits against him.[7] The structural breakdown of *To Have and Have Not* cannot, however, be attributed to external pressures. What fractured the novel was Hemingway's faulty conception of its narrative possibilities. Having already published two stories about Harry Morgan—the earlier, "One Trip Across," to appear intact as Part I of the novel—[8] Hemingway determined to amplify the counterpoint between Morgan and the "haves." Thus was Richard Gordon born and a novel aborted.

The two narrative strands stubbornly refuse to counterpoint or to cohere. Apart from the thematic weaknesses of Hemingway's plan, its unnatural pattern of episodic discontinuity is sufficiently self-defeating. For one thing, Gordon is dragged into the novel just as Morgan is about to be dragged out. Gordon and his wife appear suddenly and unexpectedly in Chapter 15—past the midpoint of the novel—at Freddy's Bar just after Morgan leaves to prepare for a smuggling expedition. The vignette of the Gordons' marital incompatibility seems at that moment neither more nor less relevant than other quick but studied glimpses of the decadents: Mr. Johnson's casual and cavalier ignoring of his debts; Fred Harrison's snobbery and malice; and Mrs. Laughton's coyly vulgar pass at Morgan. The reader justly and correctly assumes that none of these characters will reappear. Nothing about the Gordons in their brief scene warrants their reappearance. It is more than mildly surprising and disconcerting to encounter Richard Gordon again four chapters later (just after Morgan has been fatally wounded) bicycling past Morgan's wife, Marie, and utterly misreading in her countenance her inner life.

With a tawdry irony born of artistic desperation, Hemingway thrusts Gordon into the narrative at the point of its logical conclusion—Morgan's death. That death must now be delayed for another six chapters during which Morgan appears only during quick flashes as his boat is silently towed to shore. Meanwhile, the narrative center shifts to Gordon and his decline. Instead of suspense, the reader endures confusion, irritation, and, at last, embarrassment. When Morgan's boat does reach harbor and he speaks his final words, still another ending is at hand. Again, Hemingway rejects the opportunity and launches a lengthy account of disparate wasteland creatures aboard the yachts in the harbor. Not until Marie Morgan passes the drunken Gordon without recognizing him and repays his earlier irony with her own—"Some poor goddammed rummy"—does Hemingway mercifully close. "Hate and a hollow feeling" are all that remain for Marie. The poignancy of her insight is fairly stated. What diminishes its impact is that the reader has long since wearied of Hemingway's vertiginous leaps and lapses.

His random shifts in point of view add to the reader's despair.[9] The five chapters of Part I are narrated in the first person by Harry Morgan. Thereafter, all semblance of unified narrative perspective disintegrates. Conceivably, Hemingway intended, as with his structural pattern, some kind of formal orchestration, a figured bass of voices played against the dominant theme of the novel. Whatever his purpose, the result is discordant and dismal. Why, for example, does a minor character like Albert Tracy narrate, but not Richard Gordon? Why, when narrating omnisciently, does Hemingway frequently and indiscriminately allow a character to intrude as first-person narrator? And why, on at least three occasions, does he resort to interior monologue (Harry in Chapter 10, Dorothy Hollis in Chapter 24, and Marie in Chapter 26)? Virtuosity is not in itself a virtue. Although Dorothy Hollis's long inward discourse reveals Hemingway's awareness of Joyce, it does little to direct our sense of the novel's purpose (unless, of course, Dorothy's masturbating illustrates once more that one cannot—or, perhaps, can—manage alone).

Even Hemingway's control of language slackens. In the best scenes, his touch is sure and welcome, understated but eloquent in its evocation of tension (the opening scene at the bar in Havana), or of crude but compelling affection (the Morgans at home), and of mingled ebullience and anger (marlin-fishing with Johnson, and the brawling veterans at Freddy's Bar). But there are too many voices echoing dully inside the shell of self-caricature. The clash between controlled and slapdash writing produces a sullen, shrill tonality ("this thin screaming," Sinclair Lewis wrote in a review), a sort of crankiness bred of intellectual confusion and emotional discord.

Richard Gordon is the most conspicuous example of Hemingway's excesses. He is incapable of credible speech. Justifying his visits to Helène Bradley, for example, he observes: "She interests me both as a woman and as a social phenomenon . . . A writer has to know about everything. He can't restrict his experience to conform to Bourgeois standards" [140]. Poor Gordon is pushed beyond decent limits of burlesque, the more regrettable because he might have emerged, like Harry in "Snows of Kilimanjaro," as a valuable study of a failed artist and a corrupted man.[10] But instead of the depth analysis of character Hemingway produced a year earlier in "Snows," Gordon emerges only as an abstract effect without substantial cause. Only when his wife, Helen, spreads his past behavior before him—"bitter, jealous, changing your politics to suit the fashion, sucking up to people's faces and talking about them behind their backs" [186]—is there any factual evidence of what he has been like. Yet that is all, and it is scarcely enough to justify Gordon's subsequent humiliation and defeat as husband, lover, and writer—except as an arbitrary symbol of bourgeois decay and as a convenient foil to Harry Morgan.

Others serve like functions. Helène Bradley's sterile promiscuity and Dorothy Hollis's sexual solipsism contrast with Marie Morgan's fulfillment with her own husband. The yachtsmen—alcoholic, homosexual, guilt-ridden—counterpoint the honest roistering of the dispossessed veterans. But whether "have" or "have-not," all are drawn as flat creatures of theme, frozen into emblematic postures. Even those few among the affluent who escape censure—Helen Gordon and the Happy Family—earn approval as symbols rather than as characters. The "pleasant, dull and upright" family sleeps soundly aboard their yacht, their consciences as uncomplicated as the formula for the popular household product that has made them wealthy. They have done no harm and thus, even though they are capitalists, "There are no suicides when money's made that way . . ." [240]. Some of the bad people are not so bad. With Helen Gordon, Hemingway adds a corollary: a few of them may even be good. Helen's defense of religion and family may fail to establish an identity for her, but it does affirm decency as a possibility among the enemy.

Not only are such arguments as watery as the portraits, but the plea for compassion is at once too sudden and too late. Nowhere is this more evident than in Professor McWalsey's unaffected remorse at Richard Gordon's downfall (which he has sped by taking Gordon's wife). "But why," he muses as he watches the battered Gordon stumble homeward, "must all the operations in life be performed without an anaesthetic?" [221]. At that point, the reader simply does not care whether Richard Gordon gets his due with or without pain. To urge pity for Gordon and the others just three pages before Morgan speaks his last words is folly. What little thematic clarity the novel pretends to is thereby shrouded.

Not all critics would agree. Freely acknowledging the flaws in structure, style, and characterization, they insist that Hemingway's argument is crystalline. For Edgar Johnson, for example, "Hemingway reaches a logical affirmation transcending negation"; [11] for Earl Rovit, the novel "marks . . . the clear recantation of the separate peace"; [12] and for Maxwell Geismar, it is a "farewell to the solitary course he himself had been pursuing." [13] It is Harry Morgan who must bear the burden of their proof. The brief goes something like this: Morgan's brutality is offset by his honesty and courage. He can, as Carlos Baker writes, "handle his own affairs; Gordon is a kept man in a morally unkempt society." [14] But unlike earlier apprentice and exemplary heroes, Morgan rejects a "separate peace" as both inadequate and unattainable. The few who make it as individuals do so by squandering their moral inheritance and embracing the abyss of *nada*—like Gordon and the yachtsmen. For the "have-nots," like Morgan, Albert Tracy, and the veterans, the solitary quest is futile, its nobility and dignity brushed aside by destructive social and psychological forces. When Albert Tracy's widow is rescued from her fall into the harbor and cries out, "Losht my plate," Hemingway has imaged, Maxwell Geismar suggests, "our national dental plate . . . swept away by the flowing and unperturbed waters of the Gulf Stream . . . the rare and few accents of humanity's divine articulation have been reduced to a sort of grotesque mumbling." [15] A man must strike back, fighting not for peace but for victory, even if he dies in the attempt. *But he cannot wage the battle alone.* Thus, when Morgan says, ". . . a man alone ain't got no bloody f——ing chance," Hemingway signals his own rejection of the "separate peace" and acceptance of a united front.

The argument is plausible but not convincing. Its overriding weakness is its fallacious assumption about Morgan's emergent class consciousness. From the outset, Morgan's hard-boiled commitment is personal, not social. As rigorously as any of the yachtsmen, he applies the dictum of doing unto others before they do unto him. Mr. Johnson cheats him during a fishing expedition but he cheats and murders the Chinese smuggler, Mr. Sing. Morgan's excuse that he killed one man to save a dozen lacks any humanitarian significance, for he unloads the remaining Chinese refugees in Cuba, not in the United States, where he had been hired to bring them. His only concerns as he returns to Key West with $1,200 profit are that the ship bunks not betray to the customs officers any odor of his discharged human cargo, and that he might have been poisoned from being bitten by a Chinaman.[16]

On every expedition Morgan undertakes, his motive is profit, his means violence. His knowledge of social problems and class structure is negligible. All he knows or cares to discuss is that he has been cheated by men, movements, and his own government: bilked by a capitalist, betrayed by a disgruntled Cuban revolutionary, and shot by a U.S. revenue agent. Morgan's anger is against economic impotence itself, not against its specific causes. Even after he loses his arm, he admits to being "sore" but not to being a "radical." When he listens to Emilio, the young Cuban revolutionary, describe the "murderous tyranny" of capitalism and imperialism, his first thought is, "He's a radical . . . That's what he is, a radical." As the boy finishes his impassioned speech about national pride and selfless commitment, Morgan's thoughts jell: "What the hell do I care about his revolution. F—— his revolution. To help the working man he robs a bank and kills a fellow works with him and then kills that poor damned Albert that never did any harm. That's a working man he kills . . . The hell with their revolutions. All I got to do is make a living for my family and I can't do that. Then he tells me about his revolution. The hell with his revolution" [168]. A few minutes later, Morgan begins gunning down the Cubans—Emilio is his first target.

Although many of Harry Morgan's acts recall his piratical namesake, he is not a villain. "I've got no boat, no cash, I got no education . . . All I've got is my *cojones* to peddle" [147], he says. And it is precisely that spirit of the nineteenth-century frontiersman that Morgan embodies, a fusion of Western sheriff (Morgan's earlier job was as a policeman in Miami) and bad man, his violence at once a defense and a defiance of established order. He kills without a twinge of conscience but he suffers his wife's henpecking when he is late for dinner. A virile lover who moves, his wife thinks, "like some kind of animal, easy and swift . . . light and smooth-like . . ." [128], he is steadfastly faithful to his "old woman." To all who know him, he is tough and brave. He tends the wounded Negro, Wesley, ignoring his own pain. He refuses to complain about losing his arm. Yet Morgan is not a bona-fide Hemingway hero. He is, as Albert Tracy says, "a bully and he was bad spoken." But, Tracy adds, "I always liked him all right" [99]. And Morgan—like pirates, sheriffs, and old-fashioned bad men—is perversely likable for the crusty, brutal individualism that makes him, as Oscar Cargill writes, "more American than the national anthem."

Harry Morgan is a frustrated loner, a bankrupt entrepreneur. A man alone has no chance, he tells us. But the context makes clear that he would be happier if he were alone. When, for example, Morgan plans his final trip with the Cubans, he reluctantly decides to take Albert Tracy with him: "It would be better alone, anything is better alone but I don't think I can handle it alone. It would be much better alone" [105]. No militant cry for revolutionary union, this is the despairing sigh of an independent businessman forced into an unwanted partnership. It is this truth that Hemingway unwittingly acknowledges when he writes after Morgan's last words: "It had taken him a long time to get it out and it had taken him all of his life to learn it" [225]. Instead of howling outrage, Hemingway manages only an irascible grunt.

Intellectually and aesthetically confused, *To Have and Have Not* is in nearly every way a bad novel.[17] Yet it can boast a few strong scenes and an energy that drives the reader on. Delmore Schwartz's verdict may be too strong: ". . . a stupid and foolish book, a disgrace to a good writer, a book which should never have been printed." [18] But his denunciation helps to compensate for the far wilder rationalization of Hemingway's apologists. Scott Fitzgerald is absurdly kind when he writes to Hemingway that passages in *To Have and Have Not* are "right up with Dostoiefski." [19] When, however, Fitzgerald speaks of the "undeflected intensity" of these pages, he locates the single strength the novel possesses, an occasional dramatic lyricism that unsticks the fudge of intellectual pretense. For such moments, *To Have and Have Not* still deserves at least one reading.

I 2

For Whom the Bell Tolls

In Hemingway's first three novels, each of his heroes incorporates the same theme: the isolated individual must struggle desperately to learn how to hold on in a hostile or indifferent universe. That hero appears in *For Whom the Bell Tolls* as Robert Jordan, but in a different place and with a different purpose. In a sense, he has been displaced, for Hemingway's focal range here extends beyond Jordan's apprenticeship and beyond the complexities of the war in which he has volunteered to serve as a guerrilla for the Spanish Loyalists. In competition for the role of hero is Spain itself. Through the people, their language, and their land, Hemingway tries to capture the spirit of an entire nation and to dramatize its tragedy.[1] Within that tragedy—and it is here that he breaks new ground—Hemingway discerns a promise of transcendence, a unifying and sustaining spirituality that binds not only all Spaniards but all men. To reach this awareness constitutes the bulk of Robert Jordan's education; to communicate it through his thoughts and actions becomes Hemingway's purpose.

Hemingway's novel is Tolstoyan in scope but rarely in achievement. But it has many merits, and even its defects are generally interesting. Above all, it is a novel whose emotive force and integrity are never in doubt. Nor is there any question about Hemingway's instinctual commitment to the democratic spirit and his abhorrence of war, civil or other. Yet the novel falls considerably short of greatness. To some extent, Hemingway's failure in his longest, most densely populated novel is stylistic, but far more serious are his distortions of the experience he describes. Together, these technical and thematic flaws confuse and mislead the reader and, at last, diminish the novel.

Hemingway's narrative point-of-view, for example, causes difficulty. An omniscient perspective allows him a flexibility he uses on occasion to splendid advantage in the self-contained virtuoso passages: Pilar's description of killing the Fascists in her village; El Sordo's defense of the hilltop; and Andres's efforts to reach General Golz. But Jordan's is the prevailing central consciousness. Making him a college instructor of Spanish and author of a book about Spain is a plausible but not wholly persuasive ploy to erase doubts about his reliability as narrator. First of all, certain crucial episodes occur outside his ken. More important, as we shall see, he is simply too self-absorbed, too attentive to his own psychic pulse to reverberate adequately to the throbbings of those about him.[2]

➔ With structure, Hemingway fares better, counterpointing symbolic motifs of nature and technology that relate strands of plot, character, and setting to penetrating insights into life, love, and death. Many have noted that at the core of the novel is a single steel span of "solid flung metal grace"—the bridge, dramatic center of *For Whom the Bell Tolls*.[3] The bridge, Jordan reflects, "can be the point on which the future of the human race can turn" [43]. None are untouched by their encounter with the bridge—the symbol of passage between despair and hope, betrayal and trust. All action and meaning in the novel extend from the plan to destroy the bridge and the futility of its destruction.

For the guerrillas holed up in the Guadarrama, destruction of the bridge means the end of their relatively safe refuge. Destroy the bridge, Pablo prophesies in the opening chapter, and planes will come to hunt his people like prey. But the scene has another significance too. For an instant as Pablo gazes "lovingly" at his fine horses, he stands "proud and less sad-looking." Then fear and gloom again shadow his countenance: "Here am I with horses like these. And what can I look forward to. To be hunted and to die. Nothing more" [15]. Life was not always so, not before the war, when Pablo supplied picador's horses for the bull ring. Then, the dignity of man and beast made sense. But to a twin-engined bomber or a tank, horses, hills, and men are as one, merely objects to be destroyed. Pablo is a sick, frightened man, but part of his dread and despair result from the intrusion of "mechanized doom" [4] into the natural world. The bridge—itself a device of mechanics—now threatens the final holocaust.

Some of the tragic impulse in *For Whom the Bell Tolls* derives, as Allen Guttman suggests, from the sterile, repressive tyranny of machines subverting values of fertility and spontaneity identified with the earth.[5] Certainly Hemingway images this conflict, using the bridge to link the opposing forces. If the bridge fills the middle of Hemingway's canvas, the earth frames it. At the opening and at the close, Jordan lies prone on the pine-needled forest floor. There too—and always out-of-doors—he and Maria love, and their ecstasy makes the earth move. But as always in Hemingway, nature is not entirely benign. Contradictions abound. Jordan, for example, dies as well as loves in a natural setting. And if for him the smell of nature is sweetly alive—clove and raked leaves, bacon frying and bread baking—for Pilar there is also the pungent stench of death, a compost of the breath of old women, decayed flowers, and slops swept from a brothel.

Weather too tokens (as in *A Farewell to Arms*) oppositions in nature, though now it is snow rather than rain that mingles love and death.[6] An unseasonal snow threatens Jordan's mission. Yet it is across the snow that he sees Maria running toward him for a night of love during which he becomes aware that their bodies make "an alliance against death" [264]. An early hint of Hemingway's effort to transcend polarities appears in Jordan's bardic response to the snowfall. At first angered and frustrated, he soon reflects that, during a snowstorm, "it always seemed, for a time, as though there were no enemies . . . it blew a white cleanness and the air was full of a driving whiteness and all things were changed and when the wind stopped there would be the stillness" [182]. More rudimentary, Pilar says, "What rotten stuff is the snow and how beautiful it looks. What an illusion is the snow" [154].

El Sordo's fate best illustrates how nature and the machine alike ignore the poetry and the prose of human endeavor. Even as Jordan and Maria make love, El Sordo steals the horses needed to escape after the bridge is destroyed. But the horses leave prints in the snow. Jordan wakes from love to death, for he sights and must kill the Fascist scout trailing those prints. But nothing deters the cavalry, who follow hard after from tracking El Sordo to his natural fortress on a hilltop. Impregnable against land attack, the fortress crumbles and its defenders die beneath the bombs dropped from the air. Nature and technology, then, affect the form of the novel and the lives of its characters. They touch theme too, though not quite as Hemingway intends: the idealism that informs Hemingway's poetic spirit fails to alter or cancel the prosaic fatality that envelops *For Whom the Bell Tolls*.

Structure, symbol, and image combine to underscore man's isolation and doom. Even the prose—more open, relaxed, and leisurely than ever before—seems to add weight to what Hemingway had written in *A Farewell to Arms* about how the world kills not only the gentle, the good, and the brave, but also those who are none of these—although "there will be no special hurry." The formal archaism of the dialogue (at best intermittently successful) [7] suggests another time when life was simpler, personalized by "thee" and "thou," a time when human dignity seemed assured. But set against the quasi-Elizabethan pastoral exchanges between Jordan and Maria and the genteel, Old Testament solemnity of Anselmo and Fernando is the witty, racy, idiomatic vulgarity of Pilar, Agustin, and the others, a harsh reminder that the time is now, and that the Spanish earth is no more sacred or kind than any other, and its people no less vulnerable.

To the extent that *For Whom the Bell Tolls* rehearses Hemingway's familiar but always poignant sense of man's fate, the novel is relatively successful, occasionally superb. But when Hemingway tries to reconcile the struggles of lonely man with the spirit of a nation and a vision of all mankind, he drifts into a psychological smog and is soon wrapped in a philosophical mist.

Robert Jordan's politics are a striking example of this intellectual vagueness. After the war, Jordan says, he will write about his experience in Spain, "about the things he knew, truly . . ." [248].[8] Before the novel ends, he has learned enough about loving and dying to tell himself in his final moments that "the world is a fine place and worth the fighting for and I hate very much to leave it" [467]. About political truth, Jordan is less certain.[9] Bombers of both sides, for example, appear to him to be beautiful: "There's no *one* thing that's true. It's all true" [467].

It is not that Jordan is either wholly indifferent to the political complexities of the Spanish Civil War or entirely ignorant of them. But he is hardly steeped in knowledge about a cause that has led him to leave his university and risk his life on alien soil. All of which might be surprising for a young intellectual, were he not one of Hemingway's heroes. Jordan's reading in the politics of the revolution he supports is limited to a handbook of Marxism. Most of what he knows about the inner struggles raging within the Republic he picks up from Karkov, the brilliant but cynical Russian agent.[10] At first, Jordan had been attracted to the almost religious atmosphere prevalent at the headquarters of the International Brigade. Then Karkov drew him into the inner circle at Gaylord's, the hotel in Madrid from which coldly self-assured Russians deployed and disciplined the Loyalists. But the fine lines of distinction hold only casual interest for Jordan. Whether, as Karkov tells him, deviationists must be destroyed— Bukharinites and Trotskyites alike—is of little moment or use to him. Jordan, after all, fights neither as a member of the International Brigade nor as one of the regular Loyalist army, but as a guerrilla. All that really matters, he tells himself just before he dies, is that "I have fought for what I believed in for a year now. If we win here we will win everywhere" [467].

Jordan's political statements suggest an inclination toward anarchism, but Hemingway avoids defining a specific position. Most of his explicit political opinions are as negative as Harry Morgan's in *To Have and Have Not*. Early on, he answers Maria's query about his being a Communist with, "No, I am an anti-fascist" [66]. Further along, in Chapter 13, he tells himself that he has no politics, and in Chapter 26 he reflects, "You're not a real Marxist and you know it . . . Don't ever kid yourself with too much dialectics" [305]. Occasionally, he seeds a statement with a political platitude of affirmation. He believes, he says, in "Liberty, Equality, and Fraternity" as well as in "Life, Liberty, and the Pursuit of Happiness." Or more concretely (and anarchically), he believes that "all people should be left alone and you should interfere with no one" [163]. Yet Jordan knows from experience that rarely is anyone left alone, not even generals. As General Golz tells him when they plan to blow up the bridge in support of Golz's offensive, "They are never my attacks. I make them. But they are not mine . . . Always there is something. Always some one will interfere" [5]. Nevertheless, Jordan unequivocally places himself under Communist discipline, "the soundest and sanest for the prosecution of the war" [163].[11]

Jordan's political stance is neither indefensible nor—despite its vagueness—incomprehensible. But one balks at Hemingway's implied suggestion that Jordan, inspired by a special vision of transcendence, has risen above the petty vulgarities of wartime politics. Contrast Jordan for a moment with another apolitical figure in another story. "Old Man at the Bridge"—one of Hemingway's finest—tells of an old man too exhausted to flee the rebel army advancing toward the

Ebro. His sole concern is for the welfare of a cat, two goats, and four pairs of pigeons he has had to leave behind. On that Easter Sunday, the narrator says, there is nothing to do about the old man. At least, he concludes, the planes were not up that cloudy day. "That and the fact that cats know how to look after themselves was all the good luck that old man would ever have." [12]

Only two and a half pages long, "Old Man at the Bridge" sounds with subdued eloquence the themes that pervade *For Whom the Bell Tolls*, though in the novel they are less clear, less resonant. Broken, luckless, alone, the old man symbolizes what has happened to the people of Spain. About politics he knows nothing: "I am without politics . . . I am seventy-six years old. I have come twelve kilometers now and I think now I can go no further." [13] Yet, like the Major in "In Another Country," the old man is an exemplary hero who defines his humanity by his concern for others and sustains his own dignity by quiet, uncomplaining courage. It is about such people that Hemingway writes most truly in *For Whom the Bell Tolls*, as he had always written about those who know or are learning the meaning of "grace under pressure." The spirit of the old man abides in Anselmo in Hemingway's novel, but it animates most of the others as well. Certainly it inspires much of what Jordan believes and what he tries too pretentiously to be.

It may well be that this kind of personal courage—the only kind Hemingway really comprehends and writes about with conviction—is too narrow, too egocentric to reflect the communal tragedy of civil war. Obviously disturbed by this possibility, Hemingway interlards his narrative with layers of noble but vague sentiment that peel off as sentimentality. He tries to write a new tragedy about mankind, but it is the old one—about the individual—that survives. In that old tragedy, the Spanish guerrillas play a more convincing role than Robert Jordan.

Betrayed by nature, machines, and by one another, the guerrillas still cling tenaciously to life and pride in self.

Thrice-wounded, awaiting a hail of destruction from the sky, El Sordo accepts death without fear but (like Catherine Barkley in *A Farewell to Arms*) hates it as a shapeless negation he cannot even body forth as an image. About living, on the other hand, El Sordo's vision is sharp, clear, concrete. Although the hill on which he must die is a "chancre," nature is still wondrous; it *is* life, for ". . . living was a field of grain blowing in the wind . . . a hawk in the sky . . . an earthen jar of water . . . a horse between your legs . . ." [312]. Like the other guerrillas, El Sordo speaks little of politics. He fights for the Republic without question, introspection, or explanation, and he dies simply—like a bullfighter—with courage and dignity, trying to the end to kill his enemy.

El Sordo is a compendium of the virtues Hemingway admires in the Spanish personality and, by extension, in his own exemplary heroes. Most of the other guerrillas—whether gypsy or peasant—flesh out in greater detail these traits and others that amplify Jordan's conviction that there "is no finer and no worse people in the world. No kinder people and no crueler" [355]. Anselmo, for example, adds a dimension of secular sainthood. An atheist, the old man thinks in religious terms about the sin of killing a man. He kills with "a clear heart" to help the Republic, but "not with pleasure," insisting that one day all must "be cleansed from the killing or else we will never have a true and human basis for living" [196]. By no coincidence is Anselmo's counterpart a Fascist, Lieutenant Paco Berrendo, the austere young cavalryman who shoots Joaquin after the bombing raid "as quickly and as gently" as Sordo had killed his beloved horse. A devout Catholic, Berrendo loathes his blood-lusting captain, yet himself gives the order—because it is his duty—to behead the corpses of El Sordo and his men. "What a bad thing war is," he thinks as he leaves, praying. The little drama of killing by men who hate it is played to its fatal conclusion in the final paragraph of the novel, when Berrendo next appears, still "serious and grave," leading his cavalry into Jordan's gun sight.

Pablo is another matter. Yet he too is, as Jordan says, "all of them"—a compound of egotism, selfishness, and treachery. A loutish coward, he sneers at courage and seeks only survival. But as Anselmo says, Pablo "was something serious in the beginning," a leader who fought bravely and killed well.[14] Hemingway fails to make clear whether too much killing has brutalized him, whether he is simply what Jordan calls him, a *bicho raro*, or whether both are true. He achieves a tainted dignity at the close when he returns to fight at the bridge, impelled not by commitment or by loyalty but by unendurable loneliness. Whatever his motive, he is no longer a figure of humiliation as he faces Pilar squarely for the first time in months to say, "I am ready for what the day brings." One believes him as one believes Francis Macomber, and shares Pilar's feeling that "if a man has something once, always something of it remains" [391].

With Pilar, nothing has ever been lost. The most lavishly drawn of Hemingway's women, Pilar is abundant in body, mind, and heart. Not beautiful, she has loved often and well. Though her jealousy of Jordan and Maria occasionally finds harsh expression, her intent is never cruel. She is merely trying, as Jordan understands, to hold on to life. And living is Pilar's passion, for she has known—as mistress of the matador, Finitio, and of Pablo—much of dying, and of fear and courage as well. Pablo, she reflects, "was like all the bulls that Finitio had spent his life killing. But neither bull force nor bull courage lasted . . . and what did last? . . . Yes, I have lasted. But for what?" [190].

To demonstrate how, her behavior implies, in the face of barbarism, destruction, and defeat, one retains a commitment to humanity and one's self. Politically, she too is utterly simplistic: "I am for the Republic . . . And the Republic is the bridge" [53]. Intellectually, she is at once *voyant* and clairvoyant, incisively clearheaded yet superstitious, a palmist and prophetess of doom who tries to shrug off her dark art as gypsy humbug lest she frighten Jordan, whose death she foresees. Above all, Pilar is a woman of profound sensibility. For all her barbarousness of manner and expression, she is ex-

traordinarily sensitive to man's inhumanity and his latent decency. And she is quick to extend rough tenderness or mete
harsh rebuff as each is merited. Thus, she is brusque but
warm and protective toward Maria and Joaquin, caustic and
bitter to Pablo, yet forgiving when forgiveness is warranted.
Nowhere is she more clearly revealed than in her dramatic
narration of the massacre of the Fascists in her town. As
sharp-eyed and curious as a reporter and as detached as a
partisan who accepts without question that the enemy must
die, she is also sickened and saddened when men become a
mob. Bestiality and murder leave her "hollow and not well
and . . . full of shame and a sense of wrongdoing . . ." [127].

Some critics look askance at Hemingway's guerrillas as inadequate representatives of those who fought and died for the
Republic. One critic writes that no village in the Sierra of
Guadarrama would have accepted as Loyalist leaders "an old
gypsy tart" and "a horse dealer of the bull ring." [15] Another
suggests that El Sordo and Anselmo are less Spanish than lin-
eal descendants of James Fenimore Cooper's noble savages.[16]
Some truth lies in each statement. But the novel is not, as we
have seen, so much concerned with political verisimilitude as
with capturing the spirit of a people. For Hemingway, nothing in that spirit renders incompatible Cooper's Chingachgook
and the Spanish guerrilla. "All mankinde is of one Author,"
John Donne writes in his *Meditation*, "and is one volume."

Yet it would be futile to pretend that when the bell tolls
the courage of the guerrillas, it is a resounding peal honoring
the fellowship of man. Rather does it knell joylessly the doom
of proud, anarchic individualism, a familiar echo in Hemingway's fiction. What cements these people is essentially their
fierce pride in self ("What a people they are for pride," Pilar
says). This is their collectivism. They do what they must—
each in his own way—to affirm personal integrity. This is
their politics, a politics of the bull ring which, not unreasona-
bly, may be said to be no politics at all. Several of them—
Pablo, Pilar, Joaquin, Andres—are people of the *corrida*,
their ethics a product of its ritual. To this extent, *For Whom*

the Bell Tolls advances but little beyond what Hemingway had said earlier in *The Sun Also Rises, Death in the Afternoon,* and stories like "The Undefeated."

Still, there is a substantial difference Hemingway intends us to feel. The bloody sands of the arena are now all of Spain, the combatants no longer man against beast but men of the same soil pitted against one another. Without choice (there is no "separate peace" in civil war), they have become, in Donne's words, "involved in mankinde." Harry Morgan's "One man alone ain't got no bloody f——ing chance" is renewed—with added dignity and point—in Donne's "No man is an Iland, intire of it selfe." It is not death the guerrillas fear so much as it is loneliness. Pablo says, "Yesterday, all day, alone *working for the good of all* I was not lonely" [391; italics added]. Without the bond of community and cause, loneliness is an agony, even for one so serene as Anselmo. Alone, he tortures himself about the morality of killing, but at the bridge, helping Jordan, "he was not lonely nor did he feel in any way alone. He was one with the wire in his hand and one with the bridge . . . with the *Inglés* still working under the bridge and he was one with all of the battle and with the Republic . . . he was not happy but he was neither lonely nor afraid" [443].

In all this eloquence, Hemingway is groping toward a more comprehensive and affirmative vision of life than he had expressed in *The Sun Also Rises* and a clearer statement of it than he had managed in *To Have and Have Not.* Actually, even though a cosmic pessimism pervades *A Farewell to Arms,* it is imbued with the same sense of romantic idealism Hemingway strains after in *For Whom the Bell Tolls.* The difficulties that beset him here and his failure to resolve them are proportionately greater. The loneliness that unifies the guerrillas is, for example, poignant but too abstract to be more than half convincing. They linger in memory rather as trenchant portraits of individuals, whether as exemplars of courage and grace or of treachery and irresponsibility. That they fight as guerrillas further suggests their determination to avoid the mainstream of events determining the outcome of the war. Despite the pressures Hemingway applies, his Spaniards will not bend to his will. Although they are the logical bearers of his message about the brotherhood of man, he must at last let the burden fall—less logically and less successfully—on an outsider, Robert Jordan.

War is for Jordan, as for Nick Adams and Frederic Henry, a crucial part of his education. "It will be," he thinks, "quite an education when it's finished. You learn in this war if you listen" [135]. And what he learns, Hemingway insists, is congruent with the spiritual metamorphosis his Spanish mentors have undergone. Like them, Jordan has no fear of death. Yet, after Anselmo is killed, Jordan is "lonely, detached, and unelated," ready to indict man (Pablo) and nature (the snow) for the catastrophe. But hate wanes as he sees death the way the others must. Feeling closer to them, he rids himself of ego, "the always ridding of self you had to do in war. Where there could be no self" [447]. Above all, it is love that teaches Jordan that he, "with another person, could be everything" [393]. As he lives his final moments, Jordan not only reaffirms his faith in these thoughts—"You can do nothing for yourself but perhaps you can do something for another" [467]—but by sending Maria away and by staying behind to stall the enemy, he translates them into action.

Jordan's farewell to war is, then, unlike Frederic Henry's, supremely idealistic. With little more insight than Frederic into his reasons for fighting and a great deal more into the bureaucratic inefficiency and personal treachery that foredoom his cause, Jordan elects to struggle on and die for what he believes in without really understanding. He bids farewell to love too without rancor, cloaking the bitterness of reality with a mystique of spiritual oneness. Urging Maria to leave, he says, "Not me but us both. The me in thee. Now you go for us both" [464]. For the first time in Hemingway's fiction, death becomes—in both love and war—a beginning rather than an ending.

Two climaxes in love with Maria (first in the heather,

Chapter 13; again in Jordan's bedroll, Chapter 26) prepare
Jordan for the climax of war and death he endures alone on
the hill slope as the novel ends. During the first ecstasy of
love, in which the earth moves for both lovers, Jordan feels
time stop. From that instant, he is no longer aware of measured time or duration, only of eternal time, a continuously
intense *now*.[17] Into three days, seventy-two hours, Jordan realizes, he must compress all that a man who lives out a full
three score and ten might learn of life, love, and death. If
then, Jordan meditates, "there is not any such thing as a long
time, nor the rest of your lives, nor from now on, but there is
only now, why then now is the thing to praise and I am very
happy with it" [166]. Without foregoing any of the pleasures
of the flesh, Jordan achieves through his union with Maria
(who, some critics have suggested, may symbolize both Spain
and the Virgin) oneness as well with earth, man, and eternity.
After the radiant warmth of such revelation, mortality is but
a passing chill.

Some of Hemingway's most poetic writing (and overwrit-
ing) colors these passages about time and transcendence.
There can be no argument about their adding a certain depth
and dimension to an otherwise flaccid love affair. Concentrat-
ing on philosophical import distracts at least temporarily
from recognizing that Maria is less real than Jordan's sexual
fantasies about Garbo and Jean Harlow. Eternity with a creature so boundlessly and mindlessly submissive might make a
lesser man long to be translated again into time. But the
basic issues are neither Maria's credibility nor the baroque
prose. Two other matters are. First, Hemingway's excursus on
time and eternity fails to accommodate the tragedy of a nation riven by civil war. Earl Rovit argues to the contrary,
suggesting that *For Whom the Bell Tolls*, like Whitman's
"When Lilacs Last in the Dooryard Bloom'd," is a pastoral
elegy that "envelops death and temporal violence in a tran-
scendent serenity and harmony."[18] In actual fact, the reverse
is true; it is death and violence that overshadow all but a few
selected moments of quietude. One might argue further that

the tragedy of a man and that of a nation are not—even in the terms of John Donne's *Meditation*—truly analogous, especially when the men analogized are Abraham Lincoln and Robert Jordan.

And it is about Jordan himself that the second point must be made or, rather, extended, since it has already been stated in part. That he is an arbitrary, not an organic central character has been shown. In itself, this raises doubts about the dramatic validity of having such a character impose philosophical unity on the novel. A more serious doubt rises from Jordan's personality. He is too like Hemingway's other apprentices to effect a convincing leap from moral pragmatism to metaphysical pantheism. All the familiar traits are again in evidence: the obsessive concern with death and the equally compelling determination not to think about it. So too are the old escape routes—outdoor life, sex, food, and the "giant-killer," now an ever-present flask of absinthe. Yet Jordan thinks and worries more than Nick or Jake or Frederic, understandably so, for his world is more continuously violent than theirs, the imminence of death more constant. Jordan has also lived with death longer and, in certain respects, suffered its force more than they have. Like Nick Adams, Jordan was only a boy, seven years old, when he first saw violent death. For Nick (in "Indian Camp") it was a suicide; for Jordan a lynching. "You were too young for such things," Maria says. Before he finishes school, however, Jordan must endure still another trial, his father's suicide.[19]

Jordan has no difficulty following Pilar's advice not to speak of such things. "It is unhealthy," she says. Indeed, he mentions them only to Pilar and Maria, as if to talk about such matters with men would betray the discipline of the code. But he cannot so readily stop thinking about them, especially about his father's suicide. On the last night of Jordan's life, the image of his father as coward embarrasses and haunts him: "I understand it [the suicide], but I do not approve of it . . . You have to be awfully occupied with yourself to do a thing like that" [338]. Yet Jordan is wholly self-occupied, trying to behave otherwise, to behave like an earlier, braver ancestor. It is with his grandfather, who also fought in a civil war, that Jordan wishes he might talk at this moment, to learn from him what his father had failed to teach about courage. And in his final moments, suffering intensely the pain of his broken leg, Jordan once more renews his inward dialogue about suicide, calling again on his grandfather for strength. At last, Jordan musters the courage he seeks (putting aside even the "giant-killer"). "One thing well done can make—" is his last conscious thought. The rest is action —a glance at the sky, a touch of pine bark, and a finger on the trigger of a submachine gun.

Jordan's is an honorable death, fitting and proper for an apprentice hero. It represents a psychological triumph over his self-doubts and fears, and a moral victory over the Fascists, who—as he knew they would—have destroyed the tactical value of his mission. In these terms, as Philip Young writes, "this time the hero has won." [20] But Jordan's death fails to swell and fill the great circle of philosophical significance Hemingway circumscribes about it.[21] For Jordan, "any man's death diminishes me" means more narrowly than Donne intended. To share selflessly the common fate of man holds for Jordan less appeal than to die as bravely as the best among men. Hemingway's bell tolls for all men, but its deepest, most sonorous resonance honors them separately, each man alone, stranded on the island of his own lonely consciousness.

13

Across the River and Into the Trees

"Everything is much smaller when you are older" [12]. That illusion strikes Colonel Richard Cantwell, the fifty-year-old protagonist of *Across the River and Into the Trees*, as he drives beside the banks of the Tagliamento River along the well-paved road from Trieste to Venice. About thirty years earlier, during the Italian retreat in World War I, he recalls, the way seemed longer, for he had then walked most of the time. Cantwell's image of compression is not merely spatial. During these last three days of his life, he squeezes hard on time too, trying to extract the essence of the crucial events from his near and distant past.

Violence is part of the concentrate. The dusty roads of World War I have been cleared and the ditches filled. But the bridges have again been blown and adjoining houses leveled by the bombers of World War II. Death crystallizes too. "I have lived with it nearly all my life and the dispensing of it has been my trade" [220], he muses. What Cantwell remembers about how death comes is a distillate of the agonies Hemingway suffered and relived through his apprentices. Nearly all of them—Nick Adams, Frederic Henry, Harry Morgan, Harry of "Kilimanjaro," Francis Macomber, and others—come to mind in this brief passage:

Death is a lot of shit, he thought. It comes to you in small fragments that hardly show where it has entered. It comes, sometimes atrociously. It can come from unboiled water; an unpulled-up mosquito boot, or it can come with the great, white-hot, clanging road we have lived with. It comes in small cracking whispers that precede the noise of the automatic weapon. It can come with the smoke-emitting arc of the grenade, or the sharp, cracking drop of the mortar. [219]

Love is also part of what remains, the best and most vital part, the ecstasy "you might have had and instead you draw sleep's other brother" [219]. Those who love (and Cantwell has had three wives in his past), Cantwell tells his young mistress in a reprise of Frederic Henry's words to Catherine Barkley, "are more fortunate than the others. Then one of them gets the emptiness forever" [271]. And, as always, there is lonely courage, the clearheaded, unillusioned determination to live wholly, kill bravely, love passionately, and die cleanly. When Cantwell enters the back seat of his car alone and shuts the door "carefully and well," he suffers his final heart attack self-assured that he has done all he must to end as a man.

Certainly there is nothing remarkably new in any of this except that Cantwell is fifty years old, Nick Adams come to middle age. Such a portrait might of itself command interest, but on Hemingway's canvas only the background—the Venetian landscape—is memorable, its outlines and relevance clear, its colors vivid and intense. Cantwell himself fills the foreground as an overdrawn caricature, too boldly reliefed against the shadowy figures about him, too dimly recognizable as a character of fiction rather than as a blow-up of his creator.

Yet the novel is not without virtue. The brave love of a dying man for a beautiful young girl remains compelling even as it risks bathos. And although *Across the River* is least among Hemingway's novels a work of action or suspense, he creates a sense of inevitability that informs the discrete, uneventful scenes and nearly unifies them. Never for a moment does the reader doubt that Colonel Cantwell will shoot cleanly, love ardently, or die courageously. And these are the only events that fill his last weekend. All are bound together, however, as part of a ritualistic preparation for death. The "now" of the novel—the duck shoot and Cantwell's death— comprises only the opening chapter and the few brief closing chapters. The duck shooter, as Philip Young writes, "dispenses substitute deaths . . . for his own which, like those of the birds, must be perfectly accomplished, and ultimately is." [1] The rest is memory, near and remote. Yet the long flashback is also part of the ritual, for Renata's love helps Cantwell to exorcise the demons that have tormented him, to face his last encounter purged, and "to die," as Renata says, "with the grace of a happy death" [240].

Scenically, too, there is excellence. The frozen morning of the duck shoot, the views of Torcello and Burano from across the lagoon, and the deliberate, rambling "solitaire ambulante" through the streets of Venice to the market—these not only describe the external environment as Cantwell sees it but also help to define his inward response to it. Sometimes, as elsewhere in Hemingway's writing, the effect is achieved by contrasting the protagonist's response with another's. Thus, Cantwell's Italian boatman at the duck shoot is surly, insensitive to Cantwell's intense awareness of each moment of the breaking dawn; Sergeant Jackson is indifferent to Cantwell's effort to share with him the excitement of a slate-blue sea "whipped by the strong, cold wind from the mountains that sharpened all the outlines of buildings so that they were geometrically clear" [27]. Jackson's notion is that Cantwell has "been beat up so much he's slug-nutty."

Neither the boatman nor Jackson could have understood "the happiness of . . . eye and heart" Cantwell knows as he wanders the narrow Venetian streets looking at "the minor vistas, the shops and the *trattorias* and at old palaces of the city of Venice" [185]. The market itself is limned even more concretely—"the closest thing to a good museum"—and as he inhales its smells and studies its sights, Cantwell feels as if "he were enjoying the Dutch painters . . . who painted, in

perfection of detail, all things you shot, or that were eatable"
[192]. It is in such scenes that Hemingway effectively locates
the elegiac center of his narrative without the distortions of
psychological bravado or philosophical sentimentality. The
testimony of the senses is, as Tony Tanner observes about
Hemingway's writing, "the one known and knowable quantity," and must not be "pressed into generalizations . . . judgment is postponed in the interests of wonder." [2]

Were the rest of *Across the River* this good, the novel
might deserve more acclaim than it has received. Unfortunately, too much else lacks discipline and blunders off into
fulsome puffery of "Papa" Hemingway's generalizations.
Where once he had rendered a scene dramatically and objec-
tively, here Hemingway frequently intrudes flabby excesses
that undercut the desired effect. In Chapter III, for example,
Hemingway tells how Cantwell went to Fossalta, where, like
Nick Adams and Frederic Henry, he had nearly been killed
in World War I. Having determined by triangulation the
exact spot where he was wounded, Cantwell squats and re-
lieves himself. Then he completes the "monument" by bury-
ing, with the blood he had left there in his youth, his feces
and a sum of money to pay for his medals. The episode is, as
Philip Young declares, a "dazzling and apocalyptic" act of
"mingled disgust and reverence for that event of his life by
which the whole may be known, and by which it was unalter-
ably determined." [3] But it is also a passage that overreaches,
becomes pretentiously explicit, needlessly ironic, and almost
silly:

> It's fine now, he thought. It has merde, money, blood; look
> how that grass grows; and the iron's in the earth along with
> Gino's leg, both of Randolfo's legs, and my right kneecap. It's
> a wonderful monument. It has everything. Fertility, money,
> blood and iron. Sounds like a nation. Where fertility, money,
> blood and iron is, there is the fatherland. We need coal
> though. We ought to get some coal. [18–19]

Thus does a moment that approaches tragedy veer into self-
indulgent nonsense.

Such failures of taste and discretion mar the language and dialogue as well. Nowhere else in his fiction has Hemingway so carelessly abandoned his stylistic control and sunk to self-parody. Contrast, for example, the descriptions of Brett Ashley in *The Sun Also Rises* and of Renata in *Across the River:*

> Brett was damned good looking. She wore a slipover jersey sweater and a tweed skirt, and her hair was brushed back like a boy's. She started all that. She was built with curves like the hull of a racing yacht, and you missed none of it with that wool jersey. [22]

The simile of the racing yacht defines Brett's sleekness and poise precisely. All the objective details cluster about that image and are animated by it. But read the description of Renata:

> Then she came into the room, shining in her youth and tall striding beauty, and the carelessness the wind had made of her hair. She had pale, almost olive-colored skin, a profile that could break your, or any one else's heart, and her dark hair, of an alive texture, hung down over her shoulders. [80]

Here all is diffused, either by clichés—*shining* youth, a profile that breaks hearts—or by labored phrasing—the *carelessness* the wind makes of her hair, and its *alive* texture.

The writing here, lacking both assurance and competence, is merely showy, as if Hemingway had consciously forsworn his own creed that prose is architecture and that the age of the baroque is over. Elsewhere the writing becomes worse than showy: downright absurd. The lovers touch the edges of their "icy cold" martinis and feel them "glow happily all through their upper bodies" [83]. The body of the white wine is "as full and as lovely as that of Renata." Cantwell reaches "well and accurately for the champagne bucket." Their lobster is "imposing," indeed "a monument to his dead self," and Renata "chewed well and solidly on her steak."

The dialogue and description during the lovers' sexual hijinks in the lee of a gondola are scarcely more digestible. The images of battle (". . . please attack gently and with the

same attack as before," Renata urges) and of landscape
(". . . his ruined hand . . . searched for the island in the
great river with steep high banks") may attempt to reflect
Hemingway's preoccupation with death and beauty, but the
result is ridiculous. Instead of sharing the pathos and ecstasy
of a doomed idyl, one is more likely to leer at both the
sexual and the linguistic athleticism.

A similar disjunction in tonality results from the autobiographical notations scattered throughout the novel. All too
commonly, Cantwell's determined confrontation with love
and death must yield to Hemingway's equally determined
confrontation with personal foes. Sinclair Lewis is repaid for
having, years earlier, described Hemingway as puerile and
senile.[4] At a table in Harry's Bar, Lewis is seen as "an over-
enlarged, disappointed weasel or ferret," the sort of man who
"goes everywhere in Baedeker, and . . . has no taste in either
food or wine" [124]. Barely disguised as Cantwell's third
wife, Hemingway's ex-wife, Martha Gellhorn, is maliciously
though wittily denounced for her outsized ambition and minimal talent. She is, says Cantwell, "deader than Phoebus the
Phoenician. But she doesn't know it yet" [213]. The range of
obiter dicta is far more extensive than its relevance. Cantwell's views on battles, generals, admirals, politicians, and
current events do nothing to sustain sympathy for a dying
man who is, as General Stonewall Jackson said in his last moments, about to "cross over the river and rest under the shade
of trees."

However exasperating the lapses in style and tonality, the
cause of the ultimate failure of *Across the River* lies elsewhere and deeper—in the characters of Colonel Cantwell
and Renata, and in the psychological and philosophical implications of their relationship. For one thing, Cantwell is far
too obviously Hemingway's self-image of "Papa" as exemplary
hero. Frederic Henry and Robert Jordan are apprentices to
love and death, their initiation rites the substance of the novels in which they appear. Cantwell has already undergone
most of his ritual: "I have lost three battalions in my life and

three women," he says. Against those losses, he balances a zest for good living, a narcissistic consciousness of his presence and prowess, a toughness in manner, and, more apparent than real, a like toughness of mind. In these traits, he resembles most of Hemingway's heroes. The difference is that Cantwell is never perceived critically, only with indulgence and admiration. He is, as Joseph Warren Beach has observed, ". . . the oldest of all . . . avatars of Nick Adams; but one is not sure that he is actually the most adult in his attitude toward himself." [5]

It is not simply Cantwell's role in a September–May love affair that betrays him as immature. His love for the girl he perhaps too revealingly calls "Daughter" is undeniably touching. At nineteen—the same age at which Cantwell (and Hemingway) suffered his wound—Renata, whose name means "reborn," embodies the beauty and innocence he nostalgically yearns for. With her, he believes again in life even as he confronts death: "He only thought of her and how she felt and how close life comes to death when there is ecstasy" [219]. So considered, even the lovemaking in the gondola— like the escapades Hemingway recorded earlier in a hospital bed in Milan and in a sleeping bag in the hills outside of Madrid—has a poignancy that halts short of absurdity.

This much weight the relationship between Cantwell and Renata can bear. So long as they limit themselves to sensory pleasure and artless prattle, they are more or less credible and sympathetic. But when, sacrificing literary acumen and discipline for his own personal psychological needs, Hemingway freights them with a ponderous load of self-conscious symbols and significances, they collapse and sink, along with the novel. Renata is simply too fragile a creation to sustain the burden Hemingway imposes upon her. Shortly after she first appears, she makes unmistakably clear what her situation is when she asks Cantwell how he would "like to be a girl nineteen-years-old in love with a man over fifty-years-old that you knew was going to die" [91].[6] Unfortunately, Hemingway subordinates the psychology of the flesh to the philosophy of the spirit and transmutes Renata from sprite to saint. "I wish to serve you," she tells Cantwell, and indeed she does, far beyond the call of amorous duty or literary reason. Armed only with the faith and courage she has inherited from ancestral Doges, she attempts miracles and, if one has the kind of poetic faith that utterly suspends disbelief, in some measure she succeeds.

At the outset, Renata dreams of Cantwell's ruined hand as "the hand of Our Lord." Although Cantwell is never a Christ figure, he is obviously identified in Renata's mind with suffering and redemption. Once the Christian motif has been established, succeeding references, though covert, are abundant and exhortatory. Persistently, she encourages Cantwell to tell her (confess to her?) about the war: ". . . tell me true until you are purged of it." Through the purgation of telling, Renata hopes to release Cantwell from his terror, his hate, and his cynicism. Toward the close of the novel, enraged at his boatman in the duck blind, Cantwell thinks momentarily of killing him. But he has by now been purged, and he says, "Stop that . . . and think about your girl. You do not want to kill anyone anymore; ever" [291]. A moment later he continues, "Maybe I will get Christian toward the end . . . Who wants to make a bet on that?" Although Renata has not wholly converted Cantwell, she has prepared him, as she wished, "to die with the *grace* of a happy death" 7 (italics added).

To win grace, Cantwell must purge himself of two cardinal sins, pride and despair. Pride he never does quite abandon. Even after he acknowledges that it is because he has failed in his military career that he speaks ill of those who have succeeded, he rejects contrition and continues to resent those "who never fought and hold commands." Despair, however, afflicts Cantwell most profoundly and it is confrontation with its depths that he delays longest: "Let's not think about it. The hell with it. Maybe two things I will think about and get rid of them" [256]. Cantwell at last permits himself to conjure in turn the terrible memory of lifting the flattened body of a dead soldier which has been run over by passing trucks and later of watching a German dog and cat eating the body of a German soldier burned crisp by a phosphorus shell. The exorcism ended, Cantwell states that he now looks forward "to making jokes and to talking of the most cheerful things."

Curiously, Renata never directly shares in either of these crucial moments. Cantwell's most searing revelations occur while Renata lies asleep in his room. Only then does he confess—to the heedless ears of a sleeping girl and to her inanimate portrait standing against the wall. One critic interprets Renata's sleeping as consistent with the religious motif, arguing that the confession of a dying man should not be overheard.[8] By having before him, it might be added, both the girl and her portrait of two years earlier, Cantwell has access to a silent but reassuring figure in the present and a still but gentle guide during his Dantesque visit to the underworld of his past.[9]

To argue the plausibility of the Christian motif is profitless. It *is* present, less conspicuous perhaps than in this critical exposition, but apparent to any who will look for it. Its presence, however, hurts more than it helps, for it is superimposed rather than integral. For one thing, Cantwell is only remotely aware that he has been led along a path to spiritual transcendence. More important, the man who stands in the duck blind—despite the intrusive references to his newly acquired Christian humility—is neither markedly different from what he has been nor much more acutely perceptive in his understanding of himself. By making of him a semi-convert as well as an exemplary hero, Hemingway succeeds only in blunting the philosophical impact of his novel. Its dramatic and psychological force is nearly spent.

What strength remains trickles away in the coy initiation of Renata into the "Military Order of Brusadelli." As Renata has led Cantwell from experience toward innocence through her ritual of faith, so in turn she is raised from apprenticeship to exemplar. Tutored in love and "the sad science" of war, she is inducted as an honorary member, privy to the secrets of the "code," partner of those who, as Cantwell says of the only people he can love, "had fought or been mutilated" but fought on, undefeated.

Once more, however, Hemingway dissipates whatever emotive power the episode might possess. Cantwell's ritual suffers from an excess of high seriousness, Renata's from low comedy. Whereas the exemplary hero conventionally stands above and beyond cheap jibes, Brusadelli, leader of the order, is a Milanese profiteer who has "accused his young wife . . . of having deprived him of his judgment through her extraordinary sexual demands" [57]. The jest is amiable and harmless, as is much of the conversation between Cantwell and the *Gran Maestro*, headwaiter at the Gritti and another member of the Order. What is significant is that the "code" is treated with a mixture of levity and seriousness that destroys its relevance. The Supreme Secret, Cantwell facetiously tells Renata, is that "Love is love and fun is fun. But it is always so quiet when the gold fish die" [271]. Yet a moment later Cantwell responds to her query about what happens to people who love with his observation that at least "one of them gets the emptiness forever." Here, as at innumerable points in the novel, the pitch is off, the tonality irresolute. The reader shifts uncomfortably from giggling at the ridiculous to groaning at the agony of it all. And, finally, there is poor Renata, scapegoat of this horseplay, passively accepting a new role for which she is eminently disqualified by personality as well as by the logic of the plot.

Hemingway wrote to his friend Buck Lanham in 1949 that *Across the River* recapitulated themes he had used throughout his career, adding that he believed this novel was his best to date.[10] On the first count he was partially right, on the second hopelessly wrong. Cantwell is psychologically bound to his ancestors, but the bond breaks, leaving scraggy remnants of Christian and self-centered hagiography. As a result, few reviewers shared Hemingway's enthusiasm for his achievement; for many the issue was whether this novel or *To Have and Have Not* was his worst. That argument has little relevance today. Both are bad novels, though *Across the River* has a certain lyric, elegiac charm to recommend it as the better of the two. More pertinent is that in *Across the River* Hemingway sacrificed art for ego, preferring to project himself as a fully matured, exemplary hero rather than to study the far more interesting dynamism of anguish and endurance in an apprentice. He had not yet learned what he had himself taught in his first novel, that Count Mippopopoulos, though exemplary, is a minor character. When a character has suffered all, knows all, and tells all, he can be either a prophet or a bore—and Colonel Cantwell is no prophet.

14

The Old Man and the Sea

Hemingway hooked his first marlin in 1932 in the waters off Havana, twenty years before *The Old Man and the Sea* was published. During those years, Hemingway's enthusiasm for battling these magnificent fish never dulled. Nor did his admiration wane for the Cuban fishermen to whom the marlin was a way of life as well as a livelihood. Among the many fishing articles Hemingway wrote for *Esquire* in the thirties, one told the basic story of *The Old Man and The Sea*. "On the Blue Water: A Gulf Stream Letter," published in 1936, is a short essay that tells about the thrills of marlin-fishing and about an old man alone in his boat when he "hooked a giant marlin that, on the heavy sashcord handline, pulled the skiff far out to sea. Two days later the old man was picked up by fishermen 60 miles to the eastward, the head and forward part of the marlin lashed alongside. What was left of this fish, less than half, weighed eight hundred pounds. The old man had stayed with him a day, a night, a day and another night while the fish swam deep and pulled the boat. When he had come up the old man had pulled the boat up on him and harpooned him. Lashed alongside the sharks had hit him and the old man had fought them out alone in the Gulf Stream in a skiff, clubbing them, stabbing at them, lunging at them with an oar until he was exhausted and the sharks had eaten all that they could hold. He was crying in the boat when the fishermen picked him up, half crazy from his loss, and the sharks were still circling the boat." [1]

Hemingway waited another fifteen years before expanding the essay into a novel, the last printed in his lifetime.[2] The change his hero undergoes from sketch to story is at once apparent. No one brings Santiago home: he steers into harbor alone, dry-eyed and clearheaded. A composite of several actual fishermen Hemingway had known,[3] Santiago has even closer ties with the exemplary heroes of Hemingway's fiction. Like the aging mentors of the bull ring, Juan Belmonte and the "undefeated" Manuel Garcia, and like Anselmo and the other old man at the bridge, Santiago blends humility with pride. Humility is a commodity generally in short supply among Hemingway's heroes, certainly among his apprentices. When their luck (that special Hemingway *mana* that is, even more than chance, an inner fusion of spirit and skill) runs out, pride rather than humility sustains them. Most of Hemingway's younger men are proud of the carefully nurtured discipline that helps them to suppress anxiety. But it is at best a panicky pride and leads easily to flight, or bitterness, or, as with Robert Jordan, a rather shaky metaphysic. Among some of the older men, failed aspirants to exemplary status like Harry Morgan and Richard Cantwell, pride expresses itself as surliness or bravado. Among none of them is humility notable. Santiago has it, though he is too "simple" to know when or how he attained it: he knows only that "it was not disgraceful and it carried no loss of true pride" [14].

That part of luck which is happenstance has served Santiago ill for nearly three months. He has caught no fish and lost his apprentice to a luckier boat. Even the furled sail of his skiff looks "like the flag of permanent defeat" [9]. Yet the old man's body is strong, his eyes "cheerful and undefeated," his hope and confidence undimmed. "I know many tricks," he says, "and I have resolution" [23]. Some of his resolve derives from pride in his skill. No fisherman reads sky and sea with greater assurance; none drops bait straighter or more precisely. "It is better to be lucky," Santiago says. "But I would rather be exact" [32]. Like a fine bullfighter, he is methodical, patient, alert, and unshakably determined. Santiago, however, is prouder of being a man than of being an expert, of showing "what a man can do and what a man endures" [66]. To be a man is to be like Joe DiMaggio, who plays baseball superbly despite the painful bone spur in his heel. Years earlier, when Santiago and the giant Negro hand-wrestled at Casablanca, they too proved man's grace under pressure. Eyes and hands locked, blood coming from under their fingernails, they struggled sleeplessly for twenty-four hours. Though Santiago wins at last, the Negro—"a fine man and a great athlete"—is not, in the broad sense, beaten.

Neither is the marlin with whom Santiago contends for three days. At the climax of their epic contest, man and fish are as one—exhausted, suffering, but indomitable. As Santiago pulls the fish close enough to harpoon, Hemingway writes, the old man "took all his pain and what was left of his strength *and his long gone pride* and he put it against the fish's agony . . ." [93; italics added]. Santiago's pride has not deserted him, but it has been transfigured—by wonder, compassion, respect, and love. Together these comprise Santiago's humility, a humility for the most part more convincing than embarrassing, because, as Mark Schorer suggests, it is never self-conscious about granting to things in nature an independence of character as separate as Santiago's.[4] To Santiago, the sea is not merely a place or an enemy but *la mar*, a woman to be loved, however cruel she may be. And she can be cruel, as to the birds who "with their small sad voices are made too delicately for the sea" [29]. But she is what she must be, as a man is. It is the same with all living things, whether gentle like the birds and the flying fish, elegant like the green turtle, playful like the lions on the beach, or murderous like the Portugese man-of-war and the shark. With all creatures, Santiago feels some kinship as well as a humble awareness that "man is not much beside the great birds and beasts" [68].

All that Santiago, like Hemingway, has long sensed intui-
tively about life comes to dramatic climax during his engage-
ment with the marlin. It is this encounter, as he thinks, that
he was born for. After three months of failure, Santiago still
rejects rest or compromise. Instead, he elects to risk all by
reaching beyond man's reach, by going "too far out." Yet
what begins as an act of pride akin to Captain Ahab's in
Moby Dick or Kurtz's in *Heart of Darkness* is tempered at
once—as soon as the marlin takes the bait—by pity for the
creature betrayed by man's intelligence. Man and marlin are
inextricably joined by that act, "beyond all people in the
world," and, as Santiago thinks, with "no one to help either
one of us" [50]. As the struggle continues, Santiago's pity
turns to respect and at last to love. For a fleeting moment before he kills the marlin, Santiago, purged of all human pride,
is willing to die for or with the fish: "Never have I seen a
greater, or more beautiful, or a calmer or more noble thing
than you, brother. Come on and kill me. I do not care who
kills who" [92].

With that simple lyric cry, Santiago articulates an equally
simple but profound truth inherent in *The Old Man and the
Sea*. He and the fish are indeed "brothers," as are all creatures trapped in the inescapable process of living and dying.
A hook ripping its mouth, the fish endures and struggles for
its freedom; a line lacerating his back and hands, the old man
fights to deny the marlin its desire. And the sharks beat them
both. *The Old Man and the Sea* is not, as Philip Young
rightly observes, an allegory about man against nature, but a
story about the inevitable doom facing all "joined by the ne-
cessity of killing and being killed." [5] Doom is not, in Hemingway's vision, to be identified with defeat. All creatures share
doom. Knowing this breeds humility in man, the reverence
Santiago feels for the marlin alive and dead. Defeat means
yielding to doom without a struggle, abandoning, in effect,
the pride that makes it worthwhile to be a man. "You killed
him for pride and because you are a fisherman" [105], Santiago says. He kills, then, because not to do so would have

meant defeat, and "man is not made for defeat. A man can be destroyed but not defeated" [103].

Once the sharks come to mutilate the fish, Santiago thinks he has violated his luck by going out too far. A natural plaint growing out of physical and spiritual exhaustion, it is not an admission of guilt or sin or even, at last, of regret.[6] Had he not ventured alone in quest of the unknowable, Santiago could not have discovered the grandeur a man may command even in failure. It is humility that leads him to say he has gone out too far. But pride surfaces in the dream that ends the novel as once more Santiago conjures up the lions along the white beaches ("so white they hurt your eyes").[7] Those persistent memories of his youth—of grace, strength, and purity— have always goaded Santiago to conquer the unconquerable.

Writing to General Lanham about *The Old Man and The Sea,* Hemingway repeated a claim he had made earlier for *Across the River and Into the Trees:* the novel had everything in it he had always believed in. This time, he notes, the difference is that the story is simple and written as simply as he could write it. Insofar as Hemingway stays within the boundaries of simplicity, *The Old Man and the Sea* is superb. For the most part, he does, both thematically and stylistically. The narrative pattern is unexceptionable. Taut, precisely proportioned, the plot never exaggerates suspense or lingers overlong on the (almost literal) dying fall. The cadence and accent of Santiago's Spanish-English are—as in the best passages of *For Whom the Bell Tolls*—at once credible and poignant. Rarely has exposition been more lucid, description more evocative, or both so relevant to emotive and thematic force. Santiago's pride in his craft is delineated with meticulous detail. When he baits a line, "each bait hung head down with the shank of the hook inside the bait fish, tied and sewed solid and all the projecting part of the hook, the curve and the point, was covered with fresh sardines. Each sardine was hooked through both eyes so that they made a half-garland on the projecting steel. There was no part of the hook that a great fish could feel which was not sweet smelling and good tasting" [31]. The genius of the exposition shines forth in the final sentence, which—by shifting prose rhythm and vocabulary: "great fish," "sweet smelling," and "good tasting" —wrests the passage from the professional writer and restores it to the professional fisherman.

The noblest passages in *The Old Man and the Sea* work the same magic by centering consistently on Santiago's consciousness and sensibility. When Santiago dexterously guts a tuna or a dolphin for food, it is a hungry, desperate old man we recognize, not Ernest Hemingway fishing from the deck of the *Pilar*. Similarly, in the eloquent descriptions of the sea, it is the concrete sensuality of Santiago's primitive response that makes the essential poetry. He sniffs "the clean early morning smell of the ocean" and feels, through current and wind, changes in the day and night. Visually, he is keenest and most responsive. The hues of the sea, red plankton, yellow Sargasso weed, the purple filaments of the man-of-war, and the lavender stripes of the marlin—all fill the old man with wonder. Yet more wondrous and impressive is the motion of the sea and its creatures. Descriptions of the dip, slant, and dive of a man-of-war bird in pursuit of flying fish or the churning leaps of tuna animate the sense of what indeed Santiago was born for. Caught up in the lithe vitality and sinuous grace of natural movement, he is rhythmically unified with his environment. No abstract commentary can amplify the dimension of Hemingway's simple and dramatic juxtaposition of Santiago's cramped hand ("a treachery of one's own body") against the marlin's first marvelously supple leap.

Hemingway's virtuosity is not entirely without flaw. Occasionally, an image becomes too sophisticated, too literary, as when the marlin's eye looks "as detached as the mirrors in a periscope or as a saint in a procession" [96]. More jarring are those few passages in which significance—religious, poetic, mystical—is force-fed into the narrative. Santiago falls out of character when he reflects upon man's good fortune in not having to kill the sun, moon, or stars, and also when he falters into awkward ecstasy about his "true brothers" in nature. It is not that Santiago, following the tradition of the exemplary hero, should not think. Indeed he does, more than most exemplary heroes do. "Because it is all I have left," he says when the sharks strike. "That and baseball" [103]. But baseball, epitomized by Joe DiMaggio (also the son of a fisherman) and his bone spur, inspires in Santiago wholly relevant musings. Santiago's thoughts are compelling at the level of his immediate experience or through memories pertinent to that experience. But when Hemingway imposes abstractions extrinsic to the context, simplicity—the enduring power of the novel—gets mired in self-conscious sophistry.

Fortunately, Hemingway's excesses are few. *The Old Man and the Sea* is, however, baited with choice morsels of symbolism tempting some readers to extravagances of their own. Shortly after the novel was published, Hemingway teased critical imagination with this statement: "I tried to make a real old man, a real boy, a real sea, and a real fish and real shark. But if I make them good and true enough they would mean many things." [8] At once, critics spread their nets far and lowered them deep. Their haul included some indigestible blowfish (like the suggestion that the sharks symbolize critics ravaging the body of Hemingway's work) as well as more substantial fare.

Because the story abounds in religious as well as natural and pantheistic analogies, some critics have read the novel as a Christian allegory. A host of symbols lends support to the hypothesis: Santiago (St. James in English) is, as Carlos Baker writes, a man of "humility, natural piety, and compassion"; he is a fisherman and a teacher (of the young Manolin); the days he lingers at sea agonizing between humility and pride approximate in number those of Christ's sojourn in the desert; his hands are scarred, the mast he carries up the hill resembles the Cross, he assumes the posture (in sleep) of the Crucifixion, and his cry of agony—"Ay"—is, Hemingway writes, "a noise such as a man might make, involuntarily, feeling the nail go through his hands and into the wood";

and, of course, the fish itself is an ancient Christian symbol.[9]

Although Christian symbolism inspirits *The Old Man and the Sea,* the symbols do not transform it into a Christian story or allegory any more than Christian overtones alter the essential humanism of *The Sun Also Rises, A Farewell to Arms,* or *Across the River and Into the Trees.* If there is a crucifixion here, it is a man who is crucified, not a god. And it is a man for whom prayer is a superstitious sop uttered "mechanically" or "automatically," and for whom sin is beyond comprehension or belief. What Santiago dreams about is the strength and fortitude of man, not salvation. But since humanist and Christian alike share a love for man and compassion for what he must endure, a discreet reading of the symbols may show that the Christian elements serve to reaffirm the humanist theme of struggle and triumph. To force the Christian thesis beyond this point is futile. In fact, some critics have argued cogently that *The Old Man and the Sea* is more like a Greek agon than like a Christian passion. Going too far out is typical of the hero in Greek tragedy, as is his inevitable penalty for *hubris* (in this case, one critic suggests, Nemesis assumes the guise of sharks).[10]

The Old Man and the Sea is a welcome work after the disastrous *Across the River and Into the Trees.* Even a hostile critic might have been less than pleased with so ragged and crabbed an end to a distinguished career of fiction. A short book (Hemingway's only novella), but not a slight one, *The Old Man and the Sea* sounds a muted note of victory for the artist and the man. "It's as though I had gotten finally what I had been working for all my life," Hemingway wrote.[11] What had he been working for? Something more, his novels and stories suggest, than the discipline and moral stamina implicit in the "code"—almost, rather, a disengagement from mortality. Yet death and loneliness persist to the end. Too honest to alter the stark page-face of reality, Hemingway nevertheless glosses the margins. A romantic yearning for renewal— almost for immortality—attends both Hemingway's work and his life. From Nick Adams to Richard Cantwell, every hero must, like his creator, confront what he would prefer to ignore. Over the years, however, Hemingway explores paths other than the inevitable way to the insurmountable wall.

There are many trails, trails the exemplary hero usually avoids, sure they lead at last to the wall. But the apprentice persists, expending much psychic and physical energy on his quest. Jake Barnes, Frederic Henry, and Richard Cantwell survey the road to Christianity but find it impassable. All journey toward a love beyond lust, seeking what Robert Jordan calls "an alliance against death." Always they run into the dead end of mortality. From the thirties onward, the apprentice tries a broader highway where many travel, hoping to re-animate his spirit through the community of men. Again, as with Harry Morgan and Robert Jordan, the effort is vain. At last, failing with immediate experience, Hemingway groped beyond it. In his personal life, the result was nostalgia, an attempt to re-create the vitality of the past. In his art, all the early strands of Christianity and love—for nature, women, and all mankind—twine into an elementary transcendentalism, an idealized metaphysic of life within and beyond death, an ordering principle less stringent than the "code" his heroes had always needed to face *nada*. Without abandoning the "code," Hemingway sought to gentle it, to discover perhaps a "separate peace" of renewal and affirmation within the "separate peace" rooted in death and negation.

Until *The Old Man and the Sea*, most of Hemingway's later efforts in this direction failed. Sometimes the hero, like Jordan, is falsely placed; sometimes, like Colonel Cantwell, he has too much pride. Only in the symbol of the leopard frozen near the summit of Kilimanjaro does one glimpse the enduring quality Hemingway wished to project as an eternally *living* force. Even Hemingway's style often fails him in the later work, its vitality sapped by straining after eccentric effects. But in *The Old Man and the Sea* Hemingway locates at last the subject, setting, and character appropriate for what he had so long tried to express. Almost as an omen, the style is again sure, its lapses few and never fatal.

The world is still present in *The Old Man and the Sea*, but remote. Only the tourists remind us of society. And they, insensitive still as they were in *The Sun Also Rises*, are unworthy, as Santiago says, to eat the flesh of the fish he catches to feed them. There are no women (except for a photograph of Santiago's wife, removed "because it made him too lonely to see it" [16], and a picture of the Virgin of Cobre), and no men other than the boy Manolin, who appears only before and after Santiago's voyage. A shrunken world, much simplified, it has nonetheless the range of metaphor and the pertinence of parable. All of mortality is here, and courage, and love, and, for the last time, the possibility of renewal. The sea is a vast universe, but although Santiago sails alone, he feels neither isolated nor alienated. To be at one with nature is easier than with a woman or society. Hemingway's apprentices had all known this, but they were too young to forsake what must at last destroy them. Perhaps, then, one must be old and have suffered all in order to survive. But survival is not renewal. A "strange" old man, Santiago knows this and thus must journey on, still seeking an eternal "yes."

Suggesting the ritual journey as a motif in *The Old Man and the Sea*, Earl Rovit writes that Santiago "completes the fishing trip Nick began twenty-seven years earlier" [12] in "Big Two-Hearted River." One might thrust still further into the past to recall Nick in "Indian Camp" as a child, fresh from his initiation to death, trailing his hand in the water behind the boat, "quite sure that he would never die." The child apprentice has grown into the aged exemplar and, as Philip Young has said about the types of heroes in Hemingway's fiction, the gap between them has narrowed.[13] Without illusion about death or rationalization about immortality, the old man retains the psychic energy and much of the natural innocence of the child. Within Santiago, a childlike spirit—filled with curiosity, love, hope, and belief—rejuvenates the battered body and the weary mind. It is not without relevance that Santiago returns alive from his dark voyage. Other heroes—Morgan, Jordan, Cantwell—had not. Nor does Hemingway close the circle. Santiago's renewed spirit persists—despite the agony of symbolic crucifixion—in his dream of the lions, and his immortality is assured through his devoted apprentice, Manolin (a diminutive of Manuel, recalling another "undefeated" hero). Already the boy has learned much of what a man must know of love and death, pride and humility before he can venture out far enough to sight eternity.

15

Islands in the Stream

Just a few months after the critics, in the fall of 1950, had begun to fire broadsides at *Across the River and Into the Trees*, Hemingway started writing with renewed vigor and continued in a fever of energetic composition until late the next summer. In June, he wrote enthusiastically to General Lanham that he had completed the draft of four parts of a "sea novel"; three months later, he wrote again, announcing that he had completed rewriting and had pared the manuscript from 265,000 to 183,251 words.

Of the four parts, however, only one, the shortest, appeared during Hemingway's lifetime—*The Old Man and the Sea*, published in 1952. The other three appeared posthumously in 1970 as *Islands in the Stream*.[1] It comes as a shock to learn that all parts of the "sea novel" were written during the same period, for *Islands in the Stream* lacks the polish and control that distinguish *The Old Man and the Sea*. That Hemingway sensed the discrepancy in quality seems clear from the various reasons he put forward to justify delaying publication. One excuse was that high taxes would consume his profits. Another was that much "stuff in it" was still too personal to print. Or again, he wrote that the manuscript still needed, after all, much revision. In a cryptic note to a friend, Hemingway hinted also at a deeper cause, insisting that he "dreaded" writing the final section and that, as Carlos Baker paraphrases Hemingway's letter, he "even hoped at one time that he would never have to set it down." [2]

Any combination of these reasons would be cogent. The most immediately persuasive is that the book urgently needed revision. Some of *Islands in the Stream* reads well. Occasional set scenes are exciting or amusing, and many of the descriptive passages about sea, sand, and sky match his best work. More often, the novel is as painful to read as it must have been to write. Long and diffuse, it fails also to derive from its diverse accounts of experience any coherent sense of life. As a formal work of art the novel cannot survive close analysis. But there is present in the work another kind of pain too, the torment of the author, whose personal experience is almost frighteningly transparent beneath his fictional distortions. What force *Islands in the Stream* has—and it is potent—lies just beyond the boundaries of the art of fiction. It merits a short excursion after we study what happens inside the boundary line.

The three parts of the novel are only vaguely related in time or place, rather like fixed islands in a discontinuous stream of memory. The presence of the hero in the foreground and of death in the background are all that bind the sections to one another. "Bimini," the first, longest, and most readable part, tells in fifteen chapters of a summer vacation that Thomas Hudson, a famous, twice-divorced painter, spends at his island home with three young sons born of those marriages. Though Hemingway certainly intended that Hudson's consciousness unify the potpourri of pastoral, nostalgia, and high adventure that comprise "Bimini," the real impact of the section derives from its long and often dramatically moving action scenes. Since Hudson's presence is never indispensable in these episodes, his thoughts and feelings often seem—despite Hemingway's apparent intention—only remotely relevant.

One of the best of these scenes, for example, takes place aboard Hudson's yacht as his second son, David, wages a heroic battle against a huge swordfish. Though the boy's hands and back are lacerated by line and straps, he refuses to quit. At the height of the contest, speaking like a disciple of Santiago in *The Old Man and the Sea*, he says, "I don't care if he kills me, the big son of a bitch . . . Oh hell. I don't hate him. I love him" [134]. The fish escapes, but David's spirit is undaunted, his love for the creature undiminished.

Once during the struggle, Hudson tells another of his sons that "if David catches this fish he'll have something inside him for all his life and it will make everything else easier" [131]. Again, at the end of the day, Hudson sits alone thinking about his sons and the implications of their behavior during the fight with the swordfish. But however interesting Hudson's ruminations are, they fail utterly to displace the visceral impact of the recent action. What David does is more engaging than what his father thinks. To shift the focus back to Hudson, Hemingway resorts to violence—both to the niceties of plot construction and to David. Suddenly, as "Bimini" draws to a close, Hudson learns by telegram that David and his younger brother died with their mother in a car accident a few days after their return from the island.[3] From that point forward, for better or worse, Thomas Hudson is the unequivocal hero of *Islands in the Stream*.

The death of Hudson's eldest son as a fighter pilot is the central event in the single chapter of Part II, "Cuba."[4] Yet not until midway through this rambling narrative of a day in Havana does the reader learn this salient fact from Hudson's laconic reply—"He's dead"—to a bar companion's inquiry about his son. Knowing what has haunted Hudson's thoughts during the preceding day while he served on a mysterious sea patrol helps partially to account for his ramblings about cats, women, and politics. But as the day drags on, Hudson's reminiscences (shared chiefly with his cat, Boise, and with Honest Lil, the whore-in-residence at the Floridita Bar) begin to pall and his desperation turns sentimentally sottish.

The sudden arrival of Hudson's first wife (an actress serving with the USO and bearing a keen resemblance to Hem-

ingway's old friend, Marlene Dietrich) ends the damp bar-
room discourse but substitutes for it a climax as incredible as
the car accident in "Bimini." Only after the couple have returned home and enjoyed an abandoned bout of love does
Hudson's ex-wife ask about their son. Briefly, he evades and
lies, thinking to himself: "How do you tell a mother that her
boy is dead when you've just made love to her again? How
do you tell yourself your boy is dead?" [319]. Then,

> "You don't want to talk about him," she said.
> "No."
> "Why? I think it's better."
> "He looks too much like you."
> "That isn't it," she said. "Tell me. Is he dead?"
> "Sure."

Within a few minutes after this implausible exchange, they
quarrel, understand why their marriage has failed, and bid
one another an affectionate farewell as Hudson returns to sea
duty.

The final death in Hudson's family may be his own. As
skipper of his yacht—camouflaged for war duty as a marine
research vessel—Hudson leads his crew of six in pursuit of a
band of Nazi survivors from a submarine sunk off the coast of
Cuba.[5] That quest is the essential action of the twenty-one
chapters of Part III, "At Sea." Throughout the chase, Hudson
disciplines his crew as effectively as he does his own depression. With only an occasional lapse, he manages "a good job
at non-thinking" about his sons. And, until just before he is
shot, the only giant-killer Hudson drinks is tea. The task at
hand—catching the prey—is all that matters.

Unfortunately, the hunt is too often dull and overwrought,
a protracted, tedious search through the labyrinthine reefs
and keys along the Cuban coast. At the end of the chase, one
of Hudson's crew is dead, as are most of the Germans. Hudson is himself wounded seriously, probably fatally, though
Hemingway seems not yet to have decided whether to save
his hero or dispatch him.[6] Aware that he is "probably going

to die," Hudson tells himself not to worry about it, that "all your life is just pointed toward it." A moment later, however, he persuades himself that he will paint again, that "life is a cheap thing besides a man's work. The only thing is that you need it. Hold it tight. Now is the time to make your play. Make it now without hope of anything. You always coagulated well and now you can make one more real play" [464]. Yet, as the novel ends, death is again imminent. When he looks up at "the sky that he had always loved," and feels beneath him "the lovely throb" of his ship's engines, Hudson seems serenely assured about death: "He felt far away now and there were no problems at all" [466].

In a review of *Islands in the Stream,* Edmund Wilson found it difficult to describe the plot "without making it seem preposterous." [7] If the narrative often taxes either credulity or patience, Thomas Hudson is in many ways a burden upon both. He is a stiff and stifling eminence who, like Colonel Cantwell in *Across the River and Into the Trees* and Robert Jordan in *For Whom the Bell Tolls,* is always introduced honorifically by his full name, never as Hudson, never as Thomas, and certainly never as Tom. To those about him— sons, friends, women, servants, and even cats—he is without peer. Why he is so well regarded is difficult to justify from what he says or does. For the most part, he is a spectator rather than participant in the crises of the novel. He is the helmsman during the fishing and Nazi-hunting scenes, but is otherwise only peripherally involved in the action. What we know of his mind we learn essentially from his inward musings rather than from conversations with others. He communicates with the world as one who has earned a special dispensation of spiritual apartheid. Among those whom he professes to love, Boise, his cat, is the only one with whom he is wholly unguarded. Yet, if the price of Hudson's affection seems too high to bargain for, everyone in the novel is willing to pay it, even those who might share the feelings of the crewman whose words end the novel: "You never understand anybody that loves you."

Despite all this, Hemingway ceaselessly reminds us that Hudson is a man of profound emotional depth, a man who knows the pain of loneliness, the torment of love and loss, and a man who has learned that no one ever comes to terms with true sorrow. "It can be cured by death," he reflects, "and it can be blunted or anesthetized by various things . . . But if it is cured by anything less than death, the chances are that it was not true sorrow" [197]. None of this is new among Hemingway's heroes. But whereas most of them come to such knowledge after harsh and brutal experience, Hudson's past reveals nothing except success. "He had been successful in almost every way," Hemingway writes, "except in his married life" [8]. At worst, he had been, on occasion, "undisciplined, selfish, or ruthless." Why, then, his joylessness and gloomy obsession with death? Hemingway never explains. The impact of losing his sons would appear to be a more than adequate answer. But a closer look at his relationship with them makes that argument almost untenable.

Hudson's treatment of his sons is at once hieratic and hierarchic. Though the boys are youngsters enjoying a holiday, their encounters with their father are ritualistic. Conversations between them (from which profanity in the company of adults is—except with special permission—prohibited) are stilted parodies in which the boys try to sound old enough to crack Hudson's shell of paternal formality, the slight but felt distance that sets him off as high priest.

A more serious flaw in his involvement with his children is his assigning them rank and status as they mirror his own values.[8] In this contest, Andrew, the youngest, fares worst. Though he is, as Hudson frequently observes, only a little boy and does nothing really bad, Hudson adds that "There was something about him that you could not trust" [144]. Andrew lacks that intuitive delicacy of feeling and instinct for restraint Hudson (as well as Hemingway) most admires. When Andrew persists in asking about the possible outcome of his brother's struggle with the swordfish, David cries out, "Oh keep your mouth off him, please" [119]. When David

nears the physically painful climax of that battle, it is Andrew who notices and announces that his brother is crying, to
which breach of decorum Tom, Jr., retorts, "Shut up, horseman." And when David says that he really loves the swordfish, Andrew observes, "Gee . . . I can't understand that."
Though little Andrew is celebrated as a "damn genius," a fine
athlete, and an expert horseman, he is also an outsider, as
thoroughly unfamiliar with the code of the hero as, say, Robert Cohn in *The Sun Also Rises*. "He was," Hudson thinks, "a
boy born to be wicked who was being very good . . . He was
just being good while his badness grew inside him" [53].

Tom, Jr., the eldest, earns a slightly higher niche in his father's esteem. For one thing, he shares Hudson's love of
place, delighting his father with acute sensory memories of
his childhood in Paris and extraordinary recollections about
Joyce, Pound, and Ford. And yet there is something more
than slightly awry about this happy past the boy remembers
in adult terms (almost as Hemingway was to tell the story
again in *A Moveable Feast*), something too compulsive about
his rehearsal of how papa and I "used to go around together
in Paris." When Tom, Jr., says, "Tell them about when I
was little . . . I'll never get to be as good in real life as the
stories about me when I was little" [57], the voice is the son's
but the judgment is his father's. A gentle, rather passive boy,
Tom knows that he is outranked and even approves his father's choice of David as the favorite son: "I know you love
him the most and that's right because he's the best of us . . ."
[125]. Hudson's discreet rejoinder—"I've loved you the
longest"—fails to deny Tom's allegation or to win respect for
Hudson's parental tact or insight. Least of all does it appear
to justify his remorse as derived from the single fact of their
death.

At the end of the long day of fishing, Hudson ponders his
relations with his sons and concludes that, except for Tom,
Jr., "all his children had gone a long way away from him or
he had gone away from them" [143]. Curiously, Hudson fails
also to enjoy rapport with David, the son whose courage,

skill, and discipline most resemble Hudson's image of himself. David, whom Hudson regards as "a well-loved mystery," turns instead to Roger Davis, a writer, who "understands him better than his own father did" [143]. Why Roger and David are so close, Hemingway fails to say. All we learn is that David thanks Roger for something he said when David lost his swordfish, and that it is Roger who sympathetically responds, "I understand," and "I know" when the boy tries to express his love for the fish. What is clear about Roger at least is that he represents a residue of Hemingway's sense of himself (with a bit of F. Scott Fitzgerald as well) that he filtered and strained out of Hudson.

To the local bartender, the two men look enough alike to be "quarter brothers and the boys look like both of you" [155]. The fractional resemblance is minimized by substantial differences, chief of which is that Roger, like Harry in "The Snows of Kilimanjaro," is a writer who has "thrown away and abused and spent his talent" [103]. Roger's failure to write honestly is partially explained by his refusal to face unhappy endings. He has not yet accommodated, for example, to a traumatic boyhood experience in which he was unable to save a younger brother named David from drowning when their canoe overturned. "You never get over it," Roger tells Hudson, "and sooner or later I have to tell it" [76]. Instead, Roger brawls and chases women and drinks and suffers endless guilt. But though Roger has "blunted and perverted and cheapened" his talent, Hudson is convinced that "au fond he has something fine and sound and beautiful" [103]. Only such a man could serve as David's father-surrogate.

Hemingway's treatment of Hudson's sons and of Roger Davis raises questions about a writer's conflict between autobiographical and artistic demands. Conceivably, Hemingway's failure to resolve these questions to his own satisfaction contributed to his decision to avoid publishing the book. But as the novel stands, what he has done is neither psychologically nor aesthetically effective. Hudson's role as father fails to explain adequately his subsequent bitterness and drift toward death. Even if he were guilt-ridden about his manifest failure as a parent—and he is not—his reactions might well be judged excessive. One is inclined to agree with Christopher Ricks's comment that Hudson "does not really want to live whether they live or not."[9] The boys' deaths purchase too cheaply, however, the image of Hudson that Hemingway hopes to project, and the narrative deception at last cheapens the image itself.

Roger Davis must also have proved an unsettling presence as Hemingway wrote, for despite his deficiencies, he is potentially a more interesting and engaging character than Hudson. A continuing dialogue between them (their long exchanges are among the better things in the book) throughout the rest of the novel might have led Hemingway to confrontations with himself that would have been psychologically as well as dramatically intriguing. Instead, he chose the safer, simpler, but far less satisfying solution of dropping Roger altogether after the first section.

Those who supersede him as Hudson's confidants are familiar constellatory figures that orbit around Hemingway's heroes. Henry Wood, for example, recalls the lusty cynicism of Mike Campbell in The Sun Also Rises; Willie, the tough, foul-mouthed loyalty of Rinaldi in A Farewell to Arms; and Ara, the Basque, the earthy, peasant philosophy of Anselmo in For Whom the Bell Tolls. Although each is moderately interesting, none seriously competes with Hudson, whose self-discipline grows more rigorous as his spirit founders. "I never felt better," he insists when most exhausted. "I just don't give a damn." Remorse about his sons has allegedly destroyed his desire to live but not his commitment to execute his responsibilities well. "Get it straight," he tells himself. "Your boy you lose. Love you lose. Honor has been gone for a long time. Duty you do" [326]. He steers too long and stands too many unrelieved watches. Ara warns him that a man "must implement his pride with intelligence and care," and that he owes it to the others to take care of himself. But even when he yields briefly to his friends' importuning, he never relinquishes control or command. The once-welcome cocktail they urge upon him he secretly throws to the wind. As he rests, he thinks continuously of his task: "I must try to be very good. Try hard tonight, he told himself. And chase hard and good and with no mistakes . . ." [361]. These are the bravura words and deeds of a man who captains his fate, however grim, with assurance. To create this familiar portrait of the paragon among exemplary heroes, Hemingway had first to dispose of all the characters who dared undermine his paragon. What he is left with is a near caricature who has the posture rather than the stature of a tragic hero. Thomas Hudson is proof that it is possible to be too grand, too proud, too engrossed with one's self and one's fatal obsession.

Despite these shortcomings as a fictional character, Hudson does—in his resemblance to Hemingway—contribute to the compelling force the novel somehow musters. What one knows about Hemingway inevitably spills over into any reading of his work. Few will reach the end of the novel without thinking about the end of its author. Hemingway's "dread" about having to write the final section seems almost prescient, a prophecy of his concern about his own decline, despair, and death. But though a dark premonition suffuses the entire novel—a half-conscious yearning for death—energy and spirit are also present to affirm life and love. As the ambiguous ending suggests, Hemingway argues both sides but nervously evades any final resolution. A related uncertainty of tone pervades the discussions of suicide. Instead of the dour intensity with which Nick Adams ("Fathers and Sons") and Robert Jordan (*For Whom the Bell Tolls*) ponder the topic that had long haunted Hemingway, there is here an antic, comic—possibly hysterical—note. Hudson and Honest Lil inventory the techniques of suicide popular among Cubans—eating matches, drinking shoe dye or iodine, setting oneself afire—as part of her attempt to cheer him up. Elsewhere, Hudson expresses mock sympathy for a pig who swam to sea: "I'm sorry your pig committed such suicide . . . We all have our small problems." When Roger Davis tells Hudson about the suicide of his mistress and defends suicide as "logical," Bobby, the barman, quickly interrupts to lighten the mood. Gaily, he relates the story of "Suicides," a "Mechanic's Depressive" who finally drowned himself after a season of amusing everyone by promising to do so. Bobby quips that he had urged "Suicides" to "lay off or you'll never reach oblivion." After Bobby tells his story, Roger comments, "Fuck oblivion."

Suicide shadows much of Hemingway's life and fiction. Though levity is the dominant mode here, the subject occurs too often to be ignored. And it is noteworthy that the only attempt at serious discussion about suicide involves Hudson and Roger, the split images of Hemingway, Roger at first defending the act, Hudson arguing that "it would be a hell of an example for the boys."

An even better index of Hemingway's inner conflicts are Hudson's dreams, particularly the strange, unsettling one that is Chapter 3 of "At Sea." In it, the war is over, Tom, Jr., is alive, and his mother is asleep on top of Hudson: "Her hair hung down and lay heavy and silky on his eyes and on his cheeks and he turned his lips away from her searching ones and took the hair in his mouth and held it. Then with one hand he moistened the .357 Magnum and slipped it easily and sound asleep where it should be. Then he lay under her weight and with her silken hair over his face like a curtain and moved slowly and rhythmically" [343–44].[10] Later, when Hudson lays the pistol aside and is too tired to make love again, his wife urges him to accept the woman's role: "Don't try to save yourself at all. Try to lose everything and take everything too." Hudson agrees, asking only that she hold him "so tight it kills me."

Hudson's dream is a macabre nightmare idyl in which symbols of love and death coil about one another, straining without success toward reconciliation. A far cry from the exemplary hero whose masculinity (especially with long-haired women) is certain and tireless, Hudson is here enveloped by psychic weariness and indecisiveness. It is not merely that he is uncertain about his sexual identity. He seems appallingly helpless as well to separate cruelty from tenderness, or to choose between aggressive control and passive submission, between a desire to destroy and a desire to be destroyed. Even when he wakes, he cannot thrust aside the metaphoric force of his dream. As he feels the pistol holster lying between his legs, he realizes "how it was really and all the hollownesses in him were twice as hollow *and there was a new one from the dream*" [345; italics added]. The border line between nightmare and reality has grown dangerously thin for Thomas Hudson.

Life overleaps art in Hemingway's account of Hudson's dream, and it is impossible not to read into it some of Hemingway's anxiety. Nightmares do not resolve the inner turmoil they reflect, and the demons that plague Hudson's sleep continued to haunt Hemingway in the years that led to his suicide. Toward the end of the novel, after a nostalgic dream of boyhood explodes into terror, Hudson decides that "dreams aren't the solution . . . I might as well take it the same as always without any hope of anaesthetics . . . You will never have good dreams any more so you might as well not sleep. Just rest and use your head until it won't work any more, and when you go to sleep, expect to have the horrors" [384–85]. Rather than risk dreams, Hudson determines to work and to "think about something cheerful." But despite the irritatingly opaque glaze of Hudson's sure purpose and serene control, there is about the novel, as Stephen Donadio points out, "a quality of insomnia . . . an edge of desperation reminiscent of a man driving himself beyond exhaustion." [11]

If, as seems more than likely, Hudson's fears express his creator's, then both the "dread" and Hemingway's shunting aside *Islands in the Stream* to "think about something cheerful" are understandable. And if the uncompleted novel that Hemingway's wife and publisher decided to make public adds nothing to his reputation as an artist, it must still be welcomed as a valuable documentary of that artist's agonized journey toward an oblivion that had always lured and repelled him.

16

A Moveable Feast

In the Christian church, a moveable feast is one which may be adjusted in time. Easter, for example, may be moved about, as may those holidays (Lent, Pentecost) related to it. In the posthumously published *A Moveable Feast* (May 1964), Hemingway also attempts to adjust time, but on a more daring scale—not by a few days, weeks, or months, but by nearly thirty-five years. In late 1956, when porters at the Ritz Hotel reminded him, Hemingway had long since forgotten the two small trunks filled with typed manuscript and handwritten notebooks he had stored in Paris in 1928. Nearly a year passed before he began seriously to rework those notebook entries into the twenty sketches that comprise a memoir of his apprentice years in Paris (1921–26). His health had noticeably declined and his bouts of drinking and depression had increased.[1] "He found it easy to remember," Carlos Baker observes, "and hard to write." Since *The Old Man and the Sea* in 1952, he had published only a few insignificant magazine items. For most of the succeeding year, however, Hemingway worked conscientiously and well to complete the sketches that recalled more productive years, years when "we were very poor and very happy." [2]

Like *Death in the Afternoon* and *Green Hills of Africa*, *A Moveable Feast* is a minor work and an uneven one. Though it has nostalgic passages of real beauty, as well as good farce and murderous wit, its special interest is more biographical than literary. Often a reader may feel that the hero is the aging author rather than the aspiring young man who is its true center. How moveable, after all, Hemingway seems to ask, is the spring feast of youth? As in the earlier non-fiction works, an inward loneliness and a comprehensive sadness hover over his recollections. ". . . I knew that everything good and bad left an emptiness when it stopped," he wrote. "But if it was bad, the emptiness filled up by itself. If it was good you could only fill it by finding something better" [62]. Even in the joyous opening sketch that recalls his writing "The Three-Day Blow" at a "warm, clean and friendly" café in Paris, there is a hint of restiveness, of an unsated spirit: "After writing a story I was always empty and both sad and happy, as though I had made love . . ." [6]. In those early days, sadness at first passed quickly. The sea taste of oysters and the crisp flavor of cold wine helped him lose "the empty feeling" and begin "to be happy and make plans."

But hunger always returns and, indeed, functions as a central image. "There are so many sorts of hunger," his wife says to him in "A False Spring," one of the finest sketches in the book. "In the spring there are more. But that's gone now. Memory is hunger" [57]. Three decades later, her words bore even fuller meaning for Hemingway. But though his melancholy is pervasive and unmistakable, Hemingway rarely whines. Instead, he celebrates the memory of hunger as an appetite for fullness both of sense and of spirit. Eating and drinking with friends who understood the multiple implications of hunger made for an almost ritualistic love feast. Notwithstanding their poverty in the early twenties, Hemingway and his friends down an extraordinary quantity of beer, wine, and whiskey. What they thirst for, however, is more than drink. It is rather to share with agreeable companions in a clean, well-lighted place good talk about life and literature, ambition and aspiration. Even when Hemingway and Hadley cannot afford to dine out, he assures her that at their apartment (where they have neither hot water nor toilet facilities —but a fine view), "we'll have a lovely meal and drink Beaune from the co-operative . . . And afterwards we'll read and then go to bed and make love" [37].

That this rather self-parodic passage seems an echo from *A Farewell to Arms* or *Across the River and Into the Trees* is not surprising. The quasi-religious fellowship of the hungry ranges throughout Hemingway's fiction. Robert Jordan and his comrades in *For Whom the Bell Tolls* share a board, and in *The Sun Also Rises* Bill Gorton blesses the lunch he and Jake eat at their fishing site. Despite the comic tone—"Let us rejoice in our blessings. Let us utilize the fowls of the air. Let us utilize the product of the vine. Will you utilize a little, brother?" [122]—the sincerity of their communion is unquestionable. "I found," Hemingway writes in *A Moveable Feast*, "that many of the people I wrote about had very strong appetites and a great desire for food, and most of them were looking forward to having a drink" [101].

There is yet another kind of hunger an artist needs. In "Hunger Was Good Discipline," Hemingway remembers how empty he felt when all his early manuscripts were stolen at the Gare de Lyon. But he recalls too how the loss spurred him to write again. "Hunger is good discipline," he says, "and you learn from it" [75]. What Hemingway learned—and records throughout *A Moveable Feast* with pride—was that an aesthetic hunger was also healthy, and he craved to control his art. Most of the story he had told before, especially in *Death in the Afternoon* and *Green Hills of Africa*—about how he started from a "true simple declarative sentence," but soon realized (by studying the paintings of Cézanne)[3] that "writing simple true sentences [was] far from enough to make the stories have the dimensions that I was trying to put in them" [13]. And he tells again how Gertrude Stein taught him about rhythm and repetition, Sherwood Anderson to care about his characters, and Ezra Pound to settle for nothing less than the precise word. The most important lesson, however, he taught himself—to omit from his stories whatever could be omitted, so that his readers might "feel something more than they understood" [75].⁴ Omission, then, is a kind of hunger too, a corner of emptiness that staves off the dullness of surfeit.

When he describes the development of his craft or evokes the places where he wrote, where he met his friends, and where he and Hadley were happiest together, Hemingway is still the master of stylistic effect. Beyond the familiar simplicity, understatement, and precision, he achieves warmth, tenderness, and lyric grace. But *A Moveable Feast* has a larger and less attractive side, though for some readers a more lively one. When Hemingway reflects upon his fellow artists of the early twenties, he is more often than not the old "champ," defensive, brutal, ruthless. Toward a handful, admittedly, he is cordial, even grateful. Ezra Pound fares best: "the most generous writer I have ever known," and "so kind to people that I always thought of him as a sort of saint" [108]. James Joyce and Sylvia Beach; Evan Shipman, a minor poet; and Jules Pascin, a minor artist, are also treated sympathetically. They are among "the very few that were as good as spring itself" [49].

Of the others, Hemingway mangles most without mercy. His hunger in these clever but bloodthirsty portraits is for the kill. Sometimes his prey scarcely seems worth the effort, but he hunts down Hal (Harold Acton), a campy literary pest, and Ernest Walsh, a consumptive poet and editor,⁵ with savage efficiency. At the literary lions who had at one time or another clawed him, Hemingway fires dumdum bullets. Wyndham Lewis, who had ridiculed Hemingway's anti-intellectualism early in the thirties, has a "face that reminded me of a frog, not a bullfrog but just any frog" [108], and his eyes are those "of an unsuccessful rapist." Many of Hemingway's contemporaries disliked and often quarreled with Ford Madox Ford, but most of them tolerated his exaggeration and admired his talent. Indeed, Hemingway had no basis other than personal distaste to justify his laughable but heartless portrait of the oversized Ford as "an ambulatory, well clothed, up-ended hogshead" [83] who speaks and behaves like a most contemptible and ludicrous prig.[6]

In the first of three sketches about Gertrude Stein, Hemingway writes admiringly of her resemblance to a northern Italian peasant woman with "beautiful eyes . . . mobile face and her lovely, thick, alive immigrant hair . . ." [14]. At the end of the final sketch, she has become "a Roman emperor and that was fine if you liked your women to look like Roman emperors" [119]. Clearly, Hemingway did not. For years after her assault upon him in *The Autobiography of Alice B. Toklas,* they had sniped at one another. On occasion, Hemingway seemed more plaintive than angry. "It's a damned shame," he wrote in *Green Hills of Africa,* "with all that talent gone to malice and nonsense and self-praise . . . she was damned nice before she got ambitious" [65–66]. But he could also take dead aim at the heart. Joan Miró's painting, "The Farm" —which Hemingway owned—took nine months to create, he wrote in an art journal, "as long to make as it takes a woman to make a child (a woman who isn't a woman can usually write her autobiography in a third of that time) . . ." [7]

The sketches about Gertrude Stein in *A Moveable Feast* discover no new ways to pay old debts, but Hemingway does manage some ugly variations. Nothing he says about her as an artist amplifies what he had earlier said elsewhere; here he is much less harsh.[8] Her theories about language and rhythm still merit his respect, but he chides her for refusing to revise or to make her writing intelligible. As a woman, she is also rather agreeable at the outset, though she hedges on her encouragement and hospitality by charging that Hemingway belongs to a "lost generation": "You have no respect for anything. You drink yourselves to death . . ." [29]. She has few kind words for any except those who have served her interest and fewer for those whose fame challenges hers. If, for example, "you brought up Joyce twice, you would not be invited back" [28]. Such table talk is familiar enough and relatively harmless. Hemingway works his mischief in Miss Stein's boudoir, not her parlor. Broad hints of her lesbianism occur in the opening sketch: she views wives as a burden, dislikes the sexuality of "Up in Michigan," and lectures Hemingway about the comparative vices of male homosexuality and the virtues of lesbianism. Women, she argues, do nothing disgusting, and "afterwards they are happy and they can lead happy lives together" [20]. In what amounts to an uneventful but lurid and frightening closet drama (featuring Hemingway in the closet), their relationship comes to "A Strange Enough Ending," as the last sketch is called. Hemingway hears an unidentified "someone" speaking to her upstairs in her studio as he "had never heard one person speak to another; never, anywhere, ever" [118]. Miss Stein's "pleading and begging" are piteous, not at all the voice of a Roman emperor, as Hemingway images her a few paragraphs later. Hemingway leaves, and that is all—no "wow" ending, no crow of victory—except that Gertrude Stein has been annihilated.

Hemingway's reasons for destroying Gertrude Stein (who died in 1946) invite speculation. Hemingway ventures a feeble explanation, hinting vaguely about friendships of head and heart, but stops abruptly and wisely, adding, "But it was more complicated than that." It is also too complicated to be encompassed by one critic's sweeping assumption that at the core of Hemingway's hostility lay his "fear-hatred of homosexuality" and his "mixed feelings toward any kind of mother surrogate." [9] Other paths deserve exploration. It is revealing, for example, that the first sketches Hemingway prepared for *A Moveable Feast* were, in order, about writing "The Three-Day Blow" at a café, the first visits to Gertrude Stein's studio, and Ford Madox Ford.[10] Each projects Hemingway in one of his most characteristic guises—artist, friend, bully. As we have seen, he never felt secure in any of these roles, shifting rapidly from one to the other as his psychic needs demanded. Writing three decades after the people and events of his Paris years, he began as if by instinct with those recollections most likely to elicit his self-pride and self-doubt. Because Gertrude Stein had stung his pride and raised his doubts, he could not settle—even after the intervening years—for a gentle reprimand to his old friend and mentor. Having savaged Ford for less cause, he needed little encouragement to add the devastating sections about Miss Stein.

In the three sketches about Scott Fitzgerald,[11] Hemingway is deceptively sympathetic and admiring. Fitzgerald's talent, he writes as an epigraph to the opening sketch, "was as natural as the pattern that was made by the dust on a butterfly's wings." Modest about his writing, he has a shyness "that all non-conceited writers have when they have done something very fine." And when he is sober, Fitzgerald is a pleasant companion and the most loyal of friends. Whatever Fitzgerald's weaknesses, Hemingway willingly enlisted as a friend and supporter after reading *The Great Gatsby:* "If he could write a book as fine as *The Great Gatsby* I was sure that he could write an even better one" [176]. That he did not seem likely to, Hemingway blames largely on his wife, Zelda. As Hemingway's wife, Hadley, is the Catherine Barkley of *A Moveable Feast,* Zelda Fitzgerald is its Margot Macomber. Imaged as a hawk in appearance and action, Zelda ravages Fitzgerald's life, thwarting his growth as an artist and threatening his manhood.

Against this background, one might almost expect a portrait of the artist as tragic hero. Instead, Hemingway casts Fitzgerald as a sodden hypochondriac who, when he is not about to pass out, groans about imagined diseases or seeks reassurance about his sexual measurements. The scene in which Fitzgerald lies "dying" of lung congestion while Hemingway takes his temperature with a bath thermometer is hilarious—and believable. Less funny and less convincing (though probably destined to survive longer) is the anecdote about the adequacy of Fitzgerald's penis and Hemingway's knowing lecture about sexual technology.[12] Both sketches are unkind, so cleverly done that they deprive their victim not only of dignity but even of refuge in pathos. Nowhere does Fitzgerald get a chance to argue his own case against Hemingway's blunt charge that Zelda is "crazy" and "just wants to destroy you," or that his writing for the slick magazines is "whoring."

Hemingway saves until the last his deepest thrust. Visiting the Ritz bar in Paris—where Fitzgerald had been a popular figure—after World War II, Hemingway is asked by the bar chief: "Papa, who was this Monsieur Fitzgerald that everybody asks me about?" [191].

Except for the famous "long round" during which Fitzgerald forgot to ring the bell and thus allowed Morley Callaghan to floor Hemingway in a sparring match,[13] Fitzgerald had done nothing to warrant Hemingway's censure. Rather, he had done more than most at the beginning to advance his younger friend's career. Yet Hemingway merely generalizes his gratitude, failing even to mention, for example, how he used Fitzgerald's invaluable suggestions for altering the beginning of *The Sun Also Rises*. Again, it would seem that Hemingway's pride disabled his decency. An even more compelling reason lay in his curious reaction to Fitzgerald's failure. During their first trip together, Hemingway had looked forward to "the company of an older and successful writer," and to learning "much that it would be useful to know" [155]. But instead of finding a literary father figure, Hemingway found himself playing the role himself. At first it amused and pleased him, but when, over the years, Fitzgerald ignored Hemingway's injunctions about work habits, drinking, Zelda, and the rich, Hemingway grew impatient and intolerant. Failure always infuriated him, clearly because it frightened him. Now, twenty years after Fitzgerald's death, the specter of his own physical and psychic failure seemed closer than ever. As once before in "The Snows of Kilimanjaro" he had used Fitzgerald to exorcise his demon, now again he scapegoats him. No guest more deserved to share in peace Hemingway's movable feast.

In 1950, after reading a hostile review of *Across the River and Into the Trees*, Hemingway wrote to General Lanham that loneliness was a moveable feast for him.[14] At the close of his memoir, Hemingway is still a lonely man. The love and discipline that glowed in the early years vanish with the arrival of the rich, led by the "pilot fish." [15] The guests have all departed, most of them sped on their way by their host's rudeness. But though the feast is ended, hunger lingers. "I loved her and I loved no one else and we had a lovely magic time while we were alone" [210], he writes of Hadley, recalling the end of their marriage. Like a character in one of his own novels, Hemingway abandons his dream of innocence reluctantly, clinging to his vision until the facts of his life compel him to accept reality. And then memory returns as hunger.

NOTES
APPENDICES
BIBLIOGRAPHY
INDEX

Notes

Works referred to frequently are cited in shortened form after the initial, full entry:

Baker, Carlos, *Ernest Hemingway: A Life Story* as *Life*
——, *Hemingway: The Writer as Artist* as *Writer as Artist*
——, ed., *Ernest Hemingway: Critiques of Four Major Novels* as *Critiques of Four Novels*
McCaffery, John K. M., ed., *Ernest Hemingway: The Man and His Work* as McCaffery
Weeks, Robert, ed., *Hemingway: A Collection of Critical Essays* as *Critical Essays*

Life

1. See Robert O. Stephens, *Hemingway's Non-Fiction* (Chapel Hill: U. of North Carolina Press, 1968), especially Chapter 5, on Hemingway as a feudist.
2. *The Autobiography of Alice B. Toklas* (New York: Modern Library, 1933), pp. 216–17.
3. "Hemingway: Gauge of Morale," in Wilson's *The Wound and the Bow* (Boston: Houghton Mifflin, 1941), p. 226. Reprinted in *Ernest Hemingway: The Man and His Work*, ed. J. K. M. McCaffery (Cleveland: World, 1950), p. 245.
4. Introduction to *The Viking Portable Hemingway* (New York: Viking, 1944), p. xxiv.

5. The first printed reference to this famous expression appears in Dorothy Parker's profile of Hemingway in *The New Yorker* (Nov. 30, 1929, p. 31). At the close of her wide-eyed, infatuated essay, Miss Parker tells of someone at a party challenging Hemingway to define "guts." He replied, "I mean grace under pressure."

6. Quoted in Charles Fenton's *The Apprenticeship of Ernest Hemingway: The Early Years* (New York: Farrar, Straus, and Young, 1954), p. 2.

7. Hemingway wrote a long, unpublished story, "The Last Good Country," about this experience. Nick Adams and his sister are the main characters.

8. Marcelline Hemingway Sanford, *At the Hemingways: A Family Portrait* (Boston: Atlantic, Little, Brown, 1962), p. 195.

9. She had some professional success as a singer and as a painter.

10. Quoted from George Plimpton's interview with Hemingway in *The Paris Review*, 18 (Spring 1958), 74. See Emily Watts, *Ernest Hemingway and the Arts* (Urbana: U. of Illinois Press, 1971). She argues that his knowledge of painting was deep rather than broad, and that his favorite painters—especially Goya and Cézanne—shared his attitudes toward life and art.

11. The short story "God Rest You Merry, Gentlemen" and the vignette in *in our time* about two policemen gunning down two Hungarians grew out of Hemingway's apprenticeship on the *Star*.

12. "I was an awful dope when I went to the last war," Hemingway wrote to Maxwell Perkins (May 30, 1942). "I can remember just thinking that we were the home team and the Austrians were the visiting team." Quoted from Carlos Baker, *Ernest Hemingway: A Life Story* (New York: Scribner's, 1969), p. 38.

13. After he was released from the hospital in Milan, Hemingway spent a few more weeks at the front in the Italian infantry—until the Armistice. He returned home in January 1919. C. Baker, *Life*, pp. 44–46, corrects several errors in the popularly accepted version of Hemingway's war experiences recounted in Malcolm Cowley's "A Portrait of Mister Papa," *Life*, 26 (Jan. 10, 1949), 86–101. Reprinted in McCaffery, pp. 34–56. Hemingway's long and amusing letter about his wound was reprinted in his hometown newspaper; see Leicester Hemingway, *My Brother, Ernest*

Hemingway (New York: Fawcett, reprint, 1963) and Marcelline Sanford, pp. 166–69.

14. Quoted in Fenton, p. 61.

15. Philip Young, *Ernest Hemingway: A Reconsideration* (New York: Harcourt, Brace & World, 1966), pp. 164–71. Unless otherwise noted, all succeeding references to Young are to this edition.

   Hemingway wrote bitterly to General Lanham (May 23, 1953) that a study (Young's) was being published trying to prove that he was "spooked" and spent all his time acting otherwise to hide the truth. In the foreword to this book, Young recounts his difficulties in getting Hemingway to grant permission to use quoted materials from his writing. See also C. Baker, *Life*, pp. 490 ff., for an account of the obstacles Hemingway set in the path of Charles Fenton when he was working on his study of Hemingway's formative years.

16. Sanford, pp. 304–6. Leicester Hemingway, a younger brother, corroborates Marcelline's testimony that Hemingway's relations with his parents were strained after he returned from the war. His determination to write seemed to them irresponsible, and his first published stories shocked their Victorian sensibilities. Occasional "reconciliations" occurred, but the rupture, at last, was permanent. Leicester records that when their mother died in 1951, Hemingway sent their sister "a note and money, asking that she take everyone to dinner in his name, and tend to everything else that was necessary" [247].

17. Carlos Baker, *Hemingway: The Writer as Artist* (Princeton: Princeton U. Press, 1952, 1956; 3rd ed., enlarged, 1963), p. 12 and *n*. See also Hemingway's account in *A Moveable Feast*, pp. 73–75.

18. George Antheil, the composer, also arranged for the publication of four poems in a German periodical, *Der Querschnitt* ("Cross-Section") in 1924–25.

19. Ironically, Hemingway was able at this time to help Miss Stein by placing passages from her *The Making of Americans* in Ford Madox Ford's *transatlantic review*, which Hemingway helped to edit.

20. The option proved extremely important since an additional clause provided that if the second book was not accepted, the

publisher forfeited rights to the third. *The Torrents of Spring* was rejected, and Hemingway turned over to Scribner's his third book, *The Sun Also Rises*. Scribner's was his publisher for the rest of his career.

21. *Bookman*, 63 (May 1926), 262–65. Collected in *Afternoon of an Author*, ed. Arthur Mizener (New York: Scribner's, 1958), pp. 117–22.

22. See *n.* 20 above.

23. Young, pp. 60 ff., cites Hemingway's references to his father's suicide in *For Whom the Bell Tolls* and "Fathers and Sons" as further evidence of Hemingway's need to rehearse traumatic episodes of violence. C. Baker, *Life*, pp. 166–67, cites several entries about suicide from Hemingway's notebook for 1926.

24. Other non-fiction he wrote during the early thirties includes critiques of paintings by Joan Miró, Luis Quintanilla, and Antonio Gattorno, and a few pieces of social and political analysis.

25. The epigraph to this collection sets the tone. Aping the style of an old book of gaming rules, Hemingway suggests that, in the game of life, "the conditions are that the winner shall take nothing; neither his ease, nor his pleasure, nor any notions of glory; nor if he win far enough, shall there be any reward within himself." Although the collection contains two of Hemingway's most memorable stories—"A Clean, Well-Lighted Place" and "The Light of the World"—it includes also two of his most forgettable, "After the Storm" and "Wine of Wyoming."

26. *By-Line: Ernest Hemingway* (Selected Articles and Dispatches of Four Decades), ed. William White (New York: Scribner's, 1967), p. 183.

27. It was here that Hemingway met Colonel Lanham and began a friendship that lasted until his death. Hemingway wrote more than a hundred letters to Lanham during the next seventeen years, all of them now housed at the Princeton University Library.

28. See C. Baker, *Life*, pp. 393–445, for a precise account of Hemingway's wartime activities. Malcolm Cowley's narrative in "A Portrait of Mister Papa" (see *n.* 13 above) is infinitely more colorful and melodramatic, but suffers from hopeless distortions foisted on Cowley by Hemingway himself. In letters to Lanham, Hemingway makes clear that he is giving Cowley what he thinks Cowley wants, and saving the real stuff for his own use.

29. See C. Baker, *Life*, pp. 416–17. Neither place required "liberation." Hemingway and a few friends were simply the first Americans to arrive and be welcomed. The only violence was sniper fire from a roof adjoining the Travellers Club. See *By-Line*, pp. 364–83.

30. *By-Line*, pp. 340–400.

31. Although he spoke of the end of a marriage as a personal defeat, Hemingway divorced each of his first three wives at the close of a particular period of his life: Hadley at the end of his apprenticeship in Paris with the publication of *The Sun Also Rises;* Pauline at the end of the Spanish Civil War with publication of *For Whom the Bell Tolls;* Martha at the end of World War II. Each has a book dedicated to her: Hadley, *The Sun Also Rises;* Pauline, *Death in the Afternoon;* Martha, *For Whom the Bell Tolls;* Mary, *Across the River and Into the Trees.*

32. Malcolm Cowley notes that Hemingway "sometimes seems to regard writing as an exhausting ceremony of exorcism" (Introduction, *Viking Portable*, p. xii).

33. Hemingway enjoyed especially a German report that his plane had crashed on Mt. Kilimanjaro. See *By-Line*, pp. 425–69.

34. See C. Baker, *Life*, pp. 550 ff. The most graphic account of Hemingway's final months is A. E. Hotchner's in *Papa Hemingway: A Personal Memoir* (New York: Random House, 1966). Its reliability, however, is questionable; see especially Philip Young's critique, "On Dismembering Hemingway," *Atlantic Monthly*, 218 (Aug. 1966), 45–49. Young's own account in the afterword to *Ernest Hemingway: A Reconsideration* is more measured, as is Leicester Hemingway's.

35. *A Moveable Feast* was the first of Hemingway's works to be published posthumously. Nothing will appear, Young and Mann write in the preface to their inventory of Hemingway's manuscripts, that might "risk reduction of the author's stature." Among the recently published posthumous books—the novel *Islands in the Stream* as well as collections of apprentice journalism and of high-school fiction and poetry—little flatters Hemingway's image as an artist. Yet each of these works is welcome as an integral part of the yet unfinished story of the man and the artist. Still unpublished and vaulted (until the John F. Kennedy Library opens) are manuscripts of a complete novel (*Garden of Eden*), an incomplete one (*Jimmie Breen*), several short stories,

a long account of Hemingway's stint as a game warden in Africa in 1953, poems, and letters.

World, Hero, Code

1. Harvey Breit, "Talk with Mr. Hemingway," *The New York Times Book Review* (Sept. 17, 1950), p. 14.
2. Introduction to *Viking Portable*, p. viii.
3. See Harry Hartwick, *Foreground of American Fiction* (New York: American, 1934), and Sheridan Baker, *Ernest Hemingway: An Introduction and Interpretation* (New York: Holt, Rinehart, and Winston, 1967).
4. See, for example, "An Alpine Idyll," a story about a Swiss peasant who leaves his dead wife in the woodshed. When she freezes in winter, he hangs his lantern from her mouth. Another grotesque tale, "A Man of the World"—uncollected but published as one of *Two Tales of Darkness, Atlantic Monthly*, 200 (Nov. 1957)—tells of a fight in which one man has both eyes gouged out, the other man his nose bitten off. The second of the *Two Tales of Darkness*, "Get a Seeing-Eyed Dog," is less frightening than feeble, a soggy narrative of a recently blinded man who despairs of burdening his wife.

    Little has been written about Hemingway's humor, but see Jackson J. Benson, *Hemingway: The Writer's Art of Self-Defense* (Minneapolis: U. of Minnesota Press, 1969).
5. Young describes the "Hemingway hero" and the "code hero." Earl Rovit, in his *Ernest Hemingway* (New York: Twayne, 1963), talks about the "tyro" and the "tutor." Delbert Wylder, in *Hemingway's Heroes* (Albuquerque: U. of New Mexico Press, 1970), argues against the dual division, insisting that each character must be considered in a specific context. Wylder says that until Hemingway wrote *For Whom the Bell Tolls*, he had created only anti-heroes. In the final three works, there is a mythic warrior (Robert Jordan), a tyrant hero (Colonel Cantwell), and a sinning hero (Santiago). Wylder's thesis is interesting, but more rigid in its insistence than the dualistic theories.
6. Hemingway is far less tolerant of those whose sexual inclinations are aberrant. The homosexual matador in "Mother of a Queen" is a complete scoundrel; the Italian major who tries unsuccessfully to seduce his orderly in "A Simple Enquiry" has too much

unguent on his sunburned face and too much unction in his manner; the handsome young couple in "The Sea Change" part because the girl is a lesbian; and in "Mr. and Mrs. Elliot," hints of both lesbianism and impotence mark Hemingway's contemptuous treatment of this unfortunate pair.

In *Death in the Afternoon*, Hemingway writes that tales about homosexuality lack "drama as do all tales of abnormality since no one can predict what will happen in the normal while all tales of the abnormal end much the same" [180]. Nonetheless, he tells an undramatic and predictable story about an affair between two young American men in Paris. Elsewhere in *Death in the Afternoon*, Hemingway nears hysteria in his attack upon the "mincing gentry." About El Greco's "androgynous faces and forms," he asks: "Do you think that was all accident or do you think all those citizens were queer?" [204]. Goya and Velázquez serve as models for virility, but even the effeminate art of El Greco wins out over the "prissy exhibitionistic . . . withered old maid arrogance of a Gide; the lazy, conceited debauchery of a Wilde . . . the nasty, sentimental parody of humanity of a Whitman . . ." [205].

Richard Hovey (*The Inward Terrain*, pp. 17–22, 95–96) analyzes Hemingway's attitude toward homosexuality along orthodox Freudian lines. A less strained, more heterodox approach might settle upon Hemingway's hyperbolic masculinity as a possible explanation.

7. At about the same time as "The Undefeated," Hemingway published the very brief "Banal Story," which he intended as a tribute to Maera (Manuel García), recently dead of consumption. More a satiric sketch than a story, it describes a man absorbing "romance" from a popular magazine (*The Forum*) while Maera lies "with a tube in each lung, drowning with pneumonia."

8. For notable attacks on Hemingway, see Wyndham Lewis, "The Dumb Ox: A Study of Ernest Hemingway," *The American Review*, 3 (June 1934), reprinted in his *Men Without Art* (London: Cassell, 1934), pp. 17–40; D. S. Savage, *The Withered Branch* (London: Eyre and Spottiswoode, 1950), pp. 23–43; Otto Friedrich, "Ernest Hemingway: Joy Through Strength," *American Scholar*, 26 (Autumn 1957), 470, 518–30; and Robert Evans, "Hemingway and the Pale Cast of Thought," *American Literature*, 38 (May 1966), 161–76.

In "Papa and the Parricides," *Esquire* (June 1967), 162,
Malcolm Cowley writes that for many critics of Hemingway the
target is not the work but the man: "a ritual murder of the father has become a custom in the literary world."
9. In "A Situation Report," Hemingway wrote: "There is the matter of being expatriots. It is very difficult to be an expatriot at 35
minutes by air from Key West and less than an hour, faster
plane, from Miami. I never hired out to be a patriot but regu-
larly attend the wars in which my country participates and pay
my Federal taxes. An expatriate (I looked up the spelling) is,
consequently, a word I never cared for." *Look* (Sept. 4, 1956),
reprinted in *By-Line,* p. 474.

Style

1. For detailed accounts of Hemingway's use of irony, see especially Jackson J. Benson, *Hemingway: The Writer's Art of Self-
Defense;* E. M. Halliday, "Hemingway's Ambiguity: Symbolism
and Irony," collected in *Hemingway: A Collection of Critical Essays,* ed. R. P. Weeks (New Jersey: Prentice-Hall, 1962), pp.
52–71.
2. ". . . We keep it iced in the bait box with chunks of ice packed
around it. And you ought to taste it on a hot day when you
have worked a big marlin fast because there were sharks after
him. You are tired all the way through. The fish is landed untouched by sharks and you have a bottle of Ballantine cold in
your hand and drink it cool, light, and full-bodied, so it tastes
good long after you have swallowed it. That's the test of an ale
with me; whether it tastes as good afterwards as when it's going
down. Ballantine does." The writer is Ernest Hemingway, the
passage an excerpt from a letter published as an advertisement
in *Life* magazine, 31, No. 19 (Nov. 5, 1951), 91.
3. See Fenton, pp. 55–56.
4. John Peale Bishop, "Homage to Hemingway," *After the Genteel
Tradition,* ed. Malcolm Cowley (New York: Norton, 1937), p.
193. For detailed accounts of Hemingway's stylistic debts, see
also C. Baker, *Writer as Artist;* Philip Young, *Ernest Hemingway;* and Richard Bridgman, *The Colloquial Style in America*
(New York: Oxford, 1966).
5. Quoted from *A Moveable Feast,* p. 17. In an interview (*The*

Paris Review, p. 73), Hemingway added, ". . . I learned from her about the abstract relationship of words." See, too, his list of other literary "masters" cited during the interview.

6. In *Green Hills of Africa,* Hemingway continues his assault on trickery, faking, and cheating. See especially pp. 26–27.

7. Page 195. For Hemingway's sense of his debt to Twain, see my chapter on *Death in the Afternoon* and *Green Hills of Africa.* Philip Young draws close parallels between Twain's style and Hemingway's; C. Baker tones down the "influence" without denying similarities between the authors' styles.

8. "Ernest Hemingway, Literary Critic," *American Literature,* 36, No. 4 (Jan. 1965), 435. Young observes that the style tries to hold life "under the most intense and rigorous control . . . for it is savage and can get out of hand" (p. 209).

9. "The most essential gift for a good writer," he told an interviewer (*The Paris Review,* p. 89), "is a built-in, shock-proof, shit detector. This is the writer's radar and all great writers have it."

10. "The Style of Hemingway," collected in *Hemingway and His Critics: An International Anthology,* ed. Carlos Baker (New York: Hill and Wang, 1961), p. 108.

11. Page 230.

12. C. Baker's *Writer as Artist* is the most notable example of elaborate analysis of symbols. Many of Baker's suggestions are highly illuminating; others are labored, overwrought, and, occasionally, plain wrong. See also E. M. Halliday, *n.* 1 above, and Bern Oldsey, "The Snows of Ernest Hemingway," *Wisconsin Studies in Contemporary Literature,* 4 (Spring–Summer 1963), 172–98.

13. Oldsey (see *n.* 12), p. 197.

14. Robert Manning, "Hemingway in Cuba," *Atlantic Monthly,* 216 (Aug. 1965), 101.

15. "The Necessary Stylist: A New Critical Revision," *Modern Fiction Studies,* 4 (Winter 1960–61), 295.

16. Quoted in *Faulkner in the University,* ed. F. L. Gwynn and J. L. Blotner (New York: Random House, 1965), pp. 143–44. See also p. 206. Compare Leon Edel's observation that Hemingway has merely "created the artful illusion of a Style . . . an *effect* of Style by a process of evasion . . ." "The Art of Evasion," collected in Weeks's *Critical Essays,* p. 170. See, too, Young, pp. 275–77.

"Three Stories" AND *in our time*

1. In a letter to Edmund Wilson—quoted in *Shores of Light* (New York: Farrar, Straus and Young, 1952), p. 117—Hemingway wrote that he did not think his story derived from Anderson: "It is about a boy and his father and race-horses. Sherwood has written about boys and horses. But very differently . . . I know I wasn't inspired by him." Hemingway adds that Anderson's work "seems to have gone to hell, perhaps from people in New York telling him too much how good he was."
2. Edmund Wilson, "Emergence of Hemingway," in *The Shores of Light*, p. 121.
3. See Appendix A for an explanation of the relationship between *in our time* and *In Our Time*.
4. Chapters VII and X are the "germs" of the war and love stories in *A Farewell to Arms*. Chapter X appeared as "A Very Short Story" in *In Our Time* (See Appendix A).
5. Tony Tanner, *The Reign of Wonder* (Cambridge: Cambridge U. Press, 1965), p. 235.
6. See Fenton's masterly analysis of the revisions Hemingway made in transmuting a cable to the *Toronto Star* into this vignette (pp. 181–85). See also my chapter, "The Journalist, the Poet, the Satirist, and the Dramatist," pp. 73–75.
7. Hemingway had not yet seen his first bullfight when he wrote this vignette, but drew from a conversation with an artist friend, Henry ("Mike") Strater. See S. Baker, p. 20.
8. These two vignettes were based on conversations with Captain Eric Dorman-Smith of His Majesty's Fifth Fusiliers, though the portrait is not of Dorman-Smith. Hemingway was not at the scene.
9. Hemingway's source here was a conversation with Shorty Wormall, a news photographer he had quoted in earlier reports to the *Star*. See Fenton, pp. 188–89, and *By-Line*, pp. 76 ff. for Hemingway's journalistic report about European royalty.
10. Wilson, *Shores of Light*, p. 121.

Nick Adams, Master Apprentice

1. Quoted in Fenton, p. 146.
2. See Appendix B.

3. C. Baker, *Writer as Artist*, p. 131, sees Nick's story as representative of the young men of his time.

4. In *The New York Times Book Review* (July 26, 1964, p. 14), for example, Carlos Baker says that while "Indian Camp" is an invented story, "The Doctor and the Doctor's Wife" is "virtually a playback of an actual quarrel between Dr. Hemingway and a halfbreed Indian sawyer on the shore of Walloon Lake in the summer of 1912, with the youthful Ernest Hemingway as an interested onlooker. This is proved by a letter from his father to Ernest, written some thirteen years after the event."

5. See Rovit, pp. 57–58.

6. Hemingway's original title was "A Broken Heart."

7. Young argues (pp. 235–37) that Bugs, like Nigger Jim, is his master's only protector, but that what "was once amusing, or affectionate and even touching" here becomes "sinister." A more extravagant thesis is proposed by Joseph DeFalco—*The Hero in Hemingway's Short Stories* (Pittsburgh: U. of Pittsburgh Press, 1963), pp. 71–81—who describes Ad as a symbol of "father-authority," Bugs as "the hermaphroditic figure who resembles the mother," his blackness suggesting "the danger inherent in the nature of such a figure." Not really extravagant, just nonsensical.

8. Constance Cappel Montgomery, *Hemingway in Michigan* (New York: Fleet, 1966), p. 94, derives the title from Matthew 5:14, thus suggesting that the title is an ironic commentary on the people in the station café. C. Baker, *Life*, p. 606, says that Hemingway may have recalled a popular Holman Hunt print called "I am the Light of the World."

   For an analysis of the relationship between Stan Ketchel, the actual fighter, and Hemingway's character, see Matthew Bruccoli, "The Light of the World": Stan Ketchel as "My Sweet Christ," *Fitzgerald-Hemingway News Annual* (Washington, D.C.: NCR, 1969), pp. 125–29.

   In an unpublished essay, Philip Young argues that both women are lying and do not even know the correct first name of their alleged lover. Thus read, the story is extremely pessimistic, its point "really that the light of the world has gone out."

   In a preface to *The First Forty-Nine Stories*, Hemingway cites this as one of his favorites but "which nobody else ever liked." C. Baker, *Life*, p. 606, says that Hemingway wrote several letters comparing the story to Maupassant's "La Maison Tellier."

9. The best explications are in Young, pp. 48–49; C. Brooks and

R. P. Warren, *Understanding Fiction*, 2nd ed. (New York: Appleton-Century-Crofts, 1959), pp. 303–12.

10. See Rovit, p. 79. He argues persuasively that despite the force of the "interior memory" passages, "the two sections of the story never quite engage each other."

11. See Young, pp. 50–52.

12. See "The World, the Hero, and the Code," p. 24, and Young, pp. 15–20.

13. Young, p. 52.

14. Cowley, *Viking Portable*, p. xix.

15. S. Baker, pp. 36–37, notes that even today the site of Seney reminds the onlooker of a "war-burned Fossalta."

16. In *For Whom the Bell Tolls*, Hemingway finally tells the story of his father's suicide.

17. John Peale Bishop, "The Missing All," reprinted in McCaffery, pp. 302–3.

18. Rovit, p. 63. See also his analysis of structure, pp. 96–98, and style, pp. 129–31. Hemingway took his title from Marlowe's *The Jew of Malta:*

> *Thou hast committed—*
> *Fornication: but that was in another country,*
> *And, besides, the wench is dead.*

T. S. Eliot used the same passage as the epigraph for his "Portrait of a Lady," and William Faulkner refers to it in *A Fable.*

19. The reference to his wife's pregnancy parallels Hemingway's own experience, at least as Gertrude Stein recorded it in *The Autobiography of Alice B. Toklas*, p. 213: "He came to the house about ten o'clock in the morning and he stayed, he stayed for lunch, he stayed all afternoon, he stayed for dinner and he stayed until about ten o'clock at night and then all of a sudden he announced that his wife was *enceinte* and then with great bitterness, and I, I am too young to be a father. We consoled him as best we could and sent him on his way."

20. Leslie Fiedler, *Love and Death in the American Novel* (New York: Criterion, 1960), p. 306.

21. Schatz (who is based on Hemingway's eldest son, John) reappears by that nickname in *Islands in the Stream* as the son of Thomas Hudson, the hero.

Journalist, Poet, Satirist, Dramatist

1. Audre Hanneman, *Ernest Hemingway: A Comprehensive Bibliography* (Princeton: Princeton U. Press, 1967) lists 148 unpublished letters. There are currently listed holdings of unpublished letters in thirty-one libraries and private collections. Philip Young and C. W. Mann, *The Hemingway Manuscripts: An Inventory* (University Park, Pennsylvania State U. Press, 1969) cite more than three thousand pages of unpublished manuscript among 19,500 pages of manuscript in various holdings. The largest proportion of the manuscripts is held by Mary Hemingway, sole executrix.

2. Quoted in Louis Henry Cohn, *A Bibliography of the Work of Ernest Hemingway* (New York: Random House, 1931), p. 112. See R. O. Stephens, *Hemingway's Non-Fiction*, Chapter X, "Sources, Analogues, and Echoes," for a discussion of Hemingway's use of his journalistic work in his fiction.

3. *By-Line,* p. xii. Succeeding page references to *By-Line* in this chapter will appear in the text in brackets. Hemingway's earliest reporting is collected in *Ernest Hemingway: Cub Reporter*, ed. M. J. Bruccoli (Pittsburgh: U. of Pittsburgh Press, 1970).

4. In "Che Ti Dice La Patria," a weak story published originally in 1927, Hemingway ridicules conditions under Italian Fascism.

5. See Fenton, pp. 181 ff.

6. The best of these stories is "The Butterfly and the Tank," in which Loyalist soldiers at Chicote's Bar in Madrid beat, then shoot a drunkard who squirts cologne at them. It is collected in *The Fifth Column and Four Stories of the Spanish Civil War* (New York: Scribner's, 1969). The other stories—all well told but brutal—are "The Denunciation," "Night Before Battle," and "Under the Ridge." A fifth story about the Spanish Civil War, "Nobody Ever Dies"—an example of Hemingway at his tough-guy worst—was not included.

7. Foreword to the English edition of *By-Line* (London: Collins, 1968), p. 23.

8. See my chapter on *Death in the Afternoon* and *Green Hills of Africa*.

9. See "A Christmas Gift" (pp. 425 ff.) and "A Situation Report" (pp. 470 ff.).

10. *The Collected Poems of Ernest Hemingway* (Paris, n.d.). A pirated edition of 24 unnumbered pages in pamphlet binding. A similar edition, also pirated, was published in San Francisco in 1960.

11. See Fenton, p. 223, *n*. 11, for a discussion of Hemingway's relationship to imagism.

12. The original version of the poem was longer. Over the years, Hemingway offered diverse explanations of the poem—that it was a satire of literary men whose faith was temporary or expedient, and that it twitted Jean Cocteau for abandoning drugs and embracing religion. See C. Baker, *Life*, p. 596.

13. *Little Review*, 9, No. 3 (Spring 1923), 20–21. Reprinted in *Poetry: A Magazine of Verse*, 37 (Feb. 1931), 270–71. See also Fenton, p. 152, and E. Wilson in *The Shores of Light*, p. 118. Wilson quotes a letter from Hemingway stating that the poem was "a joke," written in the dining car en route to Lausanne after "a very fine lunch at Gertrude Stein's . . ."

14. See Young and Mann, *Hemingway Manuscripts*, pp. 73 ff., for the titles of the unpublished poems.

15. "Two Love Poems," *Atlantic Monthly*, 216, No. 2 (Aug. 1965), 94–100. An explanation of the circumstances surrounding the writing of each poem is given by Mary Hemingway on p. 96. Hemingway recorded "Second Poem to Mary" for Caedmon Records: *Ernest Hemingway Reading*.

16. Hemingway's introduction to the illustrated edition of *A Farewell to Arms* (New York: Scribner's, 1948), p. viii.

17. See "Life," p. 12 and *n*. 20.

18. In an unpublished essay, Hemingway later admitted that he was sorry about how he had treated Anderson. Hemingway's letters about *The Torrents of Spring* are in the Sherwood Anderson Collection of the Newberry Library in Chicago. A summary of their contents appears in R. L. White's "Hemingway's Private Explanation of *The Torrents of Spring*," *Modern Fiction Studies*, 13, No. 2 (Summer 1967), 261–63.

19. *The Nation*, 123 (July 28, 1926), 89.

20. New York *World* (May 30, 1926), p. 4M.

21. The title of the book Hemingway borrowed from a novel by Turgenev, who, in turn, drew upon an old Russian folk song.

22. Hovey, pp. 55–60, sees in this passage evidence that Hemingway's obsession with war and wounds breaks through even in a

"holiday book." The traumatic loves of Yogi and Scripps are also advanced as proof that love is sick here, as in all of Hemingway's work.

23. Part IV of *The Torrents of Spring* takes as part of its title Gertrude Stein's book, "The Passing of a Great Race and *The Making* and Marring *of Americans*" *(italics added).* Of Miss Stein, Yogi Johnson says, "Ah, there was a woman! Where were her experiments in words leading her?" [75].

24. Quoted in Robert Manning, "Hemingway in Cuba," *Atlantic Monthly* 216, No. 2 (Aug. 1965), 105.

25. S. Baker, p. 60. Caroline Gordon points out more significantly that Hemingway leaves out "a whole dimension, the supernatural," and that he treats the event with no "more eloquence . . . than a courageous but unlucky prizefighter could have called forth." "The Effaced Narrator," in *How to Read a Novel* (New York: Viking, 1957), p. 102.

26. The play—adapted by Benjamin Glazer and directed by Lee Strasberg—opened on March 6, 1940, at the Alvin Theater and ran for eighty-seven performances. Franchot Tone played Philip; Katherine Locke, Dorothy. Others in the cast were Lee J. Cobb, Lenore Ulric, and Arnold Moss. Brooks Atkinson (*New York Times*, March 7, 1940) found it "an uneven play that never recovers in the second act the grim candor of the beginning," but felt nevertheless that "it manages to make a statement that is always impressive, and sometimes poignant or shattering."

The Sun Also Rises

1. Hemingway's introduction to the illustrated edition of *A Farewell to Arms*, p. 8. See also C. Baker, *Writer as Artist*, pp. 75–76, and George Plimpton's interview with Hemingway in *The Paris Review*, pp. 78–79.

2. Fitzgerald's letter is reprinted in the *Fitzgerald / Hemingway Annual: 1970*, pp. 10–13. See also the explanatory notes by Philip Young and Charles W. Mann, pp. 1–9.

3. Quoted in Mizener, *The Far Side of Paradise*, p. 198.

4. Fitzgerald disliked Brett's prototype, Lady Duff-Twysden, and admitted that this attitude might have prejudiced his judgment. About Jake, Fitzgerald felt that Hemingway's hero was not so much like an impotent man as like one in "a sort of moral chas-

tity belt." See *The Letters of F. Scott Fitzgerald*, p. 205, and *Fitzgerald/Hemingway Annual: 1970*, p. 13.

5. Not until recent years has any writer pointed out the identities of these characters. The most detailed and interesting account— as well as the most self-consciously defensive—is Harold Loeb's *The Way It Was* (New York: Criterion, 1959). Loeb, the Robert Cohn of the novel, narrates at length his impassioned affair with Lady Duff, whom he describes as "not strikingly beautiful" but as moving among these "lost souls without losing a certain aloof splendor." Pat Guthrie (Mike) he dismisses as typical of that "fraction of the British upper class which chooses parasitism for a vocation." Ironically, it is Hemingway who emerges as the hanger-on, yearning pathetically and unsuccessfully after Lady Duff and, at last, apologizing to Loeb for his crude and belligerent actions, the outgrowth of Hemingway's frustration in the face of Loeb's amorous success. Lady Duff is alleged to have been unperturbed by her portrait, noting only that she had never slept with the bullfighter. See also B. D. Sarason, "Lady Brett Ashley and Lady Duff Twysden," *Connecticut Review*, 2, No. 2 (April 1969), 5–13. C. Baker, *Life*, pp. 179, 594, fills in other identities: Mr. and Mrs. Braddocks (Ford Madox Ford and Stella Bowen); Harvey Stone (Harold Stearns); Roger Prentiss (Glenway Wescott). For his portrait of Bill Gorton, Hemingway drew upon John Dos Passos and Bill Smith as well as Donald Ogden Stewart. See also Donald St. John, "Interview with Hemingway's 'Bill Gorton,'" *Connecticut Review*, 1, No. 2 (April 1968), 5–12; and 3, No. 1 Oct. 1969), 5–23.

6. Among Hemingway's war wounds was an infection of the scrotum, the result of bits of wool driven into his body. In an unpublished letter addressed to Philip Young, he indicated that his model was actually a young man whose penis had been shot away but whose testicles and spermatic cord remained intact. As Hemingway said in an interview in *The Paris Review* (p. 77), "he was capable of all normal feelings as a *man* but incapable of consummating them. The important distinction is that his wound was physical and not psychological and that he was not emasculated."

7. I am indebted to E. M. Halliday's "Hemingway's Narrative Perspective," *Sewanee Review*, 60 (Spring 1952), 202–18, for several insights concerning Hemingway's technique of point-of-

view. See also Rovit, p. 148, who finds Jake a "particularly opaque" narrator who is "*mostly* reliable and *mostly* sympathetic."

8. Hemingway was apparently baptized a Catholic in Italy in 1918, though there is no adequate supporting evidence for his claim that the baptism was performed by the Abruzzi priest who prayed beside him when he was wounded. For the sparse details of Hemingway's practice as a Catholic, see C. Baker, *Life*, pp. 45, 183, 185, 595.

9. *Writer as Artist*, p. 86.

10. See Arthur L. Scott, "In Defense of Robert Cohn," *College English*, 18 (March 1957), 309–14, and R. W. Stallman, *The Houses that James Built* (East Lansing: Michigan State U. Press, 1961), pp. 173 ff.

11. See J. J. Benson, *Hemingway: The Writer's Art of Self-Defense*, pp. 34–35, 42–43.

12. That Cohn is a Jew does little to assure a judicious evaluation of his personality. Although Hemingway vigorously denied any feelings of anti-Semitism, he seems to have shared with Fitzgerald, Cummings, Eliot, and others of the twenties a generalized dislike of Jews, especially of intellectuals and literary men. Several of his unpublished letters contain barbed references to Jews (including his ex-wife, Martha Gellhorn).

Note too the orthographic implications of the name of Cohn's mistress, Frances *Cline* (her real name, according to Harold Loeb, was Lily Lubow, a former secretary at *Broom*. Hemingway used only the Jewish-sounding name; the actual personality he depicts is that of Loeb's lady friend in Paris, Kitty Cannell, a dancer). See Kathleen Cannell, "Scenes with a Hero," *Connecticut Review*, 1, No. 1 (Oct. 1968), 5–9.

The anti-Semitic barbs in *The Sun Also Rises* were expunged from a Bantam paperback issued in 1949 which nevertheless advertised itself as "the complete text of the original edition— not one word has been changed or omitted." Scribner's made certain that in later editions the excised material was restored. Typical examples of Bantam's bowdlerizing: "Brett's gone off with men. They weren't ever *steers*" [original: Jews]; "Well, let him not get superior" [original: ". . . and Jewish"]. See David A. Randall, "Dukedom Large Enough," *Papers of the Bibliographical Society of America*, 56 (1962), 346–53.

13. Rovit, p. 152.

14. *Writer as Artist,* pp. 80–81.

15. *A Moveable Feast,* pp. 30–31. The origin of the expression *lost generation* occurred, Hemingway explains, when Miss Stein applied it to him and his peers after hearing her garage man use the phrase to rebuke a young mechanic who had been either dilatory or inept in repairing her Ford. An alternate version—not recounted in *A Moveable Feast*—is that Miss Stein heard it from a hotel owner as he argued that the war had forever prevented young men from becoming civilized, the deadline for that achievement being, he insisted, the age of twenty-five.

16. To Maxwell Perkins, Nov. 19, 1926. Quoted in C. Baker, *Writer as Artist,* p. 81.

17. Mark Spilka, "The Death of Love in *The Sun Also Rises*," in *Hemingway and His Critics,* p. 92.

18. Spilka, p. 87.

19. Note Cohn's reference to her as Circe; the *riau-riau* dancers who encircle her and enshrine her on a wine cask; and her discomfiture in church. Note too that Cohn, like Elpenor, falls asleep after drinking.

20. Benson, *Writer's Art of Defense,* argues that it is not just Jake's inability to have sex that goads Brett: "To her, Jake is a valuable piece of property, a home base for self-pity . . ." (p. 42).

21. The contrast between Romero and Cohn is deliberate. Earlier in the novel, Jake makes explicit Cohn's dislike of boxing and doubts that he has ever truly loved. But of Romero he observes, "He had loved bull-fighting, and I think he loved the bulls, and I think he loved Brett."

22. In *Death in the Afternoon,* Hemingway refers to Hadley's wrapping a bull's ear in a handkerchief [270]. Baker, *Life,* p. 152, says that Ordóñez had given it to her, that the handkerchief belonged to Donald Ogden Stewart, and that she put both in her bureau drawer.

A Farewell to Arms

1. See C. Baker, *Life,* p. 187. The working title was "Jimmy Breen."

2. C. Baker, *Life,* p. 201, tells of Hemingway's several rewritings before he got the ending he wanted. The "original" conclusion —a loose, generalized account of what happened to the charac-

ters after the war—has been reprinted in *Ernest Hemingway: Critiques of Four Major Novels*, ed. C. Baker (New York: Scribner's, 1962), p. 75.

3. See C. Baker, *Life*, for a detailed account of their relationship, especially pp. 47–50, 54–56, 59–61, 572, 574. Agnes was eight years older than Hemingway at the time, genuinely fond of him, but unwilling to have an affair. Though she hinted at the possibility of marriage a few years hence, she wrote to him shortly after he returned home that she had fallen in love with an Italian officer. (See "A Very Short Story." Originally, the girl's name in that story was Ag; the locale, Milan. Both were changed to avoid possible libel suits.)

4. Edmund Wilson refers to Hemingway's statement in "Hemingway: Gauge of Morale" (reprinted in McCaffery, p. 242). For critical comment on the appropriateness of the comparison, see C. Baker, *Writer as Artist*, pp. 98–100, and Rovit, p. 105.

5. The title of the novel is taken from a poem of that name by the Elizabethan poet George Peele in which he bemoans that age has deprived him of his skills as soldier and lover: "His helmet now shall make a hive for bees;/And, lovers' sonnets turn'd to holy psalms . . ." See *Oxford Book of English Verse*, p. 151.

6. Film versions were made in 1932 and 1957. W. J. Frohock writes that Hemingway's use of foreshortened time, visual appeal, dialogue, and manipulated symbols produces an "end product . . . closer to a good movie than to a conventional novel." He adds, however, that "it is still one of the few books of our time that stand entirely by themselves." *The Novel of Violence in America* 2nd ed. (Dallas: Southern Methodist U. Press, 1957), p. 176.

7. C. Baker develops an elaborate theory that equates the mountains with life, love, and home; the plains with death, war, and alienation (*Writer as Artist*, pp. 101 ff.). E. M. Halliday's essay, "Hemingway's Ambiguity: Symbolism and Irony" (reprinted in Weeks's *Critical Essays*), demonstrates the limits of Baker's "artificially rigid and unrealistic contrast."

8. Rovit suggests that Frederic's emptiness is supported by a pervasive image of a "masquerade": an American disguised in an Italian uniform is how Helen Ferguson sees him; Rinaldi as an Italian in an American uniform; and to the battle police he will seem a German in an Italian uniform. See Rovit, pp. 100–2.

9. Theodore Bardacke's "Hemingway's Women" (in McCaffery,

pp. 340–51) considers the long-haired girls and the short-haired variety. Edmund Wilson's "Gauge of Morale" (also in McCaffery) suggests that Hemingway and Kipling share a split attitude toward women—that a man is better without them, but that when he has one, "the submissive infra-Anglo-Saxon women . . . make . . . perfect mistresses" [254, n. 1]. See also C. Baker, *Writer as Artist*, pp. 109 ff. For an interesting suggestion that Faulkner's *The Wild Palms* parodies the romantic love in *A Farewell to Arms*, see E. Volpe, *A Reader's Guide to William Faulkner* (New York: Farrar, Straus, & Giroux, 1964), pp. 214–15, 230, 409.

10. C. Baker, *Writer as Artist*, p. 113.

11. In his fantasy, Frederic, standing on a balcony, sees bats flying above the houses. When the lovers actually consummate their love, a bat does fly into their room. The incident is probably intended as an ominous portent, but I doubt that it represents, as Richard Hovey suggests, "an epitomizing castration anxiety . . . centered on the wounded leg" (p. 76).

12. The timely coincidence of Frederic's wound and his discovery of love raises questions that some critics have answered with extraordinary sophistication. Stanley Cooperman, in *World War I and the American Novel* (Baltimore: Johns Hopkins Press, 1967), pp. 181–90, for example, argues that the wound shatters Frederic's sense of virility. "Only a love object . . . an erotic shadow shaped by passivity, can return . . . the initiative essential to his manhood." The object, of course, is Catherine, and their relationship is thus motivated not by love but by "an absolute psychic need." Frederic is thus less lover than patient, victim of both the "technological rape" by a shell and the Protestant view of sexuality that insists upon male virility.

Hovey also sees Frederic as a "Puritan libertine" whose wound is payment for his right to love. He reads the love affair as symbiotic, Frederic sadistically exploiting Catherine "to relieve the ennui of convalescence," Catherine masochistically escaping "the normal burdens of selfhood" (pp. 95–96).

Ingenious and partially relevant, these arguments strike me as overburdened and more appropriate for the clinician than for the critic.

13. See Donna Gerstenberger, "*The Waste Land* in *A Farewell to Arms*," *MLN*, 76 (Jan. 1961), 24–25.

14. Note the parallels between the description of the retreat on p.

205 and that in the vignette beginning "Minarets stuck up in the rain" in *In Our Time* (*Short Stories*, p. 195).

15. "Hemingway's Other Style," *MLN*, 76 (May 1961), 434–42. Reprinted in *Critiques of Four Novels*, pp. 41–46.

16. For a fuller discussion of the relationship between Hemingway and Thomas Hardy, see Daniel Fuchs, "Ernest Hemingway: Literary Critic," *American Literature*, 36 (Jan. 1965), 431–51.

17. In his introduction to *A Farewell to Arms* (New York: Scribner's, 1949), Robert Penn Warren writes, "It is, in a sense, a religious book; if it does not offer a religious solution, it is nevertheless conditioned by the religious problem" (p. xxviii).

Death in the Afternoon AND Green Hills of Africa

1. *Hemingway's Non-Fiction*, pp. 161–79.

2. Reprinted in McCaffery, p. 66.

3. *The New York Times* (Oct. 25, 1935), p. 19.

4. *New York Herald Tribune Books* (Oct. 27, 1935), p. 3.

5. In an unpublished letter to General Lanham in 1953, Hemingway writes that however wicked it may appear, he must admit that killing is what he loves most.

6. In 1947, Hemingway wrote to Lanham, after seeing Manolete fight, that bullfighting was enjoyable only between wars and that it was incapable of evoking sensations as thrilling as the sound of German tanks approaching during the night.

7. Max Eastman's "Bull in the Afternoon" sympathetically explains Hemingway's plight as that of a sensitive young man thrust into war, encouraged to be courageous, then told to abandon his blood lust. Unable to do so, he felt a continuing "obligation to put forth evidences of red-blooded masculinity . . . [evident] in a literary style, you might say, of wearing false hair on the chest" [71]. It was these final lines that precipitated the famous brawl between Hemingway and Eastman.

8. Shortly before *Green Hills of Africa* appeared, Hemingway had written for *Esquire* an article about shooting birds in which he observes, "I think they were made to shoot and some of us were made to shoot them . . ." See "Remembering Shooting-Flying: A Key West Letter," *Esquire*, 3, No. 2 (Feb. 1935), 152. Reprinted in *By-Line*, pp. 186–91.

9. Pop was in reality Philip Percival, a noted guide and hunter.

Karl was Charles Thompson, an old fishing companion from Hemingway's years at Key West. Kandisky, with whom Hemingway holds his literary conversation, was an Austrian trader named Hans Koritschoner. Hemingway's wife at this time was Pauline Pfeiffer. See C. Baker, *Life*, pp. 248–58.

10. *Shores of Light*, p. 621.

11. "A continent ages quickly once we come," he writes in *Green Hills of Africa*, adding, "The earth gets tired of being exploited . . . The machine can't reproduce, nor does it fertilize the soil, and it eats what he [man] cannot raise. A country was made to be as we found it" [284]. The efforts of the New Deal to save America won little praise from Hemingway: "Starry eyed bastards spending money that somebody will have to pay . . . Fishermen all turned carpenters. Reverse of the Bible" [191].

"The Snows of Kilimanjaro" AND "The Short Happy Life"

1. These articles—along with several other pieces of Fitzgerald's non-fiction—are collected in *The Crack-Up*, ed. Edmund Wilson (New York: New Directions, 1956), p. 69.

2. Letters to John Dos Passos (Jan. 13, 1936) and Maxwell Perkins (Feb. 7, 1936). See C. Baker, *Life*, p. 617.

3. In a letter to General Lanham (Jan. 1, 1947), Hemingway says that too many approach the rich with awe or loathing. "The Snows," he adds, is a projection of his own attitude toward them and grew from an encounter he had with a wealthy woman who invited him to tea after his return from Africa. Having read a newspaper interview in which Hemingway had spoken of his desire to return to Africa as soon as he had enough money, she made him a tempting offer that would assure him of financial security. The story, Hemingway writes, suggests what the result might have been had he accepted the lady's generosity.

4. Stung by the reference, Fitzgerald wrote Hemingway: "Please lay off me in print. If I choose to write de profundis sometimes it doesn't mean I want friends praying aloud over my corpse." In a postscript, he added, "Riches have never fascinated me, unless combined with the greatest charm or distinction." See *The Letters of F. Scott Fitzgerald*, p. 311.

When "The Snows" was reprinted in Hemingway's collected

short stories, Fitzgerald's name was changed to Julian. The story referred to is Fitzgerald's "The Rich Boy."

5. Letter to Beatrice Dance (Sept. 15, 1936), *Letters*, p. 543.

6. In the first of three Tanganyika letters published in *Esquire* (April 1934), Hemingway tells of suffering from amoebic dysentery and being flown in a two-seater biplane to Nairobi for treatment. Other details of his African adventure appear in *Green Hills of Africa*, but the antagonism toward the rich and toward marriage dates back to the 1920's, as he makes clear in the latter pages of *A Moveable Feast*.

7. Two sources provided Hemingway his material about the leopard near the summit of Kilimanjaro. In Hans Meyer's *Across East African Glaciers* (1891), the following passage occurs: ". . . at the very summit of a mountain 20,000 feet high [Kilimanjaro], we lighted on the dead body of an antelope . . . How the animal came there it is impossible to say . . . overtaken in these lofty solitudes by the fury of a mountain-storm, [it] had paid with its life the penalty of its adventurous curiosity" [183–84]. In the manuscript of "The Snows" at the University of Texas, a second, canceled, quotation follows the epigraph and is taken from Vivienne de Watteville's *Speak to the Earth* (1935), a book about her own African safari. See Robert O. Stephens's "Hemingway's Riddle of Kilimanjaro: Idea and Image," *American Literature*, 22 (March 1960), 84–87; and Robert W. Lewis's "Vivienne de Watteville, Hemingway's Companion on Kilimanjaro," *Texas Quarterly*, 9 (Winter 1966), 75–85.

8. R. W. Stallman notes that the dream of flight "is set in Roman type so as to distinguish it from the italicized passages of Harry's recollections of the past; they are not dreams." Stallman, Young, and others have also commented on the similarities between Hemingway's story and Ambrose Bierce's "An Occurrence at Owl Creek Bridge," especially in the treatment of dream and reality.

9. See Stallman's *The Houses that James Built*, pp. 193 ff., for a detailed account of the interrelationships between image and recollection in the internal monologues.

10. For some readers, the symbolism proves too self-conscious and, on occasion, inadequately integrated. Caroline Gordon and Allen Tate argue, in *The House of Fiction* (New York: Scribner's, 1950), pp. 420 ff., that the leopard, though an effective symbolic

counterpoint to Harry's rotting body and spirit, appears only once, and then in the epigraph to the story, not within the narrative itself.

11. See Oliver Evans, "'The Snows of Kilimanjaro': A Revaluation," *PMLA*, 76 (Dec. 1961), 604–6.

12. See Charles C. Walcutt, "Hemingway's 'The Snows of Kilimanjaro,'" *The Explicator*, 7 (April 1949), item 43.

13. C. Baker, *Writer as Artist*, p. 189. See also J. J. Benson, pp. 146–48, for an account of the multiple points of view Hemingway uses to achieve emotional emphasis.

14. See Warren Beck, "The Shorter Happy Life of Mrs. Macomber," *Modern Fiction Studies*, 1 (Nov. 1955), 28–37, and Sheridan Baker, p. 98, for arguments in defense of Margot. Mark Spilka, "The Necessary Stylist: A New Critical Revision," *Modern Fiction Studies*, 4 (Winter 1960–61), 289–95, refutes Beck's thesis, insisting that there "is no sign in her of deep renewal, and no support for it from Hemingway." Note, too, in the text, Margot's lack of ease when Macomber rediscovers his courage: ". . . her contempt was not secure. She was very afraid of something" [133].

15. Feeble, one of Falstaff's recruits, speaks the line in *Henry IV*, Part 2, III, ii, 253 ff. In the introduction to the anthology *Men at War* (1942), Hemingway writes of his "sudden happiness and the feeling of having a permanent protecting talisman" when, just after he was wounded in WWI, his English friend, Dorman-Smith, wrote out these lines for him at the hospital. Dorman-Smith is thus blended with Philip Percival, the guide in *Green Hills of Africa*, to create Wilson. Hemingway discusses the identities of the other characters in the unpublished "The Art of the Short Story" (*c.* 1959): "I invented [Margot] complete with handles from the worst bitch I knew (then) . . ." See C. Baker, *Life*, pp. 284, 617.

16. Hovey, pp. 119 ff., suggests an interesting comparison and contrast between Macomber and the boy Paco (a diminutive for Francis) in "The Capital of the World," published in *Esquire* in June 1936. Both are innocents killed at the moment of proving their manhood, but Paco is fearless from the outset, more nearly grown up and ready to face reality than the adult Macomber.

17. See Young, p. 69. He describes both stories as rituals, "one a ceremonial triumph over fear, the other a rite in which part of the self is destroyed."

18. In fact, as the remaining chapters will show, Hemingway's experiments rarely succeed.

To Have and Have Not

1. *By-Line*, p. 228. Until the German invasion of Russia in 1938, Stalinists took the same position toward American involvement as the isolationists. Conceivably, Hemingway might thus be regarded as a "Stalinist" at this time.
2. At the end of Clara Weatherwax's *Marching! Marching!* (1935), for example, unarmed strikers stride buoyantly and suicidally toward the fixed bayonets and machine guns of National Guardsmen. But however crushed their bodies, the spirits of those Jack Conroy called the "disinherited and dispossessed of the world" remained undaunted. "We throw the spark," one of Conroy's characters says at the close of *The Disinherited* (1933). "Sometimes it splutters and goes out, but again it will light a mighty blaze."
3. *Partisan Review*, 1, No. 1 (Feb.–March 1934), 59–60.
4. *New Masses*, 16 (Sept. 17, 1935), 9. Carlos Baker notes that Hemingway refused payment for this article on two grounds: he did not wish to profit from murder, and he had little respect for the magazine that was to print his article (*Writer as Artist*, p. 201, *n.* 9).
5. C. Baker, *Writer as Artist*, p. 201.
6. *Men Without Art*, pp. 17–18.
7. The person most maligned in the novel is John Dos Passos, upon whom Richard Gordon is modeled. See C. Baker, *Life*, pp. 298–99. Hemingway was already involved with the Spanish Civil War while working on *To Have and Have Not*. His revisions were interrupted and curtailed by his collaboration on the film script of *The Spanish Earth*, journalistic reporting for the North American Newspaper Alliance, and preparation of the speech he was to deliver to the Congress of American Writers. See also Philip Young, "To Have Not: Tough Luck," in *Tough Guy Writers of the Thirties*, ed. David Madden (Carbondale: Southern Illinois U. Press, 1968), p. 46.
8. "One Trip Across" appeared in *Cosmopolitan* in April 1934; "The Tradesman's Return" was published in *Esquire* in Feb. 1935, but was much altered in the novel.
9. See E. M. Halliday, "Hemingway's Narrative Perspective," *Se-*

wanee Review, 60 (Spring 1952), 202–18 (also collected in *Critiques of Four Novels*, pp. 174–82).

10. C. Baker suggests that Hemingway "was dramatizing a double indictment of American society for its predatory attitude towards both writers [Gordon] and individualistic men of action [Harry]."

11. "Farewell the Separate Peace," in McCaffery, p. 139.

12. Rovit, p. 71.

13. *Writers in Crisis* (Boston: Houghton Mifflin, 1961), p. 77.

14. C. Baker, *Writer as Artist*, p. 212.

15. Geismar, pp. 73–74.

16. Morgan's bigotry is racial as well as national: witness his paternal contempt for Wesley, the wounded Negro. P. Young cites two possible American sources for Harry's primitivism: Frank Norris's *Moran of the Lady Letty* (1898) and Jack London's *The Sea Wolf* (1904). See *n.* 7 above: "To Have Not: Tough Luck," p. 45.

17. C. Baker notes that Hemingway wrote to Maxwell Perkins that he did not regard it as "a real novel" (*Writer as Artist*, p. 205).

18. "Ernest Hemingway's Literary Situation," in McCaffery, p. 123.

19. Quoted from a letter to Hemingway in *Crack-Up*, p. 284.

For Whom the Bell Tolls

1. Originally, Hemingway's choice as title (among twenty-six possibilities) was *The Undiscovered Country*. While searching for his title, he read extracts from John Donne in *The Oxford Book of English Prose*. See C. Baker, *Life*, p. 348.

2. It is worth noting that for once in Hemingway's fiction the satellites outshine the star. In almost every way, the change is welcome. One tires of Jordan's dour, humorless sincerity and is grateful for Pilar's earthiness, Pablo's moodiness, and Anselmo's sweetness. Gratifying, too, is the occasional comic relief from Jordan's often interminable interior monologues. Here again it is the guerrillas who lighten the burden: the irresponsible gypsy, Rafael, who hunts hares (more real than Jordan's "Rabbit"); the foul-mouthed Agustin, who aspires to a long swim in a soup made from his enemies' *cojones;* and the ceremonious Fernando, who approves of Jordan's affair with Maria only when assured they are engaged.

3. See C. Baker, *Writer as Artist*, pp. 245 ff., and Rovit, pp. 136 ff.
4. The bombers, Jordan observes, look like sharks, but move "like mechanized doom" [87].
5. " 'Mechanized Doom': Ernest Hemingway and the American View of the Spanish Civil War," collected in *Critiques of Four Novels*, pp. 95–107.
6. See Bern Oldsey, "The Snows of Ernest Hemingway," pp. 172–98. Oldsey notes that eleven chapters in the novel are concerned with snow.
7. Arturo Barea, a Spanish critic, argues that nowhere is Hemingway more artificial than here. The language is abstract when it should be concrete, solemn when it should be simple ("Not Spain but Hemingway," in *Hemingway and His Critics*, pp. 209–11). See also Edward Fenimore, "English and Spanish in *For Whom the Bell Tolls*," reprinted in McCaffery, pp. 205–20.
8. Compare *Death in the Afternoon:* "Let those who want to save the world if you can get to see it clear and as a whole. Then any part you make will represent the whole if it's made truly. The thing to do is work and learn to make it" [278]. As early as *The Sun Also Rises*, Hemingway had expressed his sense that the Spaniards possessed a communal spirit that is less apparent among other people.
9. For accounts of *For Whom the Bell Tolls* giving particular attention to its political and social background, see Stanley Weintraub, *The Last Great Cause* (New York: Weybright and Talley, 1969); Carl Eby, *Between the Bullet and the Lie* (New York: Holt, Rinehart, and Winston, 1969); Warren French, *The Social Novel at the End of an Era* (Carbondale: Southern Illinois U. Press, 1966); and Frederick R. Benson, *Writers in Arms* (New York: New York U. Press, 1967).
10. C. Baker, *Life*, p. 343, identifies Karkov as Mikhail Koltsov, an *Izvestia* correspondent. Other identifications he suggests include Robert Merriman, a major in the International Brigade, as the prototype for Jordan; a Polish general who used the pseudonym of Walter as the original of Golz; and Hemingway's parents as the counterparts of Jordan's.
11. Hemingway's radical critics were not at all impressed. They found little to admire in a hero incapable of a lucid, informed socio-economic or political theory supporting the Loyalist cause. Nor were they happy about Jordan's (and Hemingway's) indifference to the ideals of collectivism. "And what about a planned

society and the rest of it?" Jordan asks himself, and answers, "That was for the others to do" [163].

Hemingway offended too by permitting his guerrillas a penchant for brutality and treachery usually assigned only to Fascists. Jordan makes clear that he wants to record more than Fascist brutality, about which he knows enough from his experiences behind the lines. "In stories about the war," Hemingway wrote to the Russian critic, Ivan Kashkeen, "I try to show *all* the different sides of it." *Soviet Literature*, 11 (1962), 163.

Equally objectionable to the left was Hemingway's undisguised portrait of André Marty, the French revolutionary who organized the International Brigade, as a megalomaniac, Fascistic in his obsession with his own power and point of view. Lionel Trilling writes that Marty's "protected madness . . . seals Jordan's fate." "An American in Spain," reprinted in *Critiques of Four Novels*, p. 80.

For the leftist point of view, see Alvah Bessie's review, reprinted in *Critiques of Four Novels*, pp. 90–94, and E. B. Burgum's essay, reprinted in McCaffery, pp. 320–28.

12. *Short Stories*, p. 178.

13. *Short Stories*, p. 177.

14. Pablo's 'most touted exploit—the killing of the Fascists in his village—is, however, tainted. He begins bravely enough, executing the civil guards with whatever honor such deeds allow. The rest is horror, more so because Pablo stages the slaughter as if it were a *capea*, in which a bull is turned loose to charge the people who line the streets to bait and at last to kill it. Although the *capea* lacks the form and discipline of a classic bullfight, it too involves life and death. In a later chapter (34), young Andres vividly recalls his own terror and exhilaration while grabbing the ears of an angry bull about to gore a fallen man. Pablo's *capea* has no angry bull, only terrified and defenseless Fascist townsmen, humiliated and butchered. As Arturo Barea has written, honor (*gracia*) "does not consist in killing the bull, but in knowing that he can kill you." What Pablo does, Barea adds, destroys any claim to manliness.

15. See Barea, p. 204.

16. See Trilling, p. 80.

17. See especially the opening pages of Chapter 37. The best ac-

counts of Hemingway's treatment of time are in Rovit, pp. 136–46, and F. I. Carpenter, "Hemingway Achieves the Fifth Dimension," reprinted in *Hemingway and His Critics*, pp. 192–201.

18. Rovit, p. 145.

19. See Young, pp. 111–13, for an analysis of the biographical implications of these events in Jordan's early life. See also my chapter, "Nick Adams, Master Apprentice." According to C. Baker (*Life*, p. 629), Hemingway derived his information about the lynching episode from his sister Marcelline.

20. Young, p. 114.

21. Trilling writes that, for Donne, "death is the appalling negation and therefore the teacher of the ego. For Hemingway, death is the ego's final expression and the perfect protector of the personality. It is a sentimental error from which Donne was saved by his great power of mind" ("An American in Spain," *Critiques of Four Novels*, p. 81).

Across the River and Into the Trees

1. Young, p. 115. See also "Life," p. 18, and C. Baker, *Life*, pp. 471 ff.

2. Tanner, pp. 241–43.

3. Young, p. 120.

4. See Stephens, pp. 123–24, and C. Baker, *Life*, p. 471, for an account of their feud.

5. "How Do You Like It Now, Gentlemen?" in *Hemingway and His Critics*, p. 230.

6. Hemingway's prototype for Renata was Adriana Ivancich, a young Venetian with whom he enjoyed a Platonic friendship in 1949. See C. Baker, *Life*, pp. 469–70, 476–78. Baker states that the erotic passages are comparable to those in Hemingway's unpublished *The Garden of Eden*.

7. For a detailed account of the Christian motif, see Horst Oppel's essay in *Hemingway and His Critics*, pp. 213–26. See also C. Baker, *Writer as Artist*, pp. 283 ff.

8. Oppel, p. 221.

9. C. Baker, *Writer as Artist*, pp. 285–87, interprets the portrait as a "commentary on the relationship between life and art . . . The Colonel prefers the actual, but he cherishes the art." Baker inter-

prets the emeralds Renata gives to Cantwell similarly, as symbols of a great past he is allowed temporarily to share (Baker makes no reference to the comic, sexual implications of those "family jewels" he carries for a while in his pocket). Since both the portrait and the emeralds are—like all art—inadequate substitutes for reality, Cantwell must return them and himself to the real world. The argument is desperately overwrought. See also S. Baker, *Hemingway*, pp. 121 ff.

10. Unpublished letter to Lanham, Dec. 10, 1949. Once the unfavorable reviews were in, Hemingway expressed considerable pique in several letters to Lanham written during the next nine months. *Time*, non-combatant literary critics, and even his publisher, Charles Scribner, and intimate friend Marlene Dietrich did not escape his barbs. Despite the harsh reviews, the novel remained on the best-seller list for five months; and Hemingway rejected David Selznick's quarter-million-dollar offer for film rights as inadequate.

See E. B. White's delightful parody, "Across the Street and Into the Grill," in his *The Second Tree from the Corner* (N.Y.: Harper and Row, 1954).

The Old Man and the Sea

1. *Esquire*, 5 (April 1936), 31, 184–85. Reprinted by *By-Line*, pp. 236–44.
2. In 1939, Hemingway told Maxwell Perkins, his editor, of his intention to write a long story about this fisherman (C. Baker, *Life*, p. 339), but he began work instead on *For Whom the Bell Tolls*. Hemingway began writing *The Old Man and the Sea* in January 1951 and completed the work, revisions and all, in April of the same year. His shortest novel, it totaled 26,000 words and was published in its entirety in *Life* magazine just before publication as a book. For details about the other parts of Hemingway's "sea novel," see my chapter on *Islands in the Stream, n.* 1.
3. See C. Baker, *Life*, pp. 228, 502, and Young, p. 124.
4. Mark Schorer, "With Grace Under Pressure," reprinted in *Critiques of Four Novels*, p. 132.
5. Young, p. 128. See also C. Baker, *Writer as Artist*, pp. 288–328; C. S. Burhans, "Hemingway's Tragic Vision of Man," reprinted in *Critiques of Four Novels*, pp. 150 ff.

6. "Do not think about sin," Santiago says. "There are enough problems now without sin. Also I have no understanding of it . . . and I am not sure that I believe in it" [105]. Also interesting is that each succeeding reference to going out too far diminishes in its tone of regret: "I shouldn't have gone out so far, fish . . . Neither for you nor for me. I'm sorry fish" [110]. "I am sorry that I went too far out. I ruined us both" [115]. "You violated your luck when you went too far outside" [116]. "I went out too far" [121].

7. For interpretations of the symbolism of the lions (and other symbols as well), see Keiichi Harada, "The Marlin and the Shark: A Note on *The Old Man and the Sea*," reprinted in *Hemingway and His Critics*, pp. 269–76. See also Young, p. 128, and C. Baker, *Writer as Artist*, pp. 304–11.

8. *Time* (Dec. 13, 1954). C. Baker (*Life*, pp. 505–6, 656) tells of correspondence between Hemingway and Bernard Berenson in which Hemingway insists that there is no symbolism in the novel.

   A most amusing antidote to symbol-hunting is Robert Weeks's "Fakery in *The Old Man and the Sea*," *College English* (Dec. 1962), 188–92. Weeks demolishes the realism of the story by citing a variety of technical lapses in Hemingway's descriptions of Santiago's skill as well as in his knowledge of nature. Rather than debunking for its own sake, Weeks's essay argues that the failure of realism—Hemingway's great strength—is evidence that the world view has "gone soft" and is "patently false and forced."

9. For analyses of the Christian symbolism, see especially Joseph Waldmeir's "*Confiteor Hominem:* Ernest Hemingway's Religion of Man," reprinted in *Critical Essays*, pp. 161–68; C. Baker, *Writer as Artist*, pp. 299–328; and Melvin Backman, "The Matador and the Crucified," reprinted in *Critiques of Four Novels*, pp. 135–43.

10. See Harada, *n.* 7 above, pp. 275. Rovit ties the sharks to the "symbolic inner drama of Hemingway's fiction" and reads in their presence "a symbol of the castrating mother, another figuration of Harry's hyena and Margot Macomber," p. 91.

11. *Time* (Sept. 8. 1952), 114.

12. Page 91.

13. Page 126.

Islands in the Stream

1. In *The Hemingway Manuscripts*, Young and Mann list for these four parts fourteen packets of manuscript and typescript, much of it corrected and revised. Of these, twelve contain the materials that became *Islands in the Stream*, the other two the original and corrected typescript of *The Old Man and the Sea*. The only reference to titles other than a general reference to "Sea Novel" are: (1) "The Island and the Stream"—a reference to Part I, "Bimini" in the published version; (2) "The Sea Chase"—a reference to Part III, "At Sea" in the published version.

    In letters about his work in progress, Hemingway referred to the three parts as "The Sea When Young," "The Sea When Absent," and "The Sea in Being." On the box containing the typescript of *The Old Man and the Sea*, Hemingway wrote: "There's more than that. *The Old and the Young.* A novel by Ernest Hemingway (this is one of the three books of the first volume of a three volume novel the sea, the air and the land)." Quoted in *The Hemingway Manuscripts*, p. 21.

2. C. Baker, *Life*, pp. 491–92.

3. In April 1947, Patrick and Gregory, Hemingway's sons by Pauline Pfeiffer, were injured in an auto accident. Gregory's injury was slight, but Patrick suffered a concussion and took several months to recover. See C. Baker, *Life*, pp. 460 ff.

4. John (Bumby) Hemingway, the eldest son, was a prisoner of war for six months in Germany.

5. In 1942, Hemingway used his yacht *Pilar* for anti-submarine patrols. Late that year, the crew of a German submarine was captured—but not by Hemingway.

6. In an interview with Henry Raymont in *The New York Times* (Sept. 12, 1970), Mary Hemingway commented that though Hudson is wounded, "there is a chance that he will receive medical attention and be saved."

7. "An Effort at Self-Revelation," *The New Yorker*, Jan. 2, 1970, pp. 59–62.

8. How accurately does Hemingway's portrait of Hudson's children project his feelings toward his own sons? The question is tantalizing, especially because of the psychological implications of his peremptory disposal of his fictional offspring. Was this merely a

plot device, or, as Christopher Ricks writes, are the sons "slaugh-tered for the cruellest of markets: not commercialized sentimen-tality, but authorial escape . . . so that Thomas Hudson—alias Ernest Hemingway—may get away"? Carlos Baker's extensive correspondence with family and friends suggests to him that, apart from the usual fatherly fears and irritations, Hemingway enjoyed his sons through the years (see, for example, *Life*, p. 532). My reading of Hemingway's twenty-year correspondence with General Lanham leads me to agree with Baker until the mid- and late fifties (several years after he wrote *Islands in the Stream*), when his references to Gregory (Gigi), his youngest son, who was then under psychiatric care, are gratuitously harsh and explicitly brutal. At the same time, he writes tolerantly but with mild condescension about his eldest, John (Bumby), who had entered a brokerage, and enthusiastically about Patrick (Mouse), who had become a successful professional hunter in Af-rica. By this time, of course, the boys had become men, but they seem to have fulfilled in Hemingway's eyes the promise Hudson foretold for his sons. Hemingway's sons, however, were spared to attend their father's funeral.

9. "At Sea with Hemingway," *New York Review of Books*, Oct. 8, 1970, p. 18.

10. Earlier that day, Hudson lay on the beach with his pistol be-tween his legs. " 'How long have you been my girl?' he said to the pistol." " 'Don't answer,' he said to the pistol. 'Lie there good I will see you kill something better than land crabs when the time comes' " [338–39].

11. "Hemingway," *Commentary*, 50, No. 5 (Nov. 1970), 94.

A *Moveable Feast*

1. See C. Baker, *Life*, pp. 536 ff.

2. While working on *A Moveable Feast*, Hemingway also renewed his efforts to complete *The Garden of Eden*, the long novel he had been working on for several years. See C. Baker, *Life*, pp. 540 ff.

3. See my reference to Emily Watts's *Ernest Hemingway and the Arts* (n. 10, "Life," p. 224). In an appendix, Mrs. Watts indicates all works in which Hemingway is quoted about the arts. Hem-ingway wrote appreciations of the work of Luis Quintanilla and

Joan Miró, among other artists—all published originally in catalogues.

4. The story referred to is "Out of Season," and the omission is the suicide of Peduzzi, the guide. The omission, Hemingway admits, prevented readers from understanding the story. In a letter to Scott Fitzgerald (Dec. 1925), Hemingway says the origin of the story lay in an argument he had had with Hadley, followed by an unsuccessful fishing trip. When Hemingway complained to the hotel manager about his fishing guide's drunkenness, the guide was fired and hanged himself in the stable.

5. According to C. Baker (*Life*, p. 588), the apparent reference to Walsh as an editor of the *Dial* is the result of an error in preparing the typescript of *A Moveable Feast* for publication. The reference to "this quarterly" should read *This Quarter*, of which Walsh was the editor.

6. As editor of the *transatlantic review* in the early twenties, Ford published three of Hemingway's stories: "Indian Camp," "The Doctor and the Doctor's Wife," and "Cross-Country Snow." He used Hemingway as a sub-editor of several issues and let him print part of Gertrude Stein's *The Making of Americans*, which Ford disliked (see *A Moveable Feast*, pp. 17–18). Ford printed too Hemingway's now famous insult to T. S. Eliot in a supplement to the review published on the death of Conrad: "If I knew that by grinding Mr. Eliot into a fine dry powder and sprinkling that powder over Mr. Conrad's grave Mr. Conrad would shortly appear, looking very annoyed at the forced return and commence writing I would leave for London early tomorrow morning with a sausage grinder." And in his memoirs (*It Was the Nightingale*) and in an introduction to the Modern Library edition of *A Farewell to Arms*, Ford continued to write favorably about Hemingway. See also Arthur Mizener, *The Saddest Story: A Biography of Ford Madox Ford* (New York: World, 1971), and Bernard J. Poli, *Ford Madox Ford and The Transatlantic Review* (Syracuse: Syracuse U. Press, 1967).

7. "The Farm," *Cahiers d'Art*, 9 (1934), 28.

8. Compare, for example, this passage from *Green Hills of Africa:* ". . . she never could write dialog. It was terrible. She learned how to do it from my stuff and used it in that book. She had never written like that before. She could never forgive learning that and she was afraid people would notice it, where she'd learned it, so she had to attack me" [66].

9. Quoted from Hovey, p. 217.
10. See Mary Hemingway, "The Making of a Book: A Chronicle and a Memoir," *The New York Times Book Review* (May 10, 1964), p. 27.
11. In 1956, shortly before he discovered his old notebooks, Hemingway had begun a sketch about meeting Fitzgerald. See C. Baker, *Life*, p. 539.
12. Hovey writes that Hemingway's reassuring Fitzgerald about the size of his penis was "a projection of his own castration anxiety."
13. See Morley Callaghan, *That Summer in Paris* (New York: Coward-McCann, 1963), pp. 211–21.
14. Sept. 27, 1950.
15. The "pilot fish" is John Dos Passos, who introduced Hemingway to Gerald and Sara Murphy, the "rich." For a detailed account of this unpleasant embroilment, see C. Baker, *Life*, pp. 158 ff. See also Calvin Tomkins, *Living Well Is the Best Revenge* (New York: Viking, 1971), a biography of the Murphys.

Appendix A
In Our Time

Of the eighteen untitled chapters which comprise *in our time,* (1924), sixteen appear—slightly revised and rearranged—as interchapters in *In Our Time* (1925). The other two become short stories in *In Our Time:* "A Very Short Story" and "The Revolutionist." *in our time* was published in only one, limited edition of 170 copies by William Bird in Paris early in the spring of 1924. Most readers will therefore read the vignettes either in Scribner's edition of *In Our Time* or in *The First Forty-Nine Stories.* To avoid possible confusion, I have provided two tables: the first lists the chapters as originally published in *in our time;* the second lists in parallel columns the interchapters from *in our time* and the stories they precede.

Some miscellaneous observations may also prove helpful. Answering Edmund Wilson's query about the relevance of the lowercase titling, Hemingway wrote to Wilson that he thought it "silly and affected," but that he had yielded to William Bird's determination to have it so: "That was all the fun he was getting out of it I thought he could go ahead and be a damn fool in his own way if it pleased him. So long as he did not fool with the text." (Quoted in Wilson's *The Shores of Light,* p. 122.)

In the same letter, Hemingway comments about the placement of his interchapters in *In Our Time:* ". . . that is the way they were meant to go—to give the picture of the whole between examining it in detail. Like looking with your eyes at something, say a passing coast line, and then looking at it with 15X binoculars. Or rather, maybe, looking at it and then going in and living in it—and then coming out and looking at it again. Although Hemingway added that he thought *In Our Time* had "a pretty good unity," most critics have concluded otherwise. At most, they have allowed that the interchapters, as arranged in *In Our Time,* correspond loosely to the chronology of Hemingway's personal experiences— as, for example, interchapter vi (Nick's wound) and "A Very Short Story." Clinton Burhans, however, argues that the vignettes and the stories are intimately related: ". . . the stories derive their unifying significance as detailed explorations of the premises posed in the vignettes." [1]

For an excellent account of the revisions Hemingway made as he polished the vignettes from their earliest journalistic form to their final state in *In Our Time,* see Charles Fenton's *The Apprenticeship of Ernest Hemingway,* pp. 181 ff. For complete bibliographical details about *in our time* and *In Our Time,* see Audre Hanneman's *Ernest Hemingway: A Comprehensive Bibliography,* pp. 6–11, 46, 50.

Table 1

in our time
chapter 1: "Everybody was drunk . . ."
chapter 2: "The first matador got the horn . . ."
chapter 3: "Minarets stuck up in the rain . . ."
chapter 4: "We were in a garden at Mons . . ."
chapter 5: "It was a frightfully hot day . . ."
chapter 6: "They shot the six cabinet ministers . . ."
chapter 7: "Nick sat against the wall of the church . . ."
chapter 8: "While the bombardment . . ."
chapter 9: "At two o'clock in the morning . . ."
chapter 10: "One hot evening in Milan . . ."
chapter 11: "In 1919 he was traveling on the railroads in
           Italy . . ."
chapter 12: "They whack whacked the white horse . . ."

[1] "The Complex Unity of *In Our Time,*" *Modern Fiction Studies,* 14, No. 3 (Autumn 1968) 313–328.

chapter 13: "The crowd shouted all the time . . ."
chapter 14: "If it happened right down close . . ."
chapter 15: "I heard the drums coming down the street . . ."
chapter 16: "Maera lay still . . ."
chapter 17: "They hanged Sam Cardinella . . ."
chapter 18: "The king was working in the garden . . ."

TABLE 2

In Our Time
NOTE: Short titles are used here for the vignettes from *in our time*.
"On the Quai at Smyrna" appeared originally as the introduction to the second edition of *In Our Time*.

	Interchapter	*Short Story*
		"On the Quai at Smyrna"
i	"Everybody was drunk"	"Indian Camp"
ii	"Minarets stuck"	"The Doctor and the Doctor's Wife"
iii	"Garden at Mons"	"The End of Something"
iv	"Frightfully hot day"	"The Three-Day Blow"
v	"Six ministers"	"The Battler"
vi	"Nick sat against the wall"	"A Very Short Story" °
vii	"While the bombardment"	"Soldier's Home"
viii	"At two o'clock"	"The Revolutionist" ° °
ix	"The first matador"	"Mr. and Mrs. Elliot"
x	"They whack whacked"	"Cat in the Rain"
xi	"The crowd shouted"	"Out of Season"
xii	"If it happened"	"Cross-Country Snow"
xiii	"I heard the drums"	"My Old Man"
xiv	"Maera lay still"	"Big Two-Hearted River" (Part I)
xv	"They hanged Sam"	"Big Two-Hearted River" (Part II)
	L'Envoi ("The king was working")	

° Originally Chapter 10 in *in our time*.
° ° Originally Chapter 11 in *in our time*.

Appendix B
Nick Adams

Nick Adams makes his debut in *in our time* (1924). Of the twelve subsequent stories in which he is mentioned by name, seven appear in *In Our Time* (1925), three in *Men Without Women* (1927), and two in *Winner Take Nothing* (1933). Nick is also the hero of the two unpublished stories cited below. Among the stories in which his identity is not explicit but may almost certainly be assumed, one was published in *In Our Time*, one in *Men Without Women,* and two in *Winner Take Nothing.* Table 1 below lists the stories and the volumes in which they appear. Table 2 arranges the stories roughly correspondent to Nick's chronology.

Table 1

NOTE: An ° indicates a story in which Nick's identity is assumed.
in our time (1924)
    chapter 7: "Nick sat against the wall of the church"
  ° chapter 8: "While the bombardment . . ."
In Our Time (1925)
    "Indian Camp"
    "The Doctor and the Doctor's Wife"
    "The End of Something"
    "The Three-Day Blow"

"The Battler"
* "A Very Short Story"
"Cross-Country Snow"
"Big Two-Hearted River"
Men Without Women (1927)
* "In Another Country"
"The Killers"
"Ten Indians"
"Now I Lay Me"
Winner Take Nothing (1933)
* "The Light of the World"
"A Way You'll Never Be"
* "A Day's Wait"
"Fathers and Sons"
Unpublished
"Summer People" (probably the first story written about Nick Adams)
"The Last Good Country"

Table 2

NOTE: An * indicates a story in which Hemingway uses first-person narrative point of view.

"Fathers and Sons" and "Now I Lay Me" appear twice because they refer to a past earlier than the time of narration.

Boyhood
"Fathers and Sons"
"Indian Camp"
"The Doctor and the Doctor's Wife"
"Now I Lay Me"
Adolescence
"Ten Indians"
"The Battler"
"The Killers"
* "The Light of the World"
"The Last Good Country [unpublished]"
War
Chapters 7 and 8 of *in our time*
* "Now I Lay Me"
* "In Another Country"

— "A Way You'll Never Be"
"A Very Short Story"
Postwar
— "Big Two-Hearted River"
"The End of Something"
"The Three-Day Blow"
"Summer People" [unpublished]
"Cross-Country Snow"
"Fathers and Sons"
"A Day's Wait"

Appendix C
Filmography

Between 1932 and 1962, Hollywood made a dozen attempts to translate Hemingway's fiction into film. Except in the essentially visual drama of *The Old Man and the Sea* and for a few moments at the outset of "The Killers" when the art of the camera coincides with the art of Hemingway's language, the results were essentially abortive. The film versions distort or evade Hemingway's vision of experience. In the earliest version of *A Farewell to Arms*, for example, an alternate ending allowed Catherine Barkley to survive. Twenty years later, Hollywood still insisted upon altering Hemingway's sense of reality by having an airplane arrive just in time to save Harry's life in "The Snows of Kilimanjaro." To Jake Barnes's "Isn't it pretty to think so?" a scriptwriter added Brett's "There must be a way for us."

Novels

The Sun Also Rises
> 1957, Twentieth Century-Fox. Tyrone Power (Jake); Ava Gardner (Brett); Mel Ferrer (Robert Cohn); Errol Flynn (Mike Campbell); Eddie Albert (Bill Gorton). Director: Henry King.

A Farewell to Arms
> 1932, Paramount. Gary Cooper (Frederic); Helen Hayes (Catherine); Adolphe Menjou (Rinaldi). Director: Frank Borzage.
> 1958, Twentieth Century-Fox. Rock Hudson (Frederic); Jennifer

Jones (Catherine); Vittorio de Sica (Rinaldi). Director: Charles Vidor.

To Have and Have Not

1944, Warner Brothers. Humphrey Bogart (Harry); Lauren Bacall (Mrs. Morgan). Director: Howard Hawks.

1950, Warner Brothers; retitled *The Breaking Point*. John Garfield and Patricia Neal. Director: Michael Curtiz.

For Whom the Bell Tolls

1943, Paramount. Gary Cooper (Jordan); Ingrid Bergman (Maria); Katina Paxinou (Pilar); Akim Tamiroff (Pablo). Director: Sam Wood.

The Old Man and the Sea

1958, Warner Brothers. Spencer Tracy (Santiago). Director: John Sturges.

Short Stories

"The Killers"

1946, Universal. Burt Lancaster (Ole Andreson). Director: Robert Siodmak.

"The Macomber Affair"

1947, United Artists. Gregory Peck (Macomber); Joan Bennett (Margot); Robert Preston (Wilson). Director: Z. Korda.

"My Old Man"

1950, Twentieth Century-Fox; retitled *Under My Skin*. John Garfield and Luther Adler. Director: Jean Negulesco.

"The Snows of Kilimanjaro"

1952, Twentieth Century-Fox. Gregory Peck (Harry) with Susan Hayward and Ava Gardner. Director: Henry King.

In Our Time

1962, Twentieth Century-Fox; retitled "Adventures of a Young Man." The script was prepared from a series of television adaptations A. E. Hotchner had made of about ten stories concerning Nick Adams. The cast was generally unknown and the film might also better have been so.

"The Capital of the World" was choreographed by Eugene Loring (score by George Antheil) on commission from the Ford Foundation TV Workshop and appeared on *Omnibus* in 1953, shortly before it became part of the repertory of Ballet Theater.

Selected Bibliography

Primary Sources

Only the major published works are listed here. For additional items—both published and unpublished—see the entries below for Audre Hanneman, Philip Young, and Charles W. Mann under *Secondary Sources: Bibliographical Materials*.

Three Stories and Ten Poems. Paris and Dijon: Contact Publishing Company, 1923.

in our time. Paris: Three Mountains Press, 1924.

In Our Time. New York: Boni and Liveright, 1925.

The Torrents of Spring. New York: Scribner's, 1926.

The Sun Also Rises. New York: Scribner's, 1926.

Men Without Women. New York: Scribner's, 1927.

A Farewell to Arms. New York: Scribner's, 1929.

Death in the Afternoon. New York: Scribner's, 1932.

Winner Take Nothing. New York: Scribner's, 1933.

Green Hills of Africa. New York: Scribner's, 1935.

To Have and Have Not. New York: Scribner's, 1937.

The Fifth Column and the First Forty-Nine Stories. New York: Scribner's, 1938.

For Whom the Bell Tolls. New York: Scribner's, 1940.

Across the River and Into the Trees. New York: Scribner's, 1950.

The Old Man and the Sea. New York: Scribner's, 1952.

Books Published Posthumously

FICTION

The Fifth Column and Four Stories of the Spanish Civil War. New York: Scribner's, 1969.

Islands in the Stream. New York: Scribner's, 1970.

NON-FICTION

The Wild Years, ed. Gene Z. Hanrahan. New York: Dell, 1962. A collection of 73 articles Hemingway wrote for *The Toronto Star.*

A Moveable Feast. New York: Scribner's, 1964.

By-Line: Ernest Hemingway, Selected Articles and Dispatches of Four Decades, ed. William White. New York: Scribner's, 1967.

Ernest Hemingway: Cub Reporter. Kansas City Star Stories, ed. M. Bruccoli. Pittsburgh: U. of Pittsburgh Press, 1970.

Ernest Hemingway's Apprenticeship, Oak Park 1916–1917, ed. M. Bruccoli. Washington: NCR, 1971. Uncollected early writings, Oak Park High School *Tabula* and *Trapeze.*

Secondary Sources

Bibliographical Materials

Hanneman, Audre, *Ernest Hemingway: A Comprehensive Bibliography.* Princeton: Princeton U. Press, 1967. An indispensable work that lists Hemingway's books, stories, articles, juvenilia, with full bibliographic description. Included also are brief and useful descriptions of major writings about Hemingway from 1918 to 1965. Miss Hanneman's work supersedes the excellent earlier compilations: Louis H. Cohn, *A Bibliography of the Works of Ernest Hemingway.* (New York: Random House, 1931), and Lee Samuels, *A Hemingway Check List* (New York: Scribner's, 1951).

———, "Hanneman Addenda," *Fitzgerald/Hemingway Annual: 1970,* pp. 195–218. Miss Hanneman amends her splendid bibliography by filling in omissions in the original and adding items published since 1965.

Young, Philip, and Charles W. Mann, *The Hemingway Manuscripts: An Inventory.* University Park: Pennsylvania State U. Press, 1969. A description of Hemingway's literary estate, which consists of nearly 20,000 pages of manuscript, typescript, proofs, including about 3,000 pages of unpublished material.

Beebe, Maurice, and John Feaster, "Criticism of Ernest Heming-way: A Selected Checklist," *Modern Fiction Studies*, 14, No. 3 (Autumn 1968), 337–69. Part I lists general studies of Hemingway's life and work. Part II lists discussions of individual works. This checklist supersedes the earlier compilation of 1955.

BIOGRAPHY

Baker, Carlos, *Ernest Hemingway: A Life Story*. New York: Scribner's, 1969. A major resource work, massively documented and destructive of several long-lived myths. Lacking is any significantly analytic evaluation of the inventory of facts.

Callaghan, Morley, *That Summer in Paris*. New York: Coward-McCann, 1963. An engaging reminiscence by an erstwhile colleague on *The Toronto Daily Star* and boxing partner in Paris. Contains the best account of Scott Fitzgerald's timekeeping lapse during Hemingway's "long round" with Callaghan.

Cowley, Malcolm, "A Portrait of Mr. Papa," *Life*, 25 (Jan. 10, 1949), 86–101. Reprinted in McCaffery, cited below, pp. 34–56. Despite errors (corrected in Baker's *Life*), a wonderfully readable brief account of Hemingway's career.

Hemingway, Leicester, *My Brother, Ernest Hemingway*. New York: Fawcett, reprint, 1963. Sanford, Marcelline Hemingway, *At the Hemingways: A Family Portrait*. Boston: Atlantic, Little, Brown, 1962. Each of these is a rather bland recollection, but Hemingway's younger brother and older sister corroborate tales of Hemingway's break with his family after the war.

Hotchner, A. E., *Papa Hemingway*. New York: Random House, 1966. A sensationalized and often grossly inaccurate account of Hemingway's last years.

Loeb, Harold, *The Way It Was*. New York: Criterion, 1959. A sober and defensive account of the events detailed in *The Sun Also Rises* by the Robert Cohn of that novel.

Montgomery, Constance Cappel, *Hemingway in Michigan*. New York: Fleet, 1966. Tells about the family summers in northern Michigan (1900–21) and how Hemingway used the experience in fiction.

Ross, Lillian, *Portrait of Hemingway*. New York: Simon and Schuster, 1961. Revised and enlarged version of her famous "profile" in *The New Yorker* (May 13, 1950). At once sympathetic and malicious, an ingenious effort to mix the immiscible.

CRITICISM

BOOKS

Atkins, John, *The Art of Ernest Hemingway: His Work and Personality*. Rev. ed., London: Spring Books, n.d. First published, London: P. Nevill, 1952. The first full-length English study and a disappointing one—fragmentary and vague.

Baker, Carlos, *Hemingway: The Writer as Artist*. Princeton: Princeton U. Press, 1952, 1956; 3rd ed., enlarged, 1963. An important and valuable study despite occasionally overwrought analyses and rigorous defenses of Hemingway's less defensible fiction.

Baker, Sheridan, *Ernest Hemingway*. New York: Holt, Rinehart, and Winston, 1967. A short but readable and balanced introduction.

Benson, Jackson J., *Hemingway: The Writer's Art of Self-Defense*. Minneapolis: U. of Minnesota Press, 1969. A useful study of Hemingway's techniques of irony, satire, and humor—the tough-guy style—as "defense" against emotional and linguistic superficiality and bankruptcy.

DeFalco, Joseph, *The Hero in Hemingway's Short Stories*. Pittsburgh: U. of Pittsburgh Press, 1963. Tortured analyses that collapse beneath the weight of Jungian and mythic paraphernalia.

Fenton, Charles A., *The Apprenticeship of Ernest Hemingway: The Early Years*. New York: Farrar, Straus, and Young 1954. Reprinted, Compass Books, 1958. A splendid study of Hemingway's formative years. Fenton's stylistic analyses of Hemingway's journalism and of the vignettes of *in our time* are indispensable.

Hovey, Richard B., *Hemingway: The Inward Terrain*. Seattle: U. of Washington Press, 1969. A depth-psychology study. Some of the readings are fresh and penetrating, but the total impression is one of strain and of an undue forcing of psychoanalytic theory.

Joost, Nicholas, *Ernest Hemingway and the Little Magazines: The Paris Years*. Barre, Mass.: Barre Publishers, 1968. A useful supplement to Fenton's study of Hemingway's journalistic apprenticeship, this time from the angle of relationship to the little magazines.

Killinger, John, *Hemingway and the Dead Gods: A Study in Existentialism*. Lexington: U. of Kentucky Press, 1960. Reprinted, New York: Citadel, 1965. An existential approach, narrowly conceived, broadly applied, and loosely argued. Some of the readings are most doubtful.

Lewis, Robert W., Jr., *Hemingway on Love*. Austin: U. of Texas Press, 1965. An involuted analysis of Tristan-Iseult patterns of *eros* and *agape* that sheds more light on Denis de Rougemont's *Love in the Western World* than on Hemingway's fiction.

Rovit, Earl, *Ernest Hemingway*. New York: Twayne, 1963. A solid work, perceptive and stimulating. Its chief shortcoming is an unremitting determination to locate Hemingway's roots in American transcendentalism.

Sanderson, Stewart, *Hemingway*. Edinburgh: Oliver and Boyd, 1961. Better than Atkins's book, this short English study may serve as a good elementary introduction.

Schorer, Mark, *The World We Imagine: Selected Essays*. New York: Farrar, Straus, and Giroux, 1968. Part Six contains a graceful and witty essay about Hemingway, Fitzgerald, Stein, and Anderson.

Stephens, Robert O., *Hemingway's Non-Fiction: The Public Voice*. Chapel Hill: U. of North Carolina Press, 1968. An informative and valuable study of all of Hemingway's non-fiction and, as well, its relationship to his fiction.

Watts, Emily, *Ernest Hemingway and the Arts*. Urbana: U. of Illinois Press, 1971. A long-needed and welcome study of Hemingway's use and appreciation of architecture, sculpture, and the pictorial arts.

Wylder, Delbert E., *Hemingway's Heroes*. Alburquerque: U. of New Mexico Press, 1970.

Young, Philip, *Ernest Hemingway*. New York: Rinehart, 1952. Enlarged with an introduction and afterword as *Ernest Hemingway: A Reconsideration*. New York: Harcourt, Brace, & World 1966. A new crop of psychologically oriented critics has plunged deeper than Young, but none has yet surfaced with a more substantial reading of the man or his work. Still an indispensable book.

ANTHOLOGIES OF CRITICISM

Asselineau, Roger, ed., *The Literary Reputation of Hemingway in Europe*. Paris: Minard, 1965. New York: New York U. Press, 1965. Leading scholars from Western and Eastern Europe assess Hemingway's impact on their national literature and sensibility.

Baker, Carlos, ed., *Hemingway and His Critics: An International Anthology*. New York: Hill and Wang, 1961. Nineteen interesting and valuable essays that range from overviews to analyses of specific works.

――, *Critiques of Four Major Novels*, Scribner Research Anthologies. New York: Scribner's, 1962. A useful collection of twenty articles about *The Sun Also Rises, A Farewell to Arms, For Whom the Bell Tolls,* and *The Old Man and the Sea*. Two additional essays treat of Hemingway's style.

Bruccoli, Matthew, and C. E. Frazer Clark, Jr., eds., *Fitzgerald/Hemingway Annual: 1969*—Washington, D.C.: NCR Microcard Editions. A miscellany of critical articles, hitherto unpublished materials, and incidental intelligence. The most valuable item about Hemingway to date is the publication of Fitzgerald's letter to Hemingway suggesting revisions in *The Sun Also Rises*.

Howell, John M., ed., *Hemingway's African Stories*, Scribner Research Anthologies. New York: Scribner's, 1969. Sources Hemingway may have drawn upon for "Macomber" and "Kilimanjaro," as well as various critical approaches to each of the stories.

Jobes, Katherine T., ed., *Twentieth-Century Interpretations of "The Old Man and the Sea."* Englewood Cliffs, N.J.: Prentice-Hall, 1968. Nine long essays and several shorter items that range from unreserved praise to sharp doubts about Hemingway's sincerity and authenticity.

McCaffery, John K. M., ed., *Ernest Hemingway: The Man and His Work*. Cleveland: World, 1950. The earliest critical anthology and still valuable, it contains three biographical essays (notably, Malcolm Cowley's "A Portrait of Mr. Papa") and eighteen critical pieces.

Modern Fiction Studies. Ernest Hemingway: Special Number, 14, No. 3 (Autumn 1968). In addition to seven articles, contains "A Selected Checklist" of criticism (see Bibliography).

Weeks, Robert P., ed. *Hemingway: A Collection of Critical Essays.* Englewood Cliffs, N.J.: Prentice-Hall, 1962. Sixteen penetrating essays about Hemingway's style and themes in general and as manifest in particular works.

White, William, ed., *The Merrill Studies in "The Sun Also Rises."* Columbus: Merrill, 1969. Each of the seven essays has appeared elsewhere, several of them repeatedly. What is most welcome is the inclusion of eight contemporary reviews published in 1926–1927.

CRITICAL ESSAYS

References are to general studies. For essays about specific works, see notes to individual chapters, and also—for complete coverage —the checklist (Part II) published by *Modern Fiction Studies* (see above). No comment has been appended when the contents of an essay have already been noted in my text or notes.

Aldridge, John W., *After the Lost Generation*, pp. 23–43. New York: Noonday, 1958. Doubts the validity of Hemingway's sense of life and locates only residual quality in his style. A vigorous but shallow essay.

Backman, Melvin, "Hemingway: The Matador and the Crucified," *Modern Fiction Studies*, 1 (August 1955), 2–11. Reprinted in *Hemingway and His Critics*, pp. 245–58, and *Critiques of Four Novels*, pp. 135–43. A perceptive analysis of the antagonistic yet pervasive motifs of administering and receiving death, and how, in *The Old Man and the Sea*, the two are at last synthesized.

Bardacke, Theodore, "Hemingway's Women," in McCaffery, pp. 340–51.

Beach, Joseph Warren, "Ernest Hemingway: The Esthetics of Simplicity," in his *American Fiction: 1920–1940*, pp. 97–119. New York: Macmillan, 1941. A lively introduction, especially interesting on the relationship between aesthetics and ethics.

Bishop, John Peale, "The Missing All," *Virginia Quarterly Review*, 13 (Summer 1937), 107–21. Reprinted in McCaffery, pp. 292–307. A sensitive appreciation of Hemingway's prose style, his morality in a nihilistic world.

Bridgman, Richard, "Ernest Hemingway," in his *The Colloquial Style in America*, pp. 195–230. New York: Oxford, 1966. A most valuable essay.

Brooks, Cleanth, "Ernest Hemingway: Man on His Moral Uppers," in his *The Hidden God*, pp. 6–21. New Haven: Yale U. Press, 1963. A temperate view of Hemingway's secular values and of his desperate but failing effort to substitute them for God.

Burgum, Edwin B., "Ernest Hemingway and the Psychology of the Lost Generation," in his *The Novel and the World's Dilemma*, pp. 184–204. New York: Oxford, 1947. Reprinted in McCaffery, pp. 308–28. Marxist criticism, judiciously applied.

Cargill, Oscar, *Intellectual America: Ideas on the March*, pp. 351–70. New York: Macmillan, 1941. Lively, vigorous, provocative commentary.

Carpenter, Frederic I., "Hemingway Achieves the Fifth Dimension," *PMLA*, 69 (Sept. 1954), 711–18. Reprinted in his *American Literature and the Dream*, pp. 185–93 (New York: Philosophical Library, 1954). *Hemingway and His Critics*, pp. 192–201. The first major study of Hemingway's use of time as a "perpetual now."

Colvert, James B., "Ernest Hemingway's Morality in Action," *American Literature*, 27 (Nov. 1955), 372–85. A defense of Hemingway's morality in terms of moral skepticism and empirical determination of values.

Cowley, Malcolm, "Nightmare and Ritual in Hemingway," Introduction to *Viking Portable Hemingway*. New York, 1944. Reprinted in Weeks's *Critical Essays*, pp. 40–51.

D'Agostino, Nemi, "The Later Hemingway," *Sewanee Review*, 68 (Summer 1960), 482–93. Reprinted in Weeks's *Critical Essays*, pp. 152–60. An Italian critic ventures some sharp observations about the defects of the later work, but concludes that "even his failures are not devoid of dignity and interest."

Eastman, Max, "Bull in the Afternoon," *New Republic* 75 (June 7, 1933), 94–97. Reprinted in McCaffery, pp. 66–75.

Edel, Leon, "The Art of Evasion," *Folio* 20 (Spring 1955), 18–20. Reprinted in Weeks's *Critical Essays*, pp. 169–71. A blunt attack on Hemingway's style by an eminent Jamesian; see reply by P. Young.

Evans, Robert, "Hemingway and the Pale Cast of Thought," *American Literature*, 38 (May 1966), 161–76. An interesting, though overly insistent, study of Hemingway's anti-intellectualism.

Fiedler, Leslie, *Love and Death in the American Novel*, pp. 304–9, 350–52. New York: Criterion, 1960. Reprinted in Weeks's *Critical Essays*, pp. 86–92.

Fitzgerald, F. Scott, "How to Waste Material: A Note on My Generation," *Bookman*, 63 (May 1926), 262–65. Reprinted in his *Afternoon of an Author: A Selection of Uncollected Stories and Essays*, ed. Arthur Mizener (Princeton U. Library, 1957), pp. 117–22.

Friedrich, Otto, "Ernest Hemingway: Joy Through Strength,"

American Scholar, 26 (Autumn 1957), 470, 518–30. A lusty attack on Hemingway's morality and metaphysics.

Frohock, W. M., *The Novel of Violence in America: 1920–1950*, 2nd ed., pp. 167–99. Dallas: Southern Methodist U. Press, 1957. Reprinted in McCaffery, pp. 262–91.

Fuchs, Daniel, "Ernest Hemingway, Literary Critic," *American Literature*, 36 (1965), 431–51. An important, prize-winning essay that views Hemingway's prose as an antidote to the genteel and the respectable but that is nevertheless itself literary, especially in its biblical plainness and repetition.

Geismar, Maxwell, *Writers in Crisis: The American Novel Between Two Wars*, pp. 37–85. Boston: Houghton Mifflin, 1942. Reprinted in McCaffery, pp. 143–89. A crabbed, quasi-Marxist sulking about Hemingway's "separation . . . from the common activity of his time," and insisting that he fails to plumb "the depths and nuances of his themes."

Gifford, William, "Ernest Hemingway: The Monsters and the Critics," *Modern Fiction Studies* (Hemingway Number), 14, No. 3 (Autumn 1968), 255–70. An overview of Hemingway's attitudes toward society, his style, and conflicts—and how all fuse to effect a heroic quality.

Gordon, David, "The Son and the Father: Patterns of Response to Conflict in Hemingway's Fiction," *Literature and Psychology*, 16 (1966), 122–36. A psychological analysis that argues that the hero is compelled by guilt to discover means to prove his moral superiority.

Graham, John, "Ernest Hemingway: The Meaning of Style," *Modern Fiction Studies* 6 (Winter 1960–61), 298–313. Reprinted in *Critiques of Four Novels*, pp. 183–92. An excellent study of Hemingway's style.

Halliday, E. M., "Hemingway's Narrative Perspective," *Sewanee Review*, 60 (Spring 1952), 202–18. Reprinted in *Critiques of Four Novels*, pp. 174–82; Walton Litz, ed., *Modern American Fiction* (New York: Oxford, 1963), pp. 215–27. An acute, lucid essay about Hemingway's use of first- and third-person narrative methods as they relate to his themes.

———, "Hemingway's Ambiguity: Symbolism and Irony," *American Literature*, 28 (March 1956), 1–22. Reprinted in *Critiques of Four Novels*, pp. 174–82; Weeks's *Critical Essays*, pp. 52–71.

Hoffman, Frederick J., "No Beginning and No End: Hemingway and Death," *Essays in Criticism*, 3 (Jan. 1953), 73–84. Reprinted in C. Feidelson and P. Brodtkorb, ed., *Interpretations of American Literature* (New York: Oxford, 1959), pp. 320–31. An interesting essay about Hemingway's use of death in his fiction.

Kashkeen, Ivan, "Ernest Hemingway: A Tragedy of Craftsmanship" (1935), in McCaffery, pp. 76–108. A distinguished essay by a gifted Russian critic who regards Hemingway as a superb craftsman stupefied by the *nada* induced by bourgeois society. See also a later essay, "Alive in the Midst of Death" (1956), reprinted in *Hemingway and His Critics*, pp. 162–79.

Kazin, Alfred, *On Native Grounds*, pp. 393–99. New York: Harcourt, Brace, 1942. Reprinted in McCaffery, pp. 192–204. A vigorous and invigorating essay.

Levin, Harry, "Observations on the Style of Ernest Hemingway," *Kenyon Review*, 13 (Autumn 1951), 581–609. Reprinted in his *Contexts of Criticism* (Cambridge: Harvard U. Press, 1957); *Hemingway and His Critics*, pp. 93–115; Weeks's *Critical Essays*, pp. 72–85.

Lewis, Wyndham, "Ernest Hemingway: The 'Dumb Ox,' " in his *Men Without Art*, pp. 17–40. London: Cassell, 1934.

Macdonald, Dwight, "Ernest Hemingway," in his *Against the American Grain*, pp. 167–84. New York: Random House, 1962. A witty but brutal parodic biographical account.

Moloney, Michael F., "Ernest Hemingway: The Missing Third Dimension" (1952), reprinted in *Hemingway and His Critics*, pp. 180–91. A Catholic critic responds sensitively to Hemingway's work but deplores his failure "to link up with the world of spirit."

O'Faolain, Sean, *The Vanishing Hero: Studies in Novelists of the Twenties*, pp. 112–45. Boston: Little, Brown, 1956. A trenchant appraisal of Hemingway's affirmation of human dignity.

Oldsey, Bern S., "The Snows of Ernest Hemingway," *Wisconsin Studies in Contemporary Literature*, 4 (Spring–Summer 1963), 172–98.

Paolini, Pier Francesco, "The Hemingway of the Major Works" (1956), reprinted in *Hemingway and His Critics*, pp. 131–44. An Italian critic finds stylistic and thematic harmony among the works in "the golden zone," fiction of medium length about heroes who learn to live with *nada*. A worthwhile essay.

Parker, Dorothy, "The Artist's Reward," *The New Yorker*, 5 (Nov. 30, 1929), 258–62.

Plimpton, George, "The Art of Fiction XXI: Ernest Hemingway," *Paris Review*, No. 18 (Spring 1958), 60–89. Reprinted in *Writers at Work: The Paris Review Interviews*, Second Series (New York: Viking, 1963), pp. 215–39; and in *Hemingway and His Critics*, pp. 19–37.

Savage, D. S., "Ernest Hemingway," in his *The Withered Branch: Six Studies in the Modern Novel*, pp. 23–43. London: Eyre and Spottiswoode, 1950.

Schwartz, Delmore, "Ernest Hemingway's Literary Situation," *Southern Review*, 3 (1938), 769–82. Reprinted in McCaffery, pp. 114–29.

Stein, Gertrude, *The Autobiography of Alice B. Toklas*, pp. 212–20. New York: Random House, 1933. Reprinted in McCaffery, pp. 25–33.

Tanner, Tony, "Ernest Hemingway's Unhurried Sensations," in his *The Reign of Wonder: Naivity and Reality in American Literature*, pp. 228–57. Cambridge: Cambridge U. Press, 1965.

Trilling, Lionel, "Hemingway and His Critics," *Partisan Review*, 6 (Winter 1939), 52–60. Reprinted in *Hemingway and His Critics*, pp. 61–70.

Waggoner, Hyatt H., "Ernest Hemingway," *The Christian Scholar*, 38 (June 1955), pp. 114–20. Argues that Hemingway's morality is not anti-Christian but anti-Victorian.

Warren, Robert Penn, "Ernest Hemingway," *Kenyon Review*, 9 (Winter 1947), 1–28. Reprinted as introduction to Modern Standard Authors Edition of *A Farewell to Arms* (New York: Scribner's, 1949); J. W. Aldridge, ed., *Critiques and Essays on Modern Fiction* (New York: Ronald, 1952), pp. 447–73; and M. D. Zabel, ed., *Literary Opinion in America* (New York: Harper, 1951), pp. 447–60. A major essay, in part an analysis of *A Farewell to Arms*, but also a compendium of searching insights into style, religion, ethics, and the "code."

Wheelock, John Hall, ed., *Editor to Author: The Letters of Maxwell Perkins*. New York: Scribner's, 1950. Perkins's letters to Hemingway (and to Fitzgerald, Wolfe, and others) provide fascinating insights into the editor's skill in handling prized and temperamental specimens.

Wilson, Edmund, "Hemingway: Bourdon Gauge of Morale," in his

The Wound and the Bow, pp. 214–42. Boston: Houghton Mifflin, 1941. Reprinted in McCaffery, pp. 236–57.

——, *The Shores of Light: A Literary Chronicle of the 20's and 30's,* pp. 115–24, 339–44, 616–29. New York: Farrar, Straus, and Young, 1952.

Young, Philip, "Hemingway: A Defense," *Folio,* 20 (Spring 1955), 20–22. Reprinted in Weeks's *Critical Essays,* pp. 172–74. A sprightly rejoinder to Leon Edel's attack (see above) on Hemingway's style.

——, "Our Hemingway Man," *Kenyon Review,* 26 (Autumn 1964), 676–707. In what he calls "The End of Compendium Reviewing," Young reports on thirty-two items about Hemingway published between 1960 and 1964. The comments range from admiration to outrage, and the whole piece is a hilarious—but valuable—tour de force.

Index

Bold face indicates the key discussion of the work cited.